SOCIAL CHANGE, RESISTANCE, AND SOCIAL PRACTICES

Studies in Critical Social Sciences Book Series

Haymarket Books is proud to be working with Brill Academic Publishers (http://www.brill.nl) to republish the Studies in Critical Social Sciences book series, edited by David Fasenfest, in paperback editions. Other titles in this series include:

The Apprentice's Sorcerer: Liberal Tradition and Fascism
Ishay Landa

Dialectic of Solidarity: Labor, Antisemitism, and the Frankfurt School
Mark P. Worrell

The Destiny of Modern Societies: The Calvinist Predestination of a New Society
Milan Zafirovski

Engaging Social Justice: Critical Studies of 21st Century Social Transformation
edited by David Fasenfest

The Future of Religion: Toward a Reconciled Society
edited by Michael R. Ott

Globalization and the Environment
edited by Andrew Jorgenson and Edward Kick

Hybrid Identities: Theoretical and Empirical Examinations
edited by Keri E. Iyall Smith and Patricia Leavy

Imperialism, Neoliberalism and Social Struggles in Latin America
edited by Richard A. Dello Buono and José Bell Lara

Liberal Modernity and Its Adversaries: Freedom, Liberalism and Anti-Liberalism in the Twenty-First Century
Milan Zafirovski

Marx, Critical Theory, and Religion: A Critique of Rational Choice
edited by Warren S. Goldstein

Marx's Scientific Dialectics: A Methodological Treatise for a New Century
Paul Paolucci

Profitable Ideas: The Ideology of the Individual in Capitalist Development
Michael O'Flynn

Race and Ethnicity: Across Time, Space, and Discipline
Rodney D. Coates

Transforming Globalization: Challenges and Opportunities in the Post 9/11 Era
edited by Bruce Podobnik and Thomas Reifer

Western Europe, Eastern Europe and World Development 13th-18th Centuries
edited by Jean Batou and Henryk Szlajfer

SOCIAL CHANGE, RESISTANCE, AND SOCIAL PRACTICES

EDITED BY RICHARD A. DELLO BUONO
AND DAVID FASENFEST

Haymarket Books
Chicago, Illinois

First published in 2010 by Brill Academic Publishers, The Netherlands
© 2006 Koninklijke Brill NV, Leiden, The Netherlands

Published in paperback in 2012 by
Haymarket Books
P.O. Box 180165
Chicago, IL 60618
773-583-7884
www.haymarketbooks.org

ISBN: 978-1-60846-144-8

Trade distribution:
In the US, through Consortium Book Sales, www.cbsd.com
In the UK, Turnaround Publisher Services, www.turnaround-psl.com
In Australia, Palgrave Macmillan, www.palgravemacmillan.com.au
In all other countries, Publishers Group Worldwide, www.pgw.com

Cover design by Ragina Johnson.

This book was published with the generous support of Lannan Foundation and
the Wallace Global Fund.

Printed in the United States.

10 9 8 7 6 5 4 3 2 1

Library of Congress Cataloging-in-Publication Data is available.

CONTENTS

PART III

MIGRANTS AS SOCIAL CHANGE AGENTS

NOTES ON CONTRIBUTORS

Rose M. Brewer, Ph.D. is a scholar and an activist. She is a sociologist and Professor of African American & African Studies at the University of Minnesota-Twin Cities. She writes extensively on gender, race, class and social change, publishing over 50 articles, book chapters and essays. Her most recent book is co-authored, *The Color of Wealth* (2006). The book received the Gustavus Meyer national book award as one of the 10 best books written on bigotry and human rights in 2006. For more than fifteen years she served on the board of Project South: Institute for the Elimination of Poverty and Genocide. She has also been a board member of United for a Fair Economy and is a founding member the Black Radical Congress. She is currently a co-lead of the political and popular education working group of Grassroots Global Justice Alliance. Her involvement in the U.S. Social Forum and the World Social Forum is fueled by a long term commitment to fundamental social transformation in this country and globally. She attended her first social forum in Porte Alegre, Brazil as a member of a GGJ delegation.

Krista M. Brumley is Assistant Professor of Sociology at Wayne State University. Her research interests include: social movements, gender, work, organizations, and globalization. She has extensive fieldwork experience in Mexico, and has published in Mexico her work on nongovernmental organizations and political participation in Monterrey. Her current research project explores how globalization has influenced the organizational culture at a Mexican international corporation. She has a book chapter entitled: "Gender, Class, and Work: The Complex Impacts of Globalization," that will appear in the upcoming edition of *Advances in Gender Research*.

Alejandro I. Canales was born in Santiago (Chile) and holds a Ph.D. in Social Sciences from El Colegio de México. He has been a Research Professor at the Institute of Economic and Regional Research at the University of Guadalajara, Mexico since 1998 where he has directed several research projects on Migration and Development. He was the first President of the Latin-American Population Association and is currently the Director of the Latin American Population Journal. He has been a consultant of Economic Commission for Latin-American and the Caribbean, the United Nations Fund for Population Affairs, and Secretaría General Iberoamericana. He has published widely in journals from North America, Europe and Latin America. His most recent books are *Vivir del Norte. Remesas, desarrollo y pobreza en México* (CONAPO, México, 2008), *Panorama actual de las migraciones en América Latina* (ALAP, 2006), and *Desafíos teórico-metodológicos en los estudios de población en el inicio del milenio* (El Colegio de México, 2004, co-author with Susana Lerner).

Mohammad A. Chaichian is Professor of Sociology at Mount Mercy College. He has published numerous articles on contemporary Iran, Egypt, China, urban political economy, immigration issues, and race relations. His latest book, *Town and Country in the Middle East: Iran and Egypt in the Transition to Globalization* was published in 2009 (Lexington Books).

Richard ("Ricardo") A. Dello Buono is Associate Professor and Chair of the Department of Sociology, Manhattan College. His research areas include comparative social problems and Latin American/Caribbean Studies. He has been a visiting professor at the New College of Florida, University of Havana, National University of Colombia, Autonomous University of Zacatecas and a Fulbright Professor at the University of Panama. He is co-author of *Latin America after the Neoliberal Debacle* with Ximena de la Barra (2009, Rowman and Littlefield) and co-editor of *Imperialism, Neoliberalism and Social Struggles in Latin America*, with Jose Bell Lara (2007, Brill); *Cuba in the 21st Century: Realities and Perspectives*, with Jose Bell Lara (2005, Editorial José Martí); and *Social Problems, Law and Society*, with A. Kathryn Stout and William J. Chambliss (2004, Rowman and Littlefield).

Matheu Kaneshiro is a graduate student of sociology at the University of California, Riverside. He currently studies social movements, political sociology, environmental sociology, and demography.

Kirk Lawrence is a graduate student in sociology at the University of California, Riverside. His emphases are the environment, political economy, and theory, with particular interest in the interaction of humans and the biosphere during the evolution of world-systems.

Some of his current research projects include: the development of a theory and empirical analysis of energy flow and ecological degradation in the evolution of world-systems (for dissertation); a study of upward sweeps in city and empire sizes for the last 5000 years; and, a theoretical and simulation-based model of social evolution (the latter two as a member of research groups at the Institute for Research on World-Systems at UCR).

Ligaya Lindio-McGovern, Ph.D. is a Filipina Associate Professor of Sociology at Indiana University Kokomo. A former director of Women's Studies, she is author of *Filipino Peasant Women: Exploitation and Resistance* and lead co-editor of *Globalization and Third World Women: Exploitation, Coping and Resistance*. She has also published numerous articles in several journals and book chapters in the fields of women and globalization; international labor migration; transnational social movements and social change; women and Third World development; gender-race-class stratification. She has conducted fieldwork on Filipino migrant domestic workers in Rome, Taiwan, British Columbia (Canada), Hongkong, Chicago, and in the Philippines. Currently, she is conducting research on the globalization of the health care labor market.

Irma Lorena Acosta Reveles, Ph.D. is a researcher at the Universidad Autónoma de Zacatecas, Mexico and has researched extensively on issues affecting the peasantry of rural Mexico. She is author of numerous articles and several books, including *Challenges to Rural Society at the Onset of the 21st Century* (Ed., PRODERIC and UAZ, 2008) and *The Influence of Neoliberalism on the Dialectics of the Peasantry* (Legislatura del Estado de Zacatecas and UAZ, 2003).

Israel Montiel Armas holds a degree in Political Sciences and Administration and is a doctoral student in Geography at the Universitat Autònoma de Barcelona. He is currently working as a Research Assistant at the Institute of Economic and Regional Research at the University of Guadalajara (Mexico) on a project regarding Mexican migration to the United States. His recent publications include "A world without borders? Mexican immigration, new boundaries and transnationalism in the United States", with Alejandro I. Canales; in Antoine Pécoud and Paul de Guchteneire (eds.) Migration without borders, Berghahn Books and UNESCO.

Simon Sottsas was born in Italy in 1981, where he was trained to work as software developer. Afterwards he studied political science at the universities of Innsbruck (Austria), Kent (UK) and Berlin (Germany), and got his 'Diplom' at Freie Universitaet Berlin in 2006. He has been working for the German Institute for Economic Research, the Berlin Senate Chancellery, and the German Development Service Laos. Currently he is a PhD-Student at Freie Universitaet Berlin, focusing on historical-materialist approaches for peace and conflict studies. His regional expertise encompasses above all South East Asia and the former Soviet Union republics.

A. Kathryn Stout is an Associate Professor of Criminal Justice at Southern University at New Orleans (SUNO). A scholar-activist in Chicago for many years, she moved back to her hometown of New Orleans prior to the Katrina Hurricane-flood catastrophe, giving her first hand experience with the disaster and recovery process. She is author and co-editor (with William J. Chambliss and Richard A. Dello Buono) of *Social Problems, Law and Society*, SSSP Presidential Series, Rowman & Littlefield, 2004 and other publications.

Molly Talcott is an assistant professor of sociology at California State University, Los Angeles. Her ongoing research investigates how women and youth are reshaping indigenous-led grassroots human rights movements across Southern Mexico through emergent cultural-political praxes. Her prior research on the politics of women's labor within the Colombian flower industry was published in a special issue on "Development Cultures" (2004) in *Signs: A Journal of Women in Culture and Society*.

Nicole Trujillo-Pagán, Ph.D. is Assistant Professor in the Center for Chicano-Boricua Studies and the Department of Sociology at Wayne State University. She researches Latino labor in the United States and her current work is on the recovery and construction industries in New Orleans. Her work has appeared in several anthologies on Hurricane Katrina and in the progressive magazine, *Critical Moment*. She has also collaborated with local activists, most recently the workers' center (Centro Obrero) in Detroit, Michigan.

WRITING THE RELATIONSHIP OF RESISTANCE AND SOCIAL CHANGE

Richard A. Dello Buono

Life is change,
that is how it differs from rocks,
change is its very nature
John Wyndham (1955) *The Chrysalids*

Change is eternal. Nothing ever changes.
Immanuel Wallerstein (1974), *The Modern World-System*

Since its inception, sociology has struggled to explain the relationship of resistance and social change. Early currents of non-Western sociological thought dedicated to notions of conflict and resistance can be found dating back to thinkers like Ibn Khaldun. Khaldun was born in Tunis of an Arabic family forced to relocate from Seville following the Spanish Reconquest. Among other things, the diaspora of his parents almost certainly awoke in Khaldun an academic concern over how the history of the Reconquest was being written. Notably, Khaldun explicated the need for a critical approach to social change. He emphasized the need to consider the quality of sources acceptable in studying history. Although steeped in Islamic thought, Khaldun would go on in his most famous work *Al Muqaddimah* to formulate an early, conflict approach to social change designed to universally apply across all societies.[1]

Some five centuries later, philosophers of history in the non-Islamic world were having similar problems trying to work out a systematic application of European Enlightenment thought. A substantial portion of French philosopher Auguste Comte's work was aimed at constructing a positivist understanding of what he and others of his time termed "social dynamics." But it was in the German milieu that another philosopher, Hegel, ultimately transformed Western conceptions of history into a powerful, critical system for analysis. Hegel was convinced that Western philosophy had become fairly "stupid" about history but eventually pulled itself up out of darkness with the help of non-Western

---

[1] For an English translation with annotations, see Khaldun 1958.

thought. In Hegel's own words: "Philosophy, like the arts and sciences, when through the rule of the Barbarians of Germany, they became dumb and lifeless, took refuge with the Arabians, and there attained a wonderful development; they were the first source from which the West obtained assistance (Hegel 1983: 25)."

The problem with the immense philosophical system that Hegel devised was that in practical terms, he ended up in extraterrestrial terrain. For that reason, his search for a critical method of interpreting history was relegated to elite intellectual discourse. It fell to other thinkers like Ludwig Feuerbach to apply this critical Hegelian method to Hegel's own idealist approach and bring him back to the real world. Feuerbach forced open the door to a critical Western system of dialectical historical analysis and it was ultimately Karl Marx who walked through it just a few years later.

As Marx's collaborator Frederick Engels put it:

> Then came Feuerbach's *Essence of Christianity*. With one blow, it pulverized the contradiction, in that without circumlocutions it placed materialism on the throne again. Nature exists independently of all philosophy. It is the foundation upon which we human beings, ourselves products of nature, have grown up. Nothing exists outside nature and man, and the higher beings our religious fantasies have created are only the fantastic reflection of our own essence. The spell was broken; the "system" was exploded and cast aside, and the contradiction, shown to exist only in our imagination, was dissolved. One must himself have experienced the liberating effect of this book to get an idea of it. Enthusiasm was general; we all became at once Feuerbachians (Engels 1946).

Without question, the crash of the Hegelian system at the hands of Marx and Engels produced a new era of critical social thought. Even while Khaldun had already established some five centuries earlier that human labor was at the core of explaining wealth and profit,[2] Marxian social thought took up the concept in grand Hegelian style and ran with it. An entire alternative system of political economy was born, rooted in a critical, dialectical and historical comprehension of the exploitation of human labor. This system provided a pivotal vantage point for the contemporary understanding of conflict-driven social change and remains the cornerstone of modern critical sociology.

---

[2] For an excellent summary of the political economy of Khaldun, see: Hasan 2007.

Wherever it gained influence, Marxian social thought shifted the sensibilities of sociological analysis towards a focus on social class contradictions. The class character of the state was revealed and systematically examined in a variety of camps where its social implications were now comprehended within the systemic logic of the larger political economy. Working class resistance to the structured relations of capitalist exploitation was now reconceptualized as a key part of the motor of social change.

The Crisis of Western Capitalism

> The settler which is in every one of us is being savagely rooted out. Let us look at ourselves, if we can bear to, and see what is becoming of us. First, we must face that unexpected revelation, the strip-tease of our humanism. There you can see it, quite naked, and it's not a pretty sight. It was nothing but an ideology of lies, a perfect justification for pillage; its honeyed words, its affectation of sensibility were only alibis for our aggressions...
>
> Jean-Paul Sartre (1961)
> Preface to Frantz Fanon's "Wretched of the Earth"

At the onset of the 20th Century, all signs seemed to be pointing to an impending capitalist crisis. Large waves of European immigration now replaced the previous flows of slave and indentured labor that was put to an end in the previous century. Working class movements gathered force throughout the early decades as capitalist industrialization was thrown into high gear with a nearly universal adoption of scientific management. Organized labor postured to increase the working class's share of productivity gains. Revolution broke out in Russia in the throes of a global armed conflict that consumed the core capitalist countries. In short, the stage once more seemed ripe for the collapse of capitalism.

But the eventual course taken during the 20th century proved to be quite different than what was hoped for by Marxists. Advancing capitalism eked out new paths to expansion despite a nearly fatal collapse during the 1930s. Class concessions were selectively doled out in a way that maintained sufficient working class support to carry the system through two disastrous world wars. In the end, Axis Fascism was defeated in the Second World War, paving the way for a final showdown between Western capitalism and the first serious challenge to its capitalist world hegemony waged by the Soviet bloc. The challenge soon became bolstered in the post war period by a new wave of anti-colonial and anti-imperialist movements throughout the Third World, a challenge that thrived in the space created by the bi-polar competition for global hegemony.

The lion's share of socialist and militant working class movements worldwide eventually cast their lots with the Soviet camp, only to find their hopes dashed with the implosion of the Soviet Union during the final years of the 20th Century. Leftist forces fell into disarray just as the forces of capitalist globalization that defeated the Soviet system mustered its class power to implement a global shift towards neoliberalism. By century's end, the Cold War had left organized labor in shambles and the center of gravity for systemic resistance in many advanced capitalist countries had de facto shifted towards race and gender-based civil rights struggles. At the same time, a plethora of other "new" social movements such as environmental, anti-repression, anti-interventionist and other new forms of transnational, solidarity building organizations were becoming established.

Western critical sociology likewise suffered through its late-century crisis. Left and Right-wing factions of Weberianism mostly carried the day in the United States, where Marxist sociology suffered exceptionally badly from dogmatic stagnation and ideological Cold-War fatigue. New Left currents of the 1960s had inspired a rediscovery of Marx, only to wither once more in the throes of sectarian and factional ideological warfare under the hegemony of the mainstream. Interactionism, post-modernism and social constructionism gained in popularity as evidence of a massive sociological retreat into the realm human "subjectivity" where its surviving critical edges posed no larger threat to the system.

It was in one key area, however, that critical sociology proved extremely influential, namely, in the area of global studies. In the 1970s, precisely when capitalist globalization was being thrown into high gear, sociological theory under the influence of Marxism proved to be ahead of the curve in theorizing the global world system. The birth of World-systems theory in the work of Immanuel Wallerstein (1974), along with others such as Samir Amin (1976), Giovanni Arrighi (1979) and Andre Gunder Frank (1967), offered a convincing grasp of the contours of the latest phase of capitalist expansion, reconciling the nation-centered focus of Western sociology with the increasingly self-evident global dynamic of systemic social change. Critical sociology had definitively shown its worth and entered the 21st Century in a relatively strong position.

The dynamics of mass immigration, a defining characteristic of Western capitalist industrialization in the post-slave trade era, had emerged once more as a central contradiction. The 21st Century global capitalist crisis was punctuated by the "blowback" of 9/11/01 as it set the initial tone for a new generation of critical sociologists. For its part, the capitalist state once more bared its teeth and threatened all those who voiced systemic criticism. If "you weren't with us, you were against us" and the message was dangled over academics just as it was applied more directly to the leadership of oppressed communities worldwide. The resurgence of a critical criminology pioneered by sociologists like William J. Chambliss (2001) began to make the linkage of state repression, state crime and the criminalization of diverse forms of resistance in the new world order. The identification of the "prison industrial complex" and the "Security industrial Complex" were the manifest expressions of 21st Century critical sociologists establishing continuity with the critical work of thinkers like C. Wright Mills who had largely faded from prominence nearly a half-century earlier.

Contradictory Social Practices and Emergent Forms of Resistance

The arrival of what the Christian dominated West termed the "Third Millenium" came accompanied by a diverse array of resistances. Some of these take the form of open, counter-systemic movements such as the Zapatista-led indigenous communities in Mexico. Others involve more compartmentalized forms of resistance that reflect the politics of diaspora and the struggles of peoples caught up in the web of expanding networks of global trafficking of migrants, sex workers, and even child abduction in tandem with the transnational infrastructure of inter-country adoptions. While Marx had identified the nature of "normal" exploitation under capitalist social relations, he had only hinted of the seemingly limitless forms which the commodification of human labor could assume under the global expansion of capital.

The studies that make up this volume treat some of the acute forms of these intersecting links of oppression and the resistance that grows up in response, all within the context of global capital and its present day contradictions such as ecological crisis, "disaster capitalism" and explosive migration. Matthew Kaneshiro and Kirk Lawrence argue in the opening case study chapter that the environmental justice movement has contributed to a larger, "global movement of movements." Environmental movements cut across class, race, ethnic, gender, and national boundaries in ways that are unique and strategic. The impact of these movements upon the Global Social Forums held all around the world is demonstrated in their chapter. It is precisely this kind of emerging critical articulations that must shape discussions of transnational organizing. If successful, a path is opened that can unite communities capable of spanning the global North and South divide.

One of the most dramatic events of recent years to highlight the persistent contradictions of the "South" within the Global North can be found in the aftermath of Hurricane Katrina in 2005. Its devastating impact upon the Gulf Coast of the United States and the city of New Orleans in particular provides an important glimpse at new forms of homegrown resistance. The chapter by A. Kathryn Stout takes up this case, offering a cogent statement on the dialectic of social change. She explains the process as a contradictory motion of social movement-driven resistance to state reproduction of capitalist accumulation. New Orleans provides the basis for her case study of neoliberal capitalist state neglect and abuse of an oppressed community ravaged by flooding and forced displacement. Stout, herself a native of New Orleans and survivor of the disaster, emphasizes the social movements that arose within the post-Katrina "reconstruction" and the demands of displaced peoples for the "Right to Return."

Rose Brewer makes an important contribution to the present collection with a chapter that focuses directly on the liberation struggles that are developing within the Global Social Forum process. Her work highlights the first U.S. Social Forum that took place in Atlanta, Georgia. An anatomy of transnational social movement organizing and coalition building is presented amidst the complex and overlapping contradictions that embody race, class and gender-based oppression. Brewer offers a strategic reading of the Social Forum process and its potential for contributing to emancipatory social change.

The complex relationship between forms of violence and resistance is the subject of the chapter by Simon Sottsas. Particular attention is given to the violent nature of domination and its reflection in the social production of resistance. Sottsas, writing from a European point of reference, builds off of diverse theoretical inputs such as Gramsci and Fanon with particular emphasis on social practices in the colonial and postcolonial context.

In the second part of this book, three chapters shift the focus to Mexico where the dynamics of neoliberalism have devastated the rural sectors of that country and have intensified its persistent dependency upon the United States. This fact has not been lost upon the Mexican peasantry which as remained broadly mobilized against the North American Free Trade Agreement (NAFTA) since its inception. The chapter by Irma Lorena Acosta provides a concise overview of the impact of NAFTA upon the social sectors tied to the Mexican agri cultural system. Her analysis clearly demonstrates that the so-called global food crisis associated with the high prices of foodstuffs is better understood as a global strategy of transnational corporations to heighten their profits.

Krista Brumley's chapter reminds us that NAFTA was immediately greeted with a rebellion on the part of indigenous peoples that mobilized under the leadership of the Zapatista movement. Her work further shows how non-governmental organizations (NGOs) have become an important element in the collective actions that result from contemporary resistance to neoliberalism. By focusing on the Northern Mexican city of Monterrey, she explains how NGO's gained increasing acceptance as a mode for political action that plays a contradictory role in both challenging the system and as a system-stabilizing mechanism.

Molly Talcott's chapter on resistance in southern Mexico expands the focus to include the Mexican government initiative known as Plan Puebla Panama (PPP). As a neoliberal development program, the PPP promised to focus on infrastructural modernization throughout southern Mexico and extend it through all of Central America and into Panama. Posing as a "southern" integration initiative, its main thrust was to encourage transnational corporate investment throughout the region. The PPP was met by nearly universal hostility in all of the countries contemplated by the plan, including Mexico as Talcott shows. Her work further highlights the important role played by youth and women's movements in galvanizing resistance to these NAFTA-ized, neoliberal development schemes being imposed upon the most vulnerable social sectors in Mexico.

The final part of this book explores the 21st Century contradictions that surround recent waves of migration with an emphasis on the social practices that resist its exploitative impact upon affected communities. On the one hand, resistance can be felt within the communities of migrant and displaced peoples. On the other side of the equation, racist nativism and reactionary organizations of all sorts operating within workers communities threatened by recurring economic recessions has been on the upswing. This has played a prominent role in sporadic shifts to the right within the national politics of various countries, particularly, although not exclusively, in the global North.

The chapter by Nicole Trujillo-Pagan demonstrates how the criminalization of migrants provides the basis for profits by multiple business activities associated with the "migration industrial complex." This includes those engaged in migrant trafficking, those who hire "illegal" migrants, and even those who are contracted to detain the migrants once immigration authorities choose to crack down. As Trujillo-Pagan points out, border control in the name of national security in the post-9/11 era became an obsession in the US with big winners who were positioned to reap the profits administered by two consecutive Bush Administrations.

A quite different approach is taken by Alejandro I. Canales and Israel Montiel Armas, two Mexican analysts whose piece focuses on the creation of transnational migrant communities. Their theoretical treatment of migration, punctuated by references to Mexican immigration to the US, illustrates how migrant communities can be seen as extensions of the communities residing in the country of origin. It is precisely this "postmodern" dynamic of transnationalism that seeks to build a deeper understanding of the construction of identity within migrant communities residing abroad and their role in immigration rights protests.

Ligaya Lindio-McGovern's chapter further extends the discussion of the social practices and resistance of migrants by looking at Philippine domestic service workers employed in Hong Kong, Taiwan, and the cities of Rome, Vancouver, and Chicago. Her analysis shows how the globalization of reproductive work leads to a situation where class, race and gender dynamics all intersect to create conceptual sites of resistance. She calls specific attention to how the country of origin (in this case the Philippines) actively structures the process of migration through its labor export program, creating a worldwide chain of remittances. At the same time, however, families are torn apart while the home domestic labor market becomes stunted by the drain of human resources.

Mohammad A. Chaichian's chapter caps off the collection with a focus on France where considerable resistance to assimilation has been mounted by North African immigrant communities. His analysis of gender dynamics within these Muslim immigrant and second generation communities shows how the female use of the *Hijab* (headscarf) became the catalyst for French nativist sentiments to limit the civil rights of its own citizens of North African origin or descent. This resulted in the creation of a powerful cultural symbol of resistance that is destined to come back and haunt the myopia of "enlightened" Europe. In the end, the colonial conflict once brilliantly analyzed by the likes of Franz Fanon has been brought forward into the postcolonial era as Chaichian shows how it is being waged on the backs of displaced Muslim women thrust into the role of cultural resistance.

Over five hundred years have passed since Ibn Khaldun reflected from Tunis on the nature of conflict and the pitfalls of writing human history. From a privileged family displaced from Spain to Northern Africa, he was motivated to reflect on the universal dynamics of social change. One can only wonder what Khaldun would have thought of the contemporary capitalist world. The authors who have contributed to the present volume reflect the tremendous theoretical diversity that embodies the critical tradition in sociology. In so doing, they stand on the shoulders of giants like Khaldun, Marx, Gramsci, Fanon and Wallerstein. It is now the reader's turn to take this collective contribution into their own hands and continue writing a history of resistance and a new script for liberation.

PART I

SOCIAL MOVEMENT FOR CHANGE

ENVIRONMENTALISM AND THE FAMILY OF ANTI-SYSTEMIC MOVEMENTS: TOWARD A GLOBAL MOVEMENT OF MOVEMENTS?[1]

Matheu Kaneshiro and Kirk Lawrence

This paper is not intended to be about environmentalism. Despite the nearly exclusive treatment that we give to the environmental movement, we hope that the underlying message presented here will be bigger than environmentalism as an independent movement. Environmentalism is just one of many social concerns that demand attention in the coming millennium. At the beginning of 2009, the world found itself embroiled in a resurgence of the bloody conflict against Palestinians, a global financial crisis, a continuing humanitarian catastrophe in Darfur, two unmanageable wars of United States (USA) imperialism, and intractable ethnic and gender inequalities that have plagued the history of humanity—just to name a few global problems. Issues such as climate change and environmental justice are just pieces of what could be a larger struggle for a "better world." Many of the social problems that we face today share common causes (such as neoliberal capitalism and imperialism), and activists of all varieties can benefit from mutual empathy and collaboration.

Within this context, we argue that the environmental movement can be a key actor in bringing about (or strengthening) a "movement of many movements—coalitions of coalitions," a stimulating concept used by Klein (2004). Klein argues that a movement of all varieties, from all nations, can work together to fight against the privatization of the world—the phenomenon that places profit over people. Global movements can branch out to become numerous local movements, and local movements can tie into global movements. We argue that

[1] Special thanks to Madeline Baer for her contribution to this chapter. Christopher Chase-Dunn, Ellen Reese, and the Transnational Social Movement Research Working Group (University of California, Riverside) were also indispensable for the publication of this paper. Thanks also to Sylvia Escarcega, Marc Becker, and Lauren Hunt for their help with earlier drafts. And, of course, thanks to David Fasenfest for bringing this collection of works together.

the patterns of action displayed by the environmental movement at the World Social Forum—the annual global activist conference formed as a response to the World Economic Forum—can be seen as a microcosm for the cultivation of a larger movement of movements in general. The most important assets that environmentalism has are its global reach and ability to connect with a host of other movements; two assets that are essential for the cultivation of a "movement of movements." It is not our intention to write on environmentalists as an isolate group, nor is it to write on the World Social Forum as the mother of the global anti-systemic struggle. Instead, we simply wish to use the case of environmentalism at the World Social Forum to give us a glimpse of what a global anti-systemic movement can look like, and how it can be produced.

Why the Environmental Movement?

The environmental movement is especially important because of its popularity, particularly in wealthier nations. The growth of environmentalism has been particularly easy to see in the recent years in the United States. In 2006, Al Gore inconveniently warned us of climate change in his Nobel Prize-winning documentary. In 2007, the Live Earth concert series gathered a who's who list of celebrities and musical acts to call attention to environmental issues. And in 2008, even mainstream Hollywood cashed in on the trend by releasing an entertaining social commentary housed in a movie in Wall-E. And now, it seems as if a majority of inhabitants of the United States are at least paying lip service to environmental issues (except for those who religiously consume and produce). Environmentalism is not restricted to the United States, as many environmentalist groups are found all over the world such as in Kenya's Green Belt Movement (and others, as we shall see). The academic literature also echoes the popularity of the environmental movement, demonstrating that it is one of the largest movements around the world (Johnson and McCarthy 2005, Smith 2004). Studying transnational social movement organizations, Smith (2004) writes that groups focused on environmental issues were the second most numerous in 2000 (167 organizations, representing 17% of the sample), which was second only to human rights (247 organizations, or 26% of the sample).

Environmentalism's popularity also translates into a second valuable asset, which is its political potential. There are a growing number of political institutional channels dedicated to addressing environmental issues, many of them transnational in scope (Rootes 2005). Some have argued that, of the movements emerging from the 1960s, the environmental movement has had among the most salient and enduring impact in world politics (Chase-Dunn and Babones 2006, Rootes 1999). Being so embedded within the culture and political structures of wealthier nations, environmental groups (governmental and nongovernmental alike) also have a third asset, which is their relatively vast cache of resources at their disposal. For example, Brulle and Jenkins (2008) report that USA environmental organizations operate on a collective annual budget of over $2.7 billion and have assets of more than $5.8 billion.

A fourth asset that environmentalism has (which was alluded to earlier) is its global reach. There have been three notable United Nations conferences, for example, that have been focused on addressing environmental issues (as well as other similar meetings such as in Kyoto). Not only are there a number of transnational institutions and efforts to address environmental issues, but there are also a number of grassroots forms of environmentalism found worldwide. This introduces us to the next section on environmental justice, which high-lights what is perhaps the most important key to environmentalism's power: its intersectionality with other movements. The ability to meld its goals with other movements is, we argue, what gives environmentalism so much potential to unite activists from a variety of movements.

The five valuable assets of environmentalism are exactly what make it so powerful: its popularity, political access, resources, global reach, and connections with other movements. It is because environmentalism has such powerful qualities that we argue that the environmental movement can serve as a *gateway* movement that can help to facilitate the creation of a global movement of movements. Environmentalism can get formerly complacent people interested in progressive politics, and increasingly expand in scale to cover the gamut of progressive issues from around the world. The following events may transpire in the future: environmentalism will stimulate political mobilization as a "trendy" movement (particularly in wealthier nations), and continue to introduce the newly politicized population to think about other global social problems. Global consciousness will influence those in wealthier nations to be concerned with the struggles in developing nations, diffusing resources to assist them in their struggles (though being careful *not* to subvert their autonomy). Global movements will then become a thousand local movements, and local movements will increase their ties to global politics. Together, this global multitude will re-structure the world political economy to put people above profit. These hypothetical events are admittedly lofty and difficult to imagine, though much historical change starts with a seemingly implausible idea. It is true that much of this paper will seem to glamorize global environmentalism and affiliated progressive politics, paying little attention to the competition, inconsistencies, and conflict between progressive political groups. However, it is not the intention of this paper to highlight the problems that global progressive politics faces. Instead, this paper will highlight the positives; the fact that there are cases of global social movements that have produced social "good." Whether one imagines to overturn global neoliberal capitalism or simply to bring health care to one village is not important at this moment; whether one imagines a coherent, single movement or just one local movement is similarly not important. The only thing of importance is that there are individuals and groups who are imagining and acting. This paper will focus its attention on environmentalism that flouts movement and national boundaries, serving as glimpses of what pieces of a global "movement of movements" can look like.

The Importance of Environmental Justice

Many people think of the "environmental movement" as a movement oriented toward fighting climate change, deforestation, and species extinction. Images of boisterous Greenpeace minnows confronting whalers, Sierra Club campers, and odorous tree huggers come to mind. Indeed, the mainstream environmental movement does concern itself with the indispensable goal of protecting the environment, though this movement is primarily composed of the dominant stratum of society: white and middle or upper class persons, primarily coming from more prosperous nations (Ali 2006). Mainstream environmentalists include preservationists who strive to leave natural systems untouched by humans, and conservationists who wish to manage natural resources in the best way possible for the longevity of humanity. A list of other forms of environmentalism can be found in Brulle et al. (2007).

Another important component of environmentalism is the "environmental justice" movement (EJM) (cf. Schlosberg 2004). In contrast to the NGO-dominated and nature-based environmental movement, the environmental justice movement is the relatively subordinated version of environmentalism, economically, politically, and socially. This movement is often found among the marginalized populations in less prosperous nations and is usually comprised of youth, women, and the poor (Ali 2006; Faber 2005; Taylor 2005). The EJM primarily concerns itself with social justice between *humans* on environmental issues, assuming many forms such as the right to potable water and the fight against environmental racism (the dumping of environmental hazards onto minority populations). Thus, one reason that we find so much importance in the EJM is that it gives a voice to the normally voiceless classes of society; those who often do not have the resources to present their concerns to political channels or the broader global population through mass media. A second value of environmental justice is that it is a conglomerate movement that is larger than simply "environmentalism" alone. It is essentially a cross between human rights and environmentalism, blurring the distinction between movements and bringing together different "schools" of anti-systemic movements.

Environmentalism is an issue that is larger than itself, as environmental risks have very strong implications for humanity. At their most extreme, environmental scholars argue that a society's fate is directly linked to the environment it inhabits. Neo-Malthusians (such as Ehrlich and Ehrlich 1990) argue that growing population and industrialization levels are currently degrading the environment at egregiously unsustainable levels, setting the stage for an impending social catastrophe. Chase-Dunn and Hall (2006) argue that, throughout history, entire world-systems (interaction networks between societies) have been overturned from conflict that arises from population pressures and environmental degradation. Perhaps the most popular book on this topic is Diamond's (2005) best seller *Collapse: How Societies Choose to Fail or Succeed*, which argues that environmental degradation can lead to the collapse of societies that fail to respond adequately. The ecological contradictions of capitalism increase the chance that such a catastrophe can occur, as the reckless need for capitalism to accumulate profit is driven by the exploitation of natural resources (Foster 2002, 1999, O'Connor 1998, Schnaiberg and Gould 1994).

This same dynamic can be seen today in the rising conflict (war) that results from the struggle for resources such as oil, water, and minerals (Klare 2001). Homer-Dixon (1999) argues that weak states or states with inadequate institutions for resource distribution (poor nations) are the most at risk for conflict. Many other scholars also write that wealthier nations prosper at the expense of the poorer nations— poorer nations becoming reduced to social and environmental wastelands from exploitation by the North (see Frank 2007, Hornberg 2007,

2001, and Jorgenson 2003; 2004). This body of research is important because it links environmental issues to global issues of peace and survival (which are of primary concern for many movements), and they demonstrate that much is at stake for humanity due to environmental degradation. Mainstream environmentalists tend to think in terms of climate change and rising sea levels that pose a looming threat for humanity. Climate change and rising sea levels, however, seem benign when considering that the war *today*, and the potential collapse of societies tomorrow are also at stake.

Environmentalism across Movements and across Nations

One of the most popular forms of environmental justice found in the global South (a term used to group typically poorer nations, in contrast to the global North) is the fight against the privatization and control of water. Water, being a natural resource that populations depend on for survival, is progressively becoming claimed as a commodity that can be owned. Movements in the global South include the struggle against dams in India, which endanger farming communities that have been dependent on the flow of the rivers for generations (Shiva 2003). The fight against the privatization of water exploded in the "Water War" of 2000 in Cochabamba, Bolivia.[2] The government of Bolivia, under pressure from the World Bank, effectively sold all titles to water (including ground water and rainfall) to Aguas del Tunari, a subsidiary of the United States corporation, Bechtel (Shultz 2005). Residents were charged for meter installations and water rates tripled in some locations, raising the costs of water to over a quarter of some households' incomes (Shultz 2003, Finnegan 2002). A coalition of neighborhood associations, unions, intellectuals, farmers, engineers, and environmentalists mobilized up to 100,000 people in protest against the government contract with Aguas del Tunari, eventually driving the corporation out of Cochabamba after several months of conflict (Finnegan 2002). Similar struggles for water rights can be found throughout the world, with varying levels of success.

---

[2] Many thanks to Madeline Baer for her contribution to this section.

In the global North (typically wealthier nations), a characteristically different kind of protest erupted in Seattle. In 1999, 40,000 to 60,000 protestors filled the streets to protest the World Trade Organization (WTO) conference.[3] For three days, a variety of activists from different movements and countries demonstrated tremendous amount of solidarity in protesting against the environmental degradation and social injustices that accompany global capitalism. To be sure, a common thread that connects many social problems and their respective movements is the primacy that capitalism places on the reckless accumulation of capital, as accumulation becomes more important than the environment as well as humans. It was at this event that the unification of the "Teamsters and Turtles"—linking the traditionally contentious labor and environmental movements—ignited what is now known as the "anti-corporate globalization" or "global justice movement," with environmental justice issues retaining a significant place in its platform (Buttel and Gould 2006). Although the "Teamsters and Turtles" coalition did not lead to significant salient changes in global politics, the idea of global social movement became more tangible, continuing the legacy of transnational, anti-corporate movements (Broad and Heckscher 2003).

The above cases of environmental movements in the global South and the global North are very different in their actors, content, location, and scale. However, many share important similarities. The first is that they identify a common enemy that suppresses them: neoliberal corporate capitalism. The second is that they link groups that can be classified as "environmentalist" with a host of other movements from all over the world. These cases, much like the World Social Forum, offer glimpses of a potential movement of movements that can collectively fight for a better world.

There are many benefits that can arise from collaboration with global actors. Groups in the North can gain legitimacy by allying with those in the South. Groups in the South can benefit from resource transfer, as those in the North have a wider pool of financial and technical supplies to draw from, whereas those in the South have limited resources

---

[3] Seattle by no means birthed protests against capitalism and transnational financial institutions. Such protests have long been present in the global South, and have grown in momentum and scale since the late 1970s (Smith 2004). The "Battle at Seattle" was just a cornerstone moment for the visibility of such transnational protests in the global North, receiving much publicity.

with which to campaign. Rohrschneider and Dalton (2002) find that groups in wealthier nations are more likely to supply resources such as information, technical assistance, and capital, while groups in less affluent nations are more likely to receive such resources. Groups in the global North are also are typically embedded within "open political opportunity structures," as their exercising of free speech is not met with repression by their governments. Faber (2005) argues that Southern environmentalists actively attempt to make connections with USA activists, finding promise in USA environmental organizations' greater capacity and viewing the USA government as a potential leader in defending human rights and environmental protection. Often having few resources to work with and being embedded in less responsive or more repressive regimes, some activists in the developing nations reach outside of their state in hopes that change can come from external actors (known as the "boomerang effect,") (Keck and Sikkink 1998).

Two cases in particular demonstrate the importance of cross-national and cross-movement collaboration. Rothman and Oliver (1999) write of an anti-dam movement in Brazil that began in 1979 as a locally-rooted landless peasant movement. Throughout cycles of fits, stagnation, and starts, the movement progressively expanded its struggle to include other issues. By 1989, the anti-dam movement evolved into a larger movement which included other dam resistance movements, workers' unions, political parties, and (begrudgingly) transnational environmental movements, as doing so was beneficial in the wider resource-base it afforded. A similar case can be found in the Bhopal chemical gas leak in 1984. Little progress had been made in addressing the health concerns of the victims of the chemical leak after ten years of campaigning. Victims faced a recalcitrant political climate and lacked effective skills of research and logistical organization. Groups such as Greenpeace and Amnesty International provided expertise and publicity to help create institutions that addressed the health needs of the survivors (Zavestoski 2006). These two cases demonstrate that groups in the global South can increase their efficacy when working alongside transnational actors.

Crossing national and movement lines may not only be a question of convenience and expediency, but it may also be an issue of necessity. Even well-resourced NIMBY campaigns in the global North (such as those against neighborhood incinerators) find themselves needing to identify with larger social issues in order to be successful (Walsh et al. 1993). Environmentalism is not an isolate issue, nor is it one that can be confined to one locality. The global political economy affects all persons, allowing powerful actors to make far-reaching decisions that affect distant lands (Jorgenson 2006, Rootes 2005). A global problem warrants a globally-minded solution.

The World Social Forum and Global Activism

The World Social Forum (hereafter referred to interchangeably with the "WSF") is a cross between a movement and an open deliberative space, where activists from around the world gather to discuss social issues to whatever capacity they choose. Drawing from tens to hundreds of thousands of activists annually, the WSF has arguably become the epicenter for the global left's attempts to bring about another world. As global institutions such as the United Nations and World Bank retain egregious deficits of democracy, the WSF attempts to be a voice for the *people*, striving to engage participants in an honest, organic, and participatory democracy—insofar as it has the capacity to do so.

Needless to say, it is easy to be skeptical of the claim that the World Social Forum will usher in a global movement of movements that changes the world. Fulfilling such a lofty goal is incredibly difficult. However, regardless of one's opinions on the future of the World Social Forum, one cannot deny that, at the very least, it exposes activists to one another. In doing so, it allows a plethora of movements from around the world to network, organize, and reconceptualize the very mission of their movements. Even the fulfillment of this minimal goal makes the WSF tremendously important, and perhaps indispensable, in its ability to link activists together.

The following data were gathered by the Transnational Social Movement Research Working Group at the University of California-Riverside. Surveys were collected from 639 participants in 2005 (in Porto Alegre, Brazil), and 535 in 2007 (in Nairobi, Kenya).[4] The surveys

---

[4] In order to better capture the diversity of the forum participants, we used three languages in Brazil (English, Spanish, and Portuguese) and five languages in Kenya (English, Spanish, Portuguese, French and Swahili). To ensure proper translation, we had a second translator back-translate the survey into English to identify errors, and then requested that changes be made accordingly. Our research team was dispersed in a variety of locations including the registration line, the opening march, workshops, cultural events, and solidarity tents to sample as many participants as possible from numerous sites. Evidence of our sample's validity is exemplified in the similarity of our findings with those of IBASE, a group that conducts research on the WSF using

captured respondents' demographic characteristics, political attitudes, and movement affiliations. Other ethnographic findings were conducted by one author of this paper, who attended the World Social Forum in 2009 (in Belem, Brazil). Data from Figure 1 and Table 2 excluded individuals who were not involved in any movements.

Characteristics and Opinions of Participants at the World Social Forum

The composition of World Social Forum participants is clearly biased toward the host country. The disproportionate South/Central American representation is largely due to the hosting of the 2005 WSF in Brazil, and the large African representation from the 2007 WSF in Kenya, as seen on Table 1. Rather than being a deficit for the representation of the "global left," we find that the placement of the WSF in different regions in the global South is a key to ensuring a broad representation of participants. In other words, hosting the WSF in Kenya allows for the attendance of individuals who would normally not have the resources to attend if it were hosted in Western Europe, for example. Even with this sampling bias, there is a considerable representation of activists from around the world (Western Europe, North America, and Asia). Similarly, we find that members of poor (peripheral), wealthy (core), and in-between (semiperiphery) nations are represented at the WSF, affording representation from several different perspectives.

The important finding in Table 1 is simply the non-finding. We find that, for the most part, environmentalists at the WSF are not statistically different from non-environmentalists on a vast majority of the survey questions.[5] Instead, the environmental movement at the World

---

stratified samples of people using the registration database. Although our findings align closely, our respondents tended to be slightly more diverse in terms of their nation of residence and race/ethnicity than found by IBASE (see Reese et al. 2009).

[5] A few exceptions can be found in which environmentalists differ from non-environmentalists, though these are few and minor. Questions on demographics (e.g. race), protest frequency, and purposes for attending the Forum are among those that are different. Ideologically, the groups are not in contradiction. Differences, however, can be found across world systems lines, particularly in the desire for WSF environmentalists in peripheral nations to be more *reformist* in their approach to global change, rather than being more *radical* as are those in the core and semiperiphery (Kaneshiro et al. forthcoming).

Table 1. World Social Forum Survey Results

	Environmentalists n = 245 (24.5% of sample)	Non-Environmentalists n = 754 (75.5%)		Environmentalists n = 245	Non-Environmentalists n = 754
Geopolitical region of origin[1]			*World Trade Organization*		
South/Central America	47.6	45.0	Negotiate	26.8	32.3
Western Europe	14.2	14.3	Replace	51.3	43.9
North America	9.0	8.4	Abolish	21.9	23.8
Asia	9.9	6.0	*What level would best solve global problems?*		
Africa	18.5	26.0	Communities	56.5	54.2
Oceania	0.9	0.3	Nation states	8.8	10.4
World system position[2]			International/global	34.7	35.4
Core	24.5	23.3	*Democratic world government?*		
Semiperiphery	53.2	48.0	Good idea and possible	37.6	35.0
Periphery	22.3	28.7	Good idea but not possible	38.0	40.0
Capitalism should be…			Bad idea	24.5	25.0
Reformed	46.4	46.3			
Abolished and Replaced	48.5	50.1			
Neither	5.1	3.7			

[1] South/Central America includes Mexico.
[2] Based on Kentor's (2000) country positions in the world economy. Cutoff points were set at 2.00 between core and semiperipheral countries, and −0.89 the cutoff between semiperipheral and peripheral countries.

Social Forum is a colorful, complex assemblage that shares most of its characteristics with the rest of the participants of the WSF. This suggests that environmentalism has the potential to link with different types of activists without confronting distinctive ideological divisions. Conversely, those involved in other movements did tend to differ from the rest of the WSF population in their ideological beliefs (results not shown, but will be explored in further research).[6] The peace movement,

---

[6] Of eighteen social movements, only three other movements did not significantly differ from the rest of the WSF population on the variables provided in Table 1. These movements were, surprisingly, Slow Food/Food Rights, National Liberation,

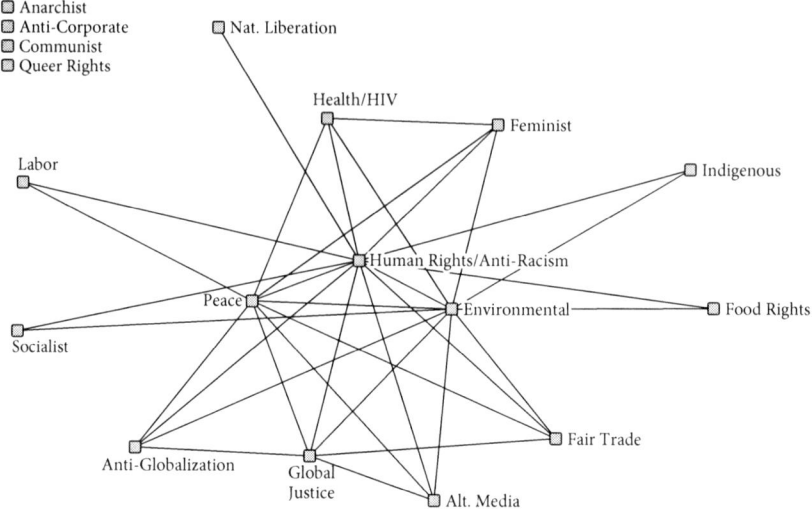

Figure 1. The Network of Movements*

* A cutoff point of 0.5 standard deviations above the mean number of cross-movement affiliations was used to identify a "tie." This translated into 42 individuals involved in tied movements, out of a total sample size of 988. This network differs from previous networks (Chase-Dunn and Kaneshiro 2009) in two ways: we compiled the 2005 and 2007 surveys into one data set; and we did not use the diagonals in the matrix to calculate the standard deviation. In other words, the total number of respondents involved in the [human rights] movement—which would increase the standard deviation substantially—was not used to calculate the standard deviation. All algorithms used cross-movement affiliations exclusively.

for example, was significantly more favorable to capitalism, was more prevalent in wealthier nations, and was more prevalent in Western Europe and North America than the rest of the WSF population. Environmentalists, thus, can serve as the mediators between actors in a movement of movements. The beliefs worked out within the environmental movement are the same that are worked out between groups in the rest of the WSF population. In short, the environmental movement can be seen as a microcosm for the global left as a whole; the flexibility, divisions, and geographical dispersion of environmentalists are reflected in the larger WSF population. Environmentalists are thus in a particularly favorable position to work alongside, find common ground, compromise, and unite with other movements.

---

and Anarchist, though these featured small sample sizes and significant variables at the .10 level.

The findings on Table 1 warrant some attention. One ideological debate that the WSF faces is on the future of capitalism. Just under half of the participants argue that capitalism should be reformed, while the other half argues that it should be abolished and replaced with an alternate system. Most participants believe that the World Trade Organization should either be replaced or abolished (rather than negotiated with). To what capacity capitalism should be reformed, and what kind of system should replace capitalism are important topics to be addressed in further research. What is clear, however, is that significant changes must be made to the global economy. As for political action, over half believed that the grassroots was the preferable path through which to enact global change. A third believed that the international/global level was the most important avenue for attack. Thus, we find that there is a healthy representation of proponents for both

Table 2. Size and Connectedness of Movements**

	Active Membership n = 997–999	Average number of cross-movement affiliations, per individual
Human Rights/ Anti-Racism	297	3.54
Environmental	245	3.43
Peace	194	4.23
Global Justice	171	3.96
Fair Trade	132	4.78
Alternative Media	192	3.28
Feminist	136	5.27
Health/HIV	150	3.82
Anti-Globalization	130	4.52
Socialist	146	3.49
Labor	131	3.73
Slow Food	85	5.40
Indigenous	83	5.31
Anti-Corporate	68	5.44
National Liberation	65	5.12
Queer Rights	60	4.95
Communist	62	4.28
Anarchist	26	5.46

** Movements are listed in order of "multiplicative coreness," or centrality within the network (the movements holding the most important positions within the network). The total sample size for each of the movements was 997–999. Thus, the "valid percent" of the sample that affiliated a listed movement is simply the active membership divided by 10.

essential paths for change, though a slight majority would go to grass-roots activism. A democratic world government seems to be heavily favored by those in the WSF—though half of those favoring one do not believe that this is actually a possibility.

A Network of Movements[7]

Even if all participants at the World Social Forum are not united in all of their goals, it is promising to note that there is evidence of cross-movement collaboration. Although some movements lie outside of the network in Figure 1 (for their failure to meet the .5 standard deviation threshold), there were no movements that shared fewer than three actors with another movement (affiliation matrix not shown). In fact, the average number of activists that were shared between movements was 31.7! On average, each activist was involved in 3.3 movements. Activists routinely cross movement lines and are struggling on multiple fronts; no movement stands alone.

The second most connected movement within the network of movements is the environmental movement (behind the human rights movement). This means that the ability for the environmental movement to unite activists for a campaign, convey information, or distribute resources across movement lines is particularly high. This finding also demonstrates that environmentalism is enmeshed with a host of other social issues, making environmentalism inextricably linked to health politics, for example. Retaining such an important node within the network of actors affords the environmental movement much power if environmental organizations were to decide to broaden their horizons and work alongside others.

---

[7] For a more in-depth analysis of the network of movements, see Chase-Dunn and Kaneshiro (2009). Slightly different questions are raised, such as "what causes the changes in the network of movements over time?" In the other chapter, the data are disaggregated over time, whereas here the surveys are combined. This current approach considers the totality of actors, with a sizable proportion from Brazil (in the "semiperiphery," using world systems terms) and Kenya (periphery) represented in the same data set, allowing for a broader diversity of cases. For Figure 1 and Table 2, individuals who were nots actively involved in any movement were excluded from the analysis.

Although the environmental movement holds a particularly strong node within the network of movements, one can also observe that cross-movement linkages are not exclusive to environmentalists. Table 2 demonstrates that, on average, individuals in the environmental and human rights movements are actually *less* connected than other movements. Less popular movements tend to be more likely to share activists between other movements, demonstrating their flexibility (and perhaps need) to associate with other, larger movements. The greatest factor that makes the environmental movement so strong within the network of movements is simply its size; since membership is so high, the absolute numbers of individuals with cross-movement linkages are also high. Individuals in popular movements (with presumably greater resources) thus show greater room to expand their frames to incorporate the goals of other movements.

Evidence of Collaboration

Survey results indicate that 46.2% of our sample attended the WSF to network, and 30.7% to organize. A sizable portion of activists reported an intention to connect with others and collaborate with others on campaigns at the WSF. Writers refer to this process as *scale shift*, in which actors share information, create new ties with actors, identify with each others' struggles, and expand their movements' objectives to unite under a shared cause. Scale shift allows movements to gain strength through collaboration with others in new, collective struggles (Reitan 2006, Tarrow and McAdam 2005).

The global reach of the World Social Forum is a great asset for cross national collaboration. This can allow for external actors with more resources to campaign on behalf of oppressed individuals who are embedded in regimes with few political opportunities (the "boomerang effect," Keck and Sikkink 1998). Our surveys suggest that this practice occurs, as 48.6% of our survey belonged to an organization that was "international in scope," reaching beyond state boundaries to bring change. Two short ethnographic cases (drawn from field notes) found at the 2009 World Social Forum will illustrate the points that have been argued throughout this chapter: that activists at the WSF cross movement and state lines.

The placement of the 2009 WSF in a city planted in the Amazon forest was particularly conducive to bringing representation from indigenous peoples from South America. Organizers secured spaces for numerous tents dedicated to indigenous issues such as Peoples of the Forest Tent, Sister Dorothy Tent,[8] and the Indigenous Tent. At any given time the Indigenous Tent drew between 75 and 200 people (and up to as much as 500) in the audience, with panelists from a number of countries including Brazil, Colombia, Peru, South Africa, and Italy. A common grievance was agribusiness' threatening the very lives of the indigenous people; agribusiness contributes to land dispossession and the displacement of communities, pollution of water supplies, deforestation, and the complete overturning of (previously sustainable) economies. Here one sees the intersection between environmentalism, indigenous rights, and basic human rights. The linking of environmental issues with other movements was a ubiquitous theme found in the self-managed activities, the Environmental Tent, Human Rights tent, and even the World of Work Tent (which is notable considering that labor activists have a history of tension with environmental activists, Obach 2004). Further in-depth examples of cross-movement and cross-national collaboration would make this analysis overly repetitive.

A particularly inspiring panel was organized by Via Campesina, an international movement that represents peasants, small farmers, and landless people for the rights to food sovereignty and sustainable farming. Via Campesina is itself a conglomerate movement, linking together indigenous rights, slow food, anti-corporate capitalism, feminism, and environmentalism. The participants on this panel came from Haiti, Mozambique, and Palestine, representing peoples as diverse as the movement itself. Much of the attention, however, was centered on solidarity and empathy on behalf of the near apartheid and ethnic cleansing conditions of Palestine. Although the Palestinian crisis

---

[8] An interesting case in its own right, as the Sister Dorothy Tent was named after a former teacher in ecumenical schools in the United States who worked in the Amazon for social and political justice in the Amazon—including preventing further environmental degradation, fighting for the rights of indigenous peoples and rural poor, providing education, and fighting against agribusiness. Her case clearly embodies a transnational environmental justice movement that encompasses many movement fronts. She was assassinated in 2005 by ranchers; only one of the ranchers has been arrested (very recently), and the hit men took the fall for the other rancher who remains free.

is normally viewed as a national sovereignty and human rights issue, the panelists highlighted the environmental/agricultural dimensions of the conquest of Palestinian territory (perhaps to frame their struggles closer to those of Via Campesina). Israel's appropriation of the water resources in the territory in 1967 and the more recent burning of fields of crop land and olive trees (a staple for the Palestinian economy) were among atrocities committed against the Palestinians that were mentioned. The representative from Mozambique insisted that we all fight on behalf of the Palestinians, leading chants of "Viva Palestina!" He argued that the liberation of Zimbabwe and elimination of apartheid in South Africa during the 1970s and 1980s would not have been possible without the help from Mozambique (which was facing its own host of problems at the time—including an ongoing civil war). Just as Mozambique's support was indispensable for the outcome of those two countries, international support is pivotal for the future of Palestine. Many social problems, he insisted, demanded international responses, and it is all of our duties to fight on behalf of our brothers and sisters in distant lands. The problems facing the world are clearly larger than environmentalism, slow food, anti-imperialism, feminism, and even human rights. In many ways, we are all part of the same simple struggle: the struggle for a better world.

In Conclusion: A Utopian Plea for the Future

We wish to echo Faber (2005), who also recognizes the importance of the environmental justice movement. He argues that environmental justice is the most socially powerful form of environmentalism that can mobilize new activists (particularly those of color and the poor), foster greater democracy through grass-roots activism, connect the grassroots to national and international levels of environmental activism, build coalitions with other progressive social movements, and pressure for changes in international policy (Faber 2005: 62). We are in agreement with this statement. But we also want to take it a step further by positing that environmentalism, along with human rights, can potentially "lead" activists of *all* varieties in the global left to pressure for change. Its resources (economic, political, and ideological), popularity, universality, and malleability are all assets that are crucial for ushering in a new world. Before environmentalists can help to usher in a coherent global anti-systemic movement, however, there are three lessons that must be learned.

Lesson 1: Humble the self and learn from others. Not all environmentalists are like those found at the World Social Forum. There are several types of environmentalists—many of them as closed-minded as the followers of any other ideology. In order to link to broader campaigns, environmentalists must look beyond their own movements and see the connections they have with other activists. The mainstream environmental movement must understand that building sustainable communities and reversing deforestation are the same goals that indigenous people from all over the world have (for far more urgent reasons). Environmentalists can learn from global justice activists, who insist that practices such as corporate social responsibility, green capitalism, and carbon trading are merely masks of legitimacy for bulldozing the Earth (cf. Buttel and Gould 2006). Environmentalists can listen to peace activists and connect war and imperialism directly to the destruction of the earth. In short, no movement monopolizes a particular issue, as all social problems are interconnected. Environmentalism must transcend fluorescent bulbs and soy lattes and join the struggle for basic human rights.

Lesson 2: Organize and join other struggles. Interconnected social problems demand interconnected social actors—from different movements and nations. In other words, a global movement of movements may be necessary to bring about environmental (and humanitarian) change. As argued throughout this paper, environmentalists are in a good position to act as a unifier of disparate struggles and a solidifier of a larger struggle for social justice. In doing so, however, *environmentalists must avoid the desire to lead other movements.* In a world of innumerable social problems, environmentalists should not place their personal agendas over those of others in collective campaigns. This is a particularly sensitive issue within environmentalism itself, as larger, whiter, and more mainstream environmental organizations have had a history of subverting the wills of smaller environmental justice campaigns (evidenced in the tension between two actors at a United States Social Forum panel, personal field notes).[9] Working across movement

---

[9] One panel at the USSF featured environmental justice activists (most of them African American) fighting local struggles against environmental racism in underprivileged communities. During a question and answer period, an older, white representative from a large, mainstream environmental organization suggested that smaller

and national boundaries must respect the autonomy and needs of other activists.

Lesson 3: Be gracious. Money is a very touchy topic for people, but environmentalists from larger organizations in wealthy nations must be willing to transfer their resources across nations. Even smaller environmental organizations in the United States must remember that environmental issues are far more egregious in places such as Haiti, and that the dollar will go much further in such underdeveloped nations. Keeping a global perspective is not only a selfless act of empathy, because their problems become our problems. The deforestation of South America for soy bean cultivation depletes the supply of oxygen that the United States breathes. The diffusion of resources called for need not exclusively be monetary (though much financial capacity is dearly needed). Information, expertise, logistical planning, contacts, grant resources, petitions, and old computers and telephones are just a few other examples of resources that can be transferred.

Naomi Klein (2004) refers to a "movement of many movements—coalitions of coalitions" as a collective of movements that all, at their core, fight against the commodification and privatization of everything in the world. Global movements should become thousands of local movements, and local movements should link to global movements—all while maintaining the diversity and integrity of many local decisions and not imposing a particular ideology upon another. This is a great beginning. The grassroots and global activists can learn from one another, and each can engage in both forms of politics. Unfettered neoliberal capitalism can be a target that all can agree on, as it is undoubtedly at the heart of many of our collective social problems.

---

groups should tie in with larger organizations to put pressure on the state and nation (rather than just the communities), as doing so would be the only way to enact lasting change. One panelist in particular was vocally and fervently against the idea. As the pleas for collaboration were reiterated, the panelist's response was very heated, as she stated that the white audience member came from a privileged position in which racial politics were not understood. She further explained that the history of collaboration with larger groups only led to the disempowerment of the local, grassroots struggles, as the larger organizations overtook the smaller organizations' agendas and disregarded their voices during meetings. The audience seemed very sympathetic to her complaints as the room erupted in applause. It should also be mentioned that I (Kaneshiro) personally found that a vast majority of environmentalists at the USSF were involved with smaller organizations, and I heard similar skeptical remarks of larger organizations in later panels.

However, (theoretically) abolishing capitalism will not be a panacea. Political corruption, patriarchy, and racism, for example, will not meet their ends. The struggle for a better world is larger than the struggle against the towers of capitalism, although this is a good start.

What does all of this mean about the movement of movements? We do not know. We realize the potential that environmental and human rights organizations can have toward cultivating a global movement of movements. However, we also realize that environmental organizations are not the keys to solving the world's problems, the World Social Forum is not the voice of the world, and the logistical loads of successfully executing a single movement of movements make it hard to imagine. Furthermore, social movement organizations often work at cross-purposes, holding very different agendas while bitterly competing for the same resources. A global movement of movements *should* be cultivated, though we should not count on this potential movement to be the only actor that brings about sorely-needed global change. Activists should also not rely on others to bring about change in the world, as doing so will only absolve one's self of the responsibility to bring about change. The environmental movement is not just some 501(c)3 organization that does our work for us. *We* are the environmental movement.

What we are trying to say is that the first step in bringing about a global movement of movements is to become the movement. In the end, the most important thing that we can do is simply do the best that *we*, as individuals, can do. Only then can we be able to fight on a single front with similar activists from around the world. We should not count on environmental organizations to humble themselves and learn from others. We must humble ourselves. Environmental organizations should not be the only actors responsible for uniting activists from around the world. We must become those activists. And it is not the duty of environmental organizations to single handedly fund activist campaigns around the world. We must give at least some of our resources to movements that need them most. Only after this happens would we be able to ask the same from the organizations that allegedly represent us. Before we can expect a movement of movements to arise, we must create our own movement of movements within ourselves, and perhaps our own little actions can collectively "strike at the heart of Empire" (Hardt and Negri 2000). On the tombstone of an unknown monk reads,

When I was a young man, I wanted to change the world.
I found it was difficult to change the world, so I tried to change my nation.
When I found I couldn't change the nation, I began to focus on my town.
I couldn't change the town and as an older man, I tried to change my family.
Now, as an old man, I realize the only thing I can change is myself, and suddenly I realize that if long ago I had changed myself, I could have made an impact on my family.
My family and I could have made an impact on our town.
Their impact could have changed the nation and I could indeed have changed the world.
(Unknown, 1100)

NEW ORLEANS AND THE DIALECTICS OF POST-KATRINA RECONSTRUCTION

A. Kathryn Stout

For a majority of Americans, the events of September 11, 2001 represented the abrupt beginning of a whole new era marked by deepening military involvement, a heightened security state and a prolonged economic dislocation. For those of us living in the New Orleans area, a traumatic second wave came with the arrival of Hurricane Katrina in August 2005. The disaster uprooted every aspect of our lives and so we were especially ill-equipped to deal with the "relief efforts" that would soon reach proportions of another disaster in its own right.

Even before the waters had completely receded, the official response to the catastrophe was being viewed as a mostly bungled affair. Riddled with faulty planning and a clear lack of preparedness by the Federal Emergency Management Agency (FEMA), the situation unfolded in a fury of bureaucratic ineptitude and a deeply flawed inter-agency coordination of emergency responses. The whole process would eventually blend into a perverse medley of government indifference and greedy business opportunism.

Many critical theorists have analyzed the far-reaching implications of the events of 9/11, showing how it served in so many ways to justify a reordering of domestic and international politics. In this chapter, I assert that something very similar happened after Katrina attacked the Gulf Coast region. Though more localized in its scope, it was all pervasive in its impact over the surrounding area. Critical sociology has only recently begun to turn its attention to the skewed, militaristic, and elite interests-driven response to the Katrina recovery and subsequent rebuilding process. Scott and Katz-Fishman (2007: 2) discuss the "creative chaos" harnessed when the capitalist establishment allows a preventable disaster to unfold in order to pave the way for a round of unscrupulous profiteering. Naomi Klein (2007) refers to "disaster capitalism" as the modality of utilizing either natural or humanly created disasters to accelerate the violent imposition of neoliberal capitalism in stubborn, more resistant areas of the world where cultural obstacles confront capitalist expansion. This is indeed the case in New Orleans where "deep South" culture has long defied a smooth shift to "McDonaldized" development.

As in other areas, organized resistance to neoliberal impositions in New Orleans suggests a dialectic that inevitably places new demands on the system as it plays out over time. To fully capture this historical process, critical sociologists must not only grasp the social class character of "disasters" and their political utilization by the state, but also interpret the influence that emergent social movement activity may exert from time to time in challenging the profit-driven logic of capitalist expansion. In this chapter, I present some theoretical suggestions about how these issues can be placed under analysis in view of the contradictory dynamics that are unfolding in post-Katrina New Orleans.

Understanding Capitalist State and Social Movement Responses to Natural Disasters

Natural disasters can provide textbook examples of how the cumulative structures of social *injustice*, particularly in social service delivery, can conspire to leave people unprotected, unassisted and unaccounted for (Stout and Dello Buono, 2008). This well-known sociological fact has long been apparent in the Third World where international relief agencies work with "vulnerability maps" to warn of impending disasters in regions of identifiable risks (Disaster Resource Network 2007). Natural scientists generally seek to predict how the accumulating effects of long term trends and/or a sudden wave of predictable adverse conditions can trigger a catastrophic loss of life and large scale impact upon human populations. From Sumatra to Guatemala, the abrupt and devastating forces of nature associated with tsunamis, hurricanes, volcanic eruptions, and others have produced dramatic dislocations of entire communities that invariably affect the poorest social sectors in a disproportionate manner.

A similar pattern has prevailed in the more developed countries and has been especially pronounced in the "underdeveloped" regions within them. The resulting social consequences of these natural disasters have been well-documented by memorable case studies that seek to detail the "chain reaction" of social devastation that accompanies the physical damage caused by "natural" disasters. In the widely read study *Everything in Its Path: Destruction of Community in the Buffalo*

Creek Flood, Kai Erickson (1978) brilliantly explored the sociological effects of community dislocation. His vintage interactionist approach illustrated the detached stance of mainstream social constructionism and the liberal emphasis on the "destruction of community." Such studies have always seemed more concerned with explaining the processes of social bonding rather than forming a critical analysis of the sort that could inform a just social response.

The overall attention dedicated to disasters has steadily grown in mainstream sociology. This is probably due, in part, to the large increase in "official" cases in countries like the United States where well over 400 were declared in 2008 alone (Brunsma 2008). Prior to its culmination in social constructionism, mainstream disaster research often adopted a functionalist approach that extolled the myth that the quality of social investigation in this area is generally enhanced by a "detached, neutral stance" (Quarantelli, Lagadec and Boin 2006). Critical sociologists, in contrast, have long emphasized the inherent limitations of this kind of methodological orientation. Beginning with the work of C. Wright Mills, value engaged sociology became the preferred option for more structurally informed approaches and has remained influential throughout the field. An important step in mainstreaming these radical/critical approaches dates back to Robert "King" Merton whose migration from orthodox functionalism led him towards a more structural sociological approach of the sort that ultimately ascended to the throne of mainstream disaster research (Merton 1968).

It was from this complex starting point that the "structural vulnerability" approach to disaster research became embodied with a liberal concern with social inequalities. Such approaches sought to establish a coherent statement of relationships between structured social inequalities and the key variables of patterned risk, differential harm and variable prospects for social recovery (e.g., Albala-Bertrand 1993; Corotis and Enarson 2004). The emphasis is placed on showing that excessive social inequalities create untenable risks and exceptional precarious situations that surface under adverse conditions to create differentiated, disastrous outcomes in otherwise "preventable" situations. Additional attention is given to the forces of urbanization and population shifts that fuel the drive to put competition, production and efficiency over safety concerns (Hazma and Zetter 1998).

More radical theorists remained unsatisfied with this liberal approach. In an influential piece written in the 1970s by Molotch and

Lester (2004), critical sociology was charged with reading through the power-structured discourses of mainstream news media. This more critical and value-engaged brand of constructionism carried with it the conscious aim of demonstrating the urgent need for a radical restructuring of social inequalities. The contribution of Molotch and Lester was to point out the need for more radical methodologies so as to critically reinterpret "accidents" such as massive oil spills in the light of the larger environmental practices of corporate capitalism and its ideological portrayal in the mass media. In more recent decades, the role of the mass media has been increasingly viewed as an important part of analyzing the social consequences of disasters, referring to concepts such as the "social amplification" of catastrophes (Brunsma 2008: 983; Quaranteli et al. 2006). This renewed interest in the framing activities of mass media is an extension of concerns first established earlier by other critical theorists and further demonstrates the mainstreaming of social constructionism in the field of disaster research.

In seeking to develop a more systemic approach in my work, I have opted for a more dialectical framework of social problems analysis (see Stout, Dello Buono and Chambliss 2004) that can help reorient critical sociological approaches to problems like disasters. The aim is to more clearly spell out the political economic determinants that conspire to preclude any real possibility for a comprehensive program for disaster preparedness and response programs. I am particularly interested in exploring the utility of a dialectical framework in analyzing the reconstruction process that began with the August 2005 impact of Hurricane Katrina on the Gulf Coast region of the United States.

The analytical approach advocated in this work is based on a critical, structural contradictions model rooted in contemporary political economy, modified by inputs from a critical sociology of law and social movements theory (Chambliss 2004; Stout 2004; Dello Buono, 2004). As suggested earlier, this framework was influenced by a growing disenchantment with social constructionism and its overly subjectivistic orientation. While there is no question that social constructionism transformed the contemporary landscape of sociology, criminology and legal studies, we now know there are serious limitations to its critical reach. Indeed, many theorists schooled within the social constructionist tradition have recognized in their own work the need for including a processual analysis of structured power relations. Prominent among the paradigmatic limitations of mainstream constructionism is an inability to adequately conceptualize the relationship between the legal order, the state and social movements in an era of rapidly changing, globalized capitalist development.

In this light, the theoretical challenges of constructing a critical sociological framework revolve around the need to nestle social problems as they develop within the larger and historically evolving political economy. There is also an urgent need to account for the impact of organized social resistance on the dominant political and economic logic. This challenges us to build a more integrated model that incorporates the dynamics of social movements as they interact with the state (Stout 2004).

As I have argued elsewhere (Stout 1989: 110–111), social movements are essentially organized expressions of resistance generated in response to social contradictions and state policies and institutions which attempt to mediate contradictory social forces. It is always important to remember that organized resistance as a product of such dynamics tends to unfold at uneven rhythms and contain only the potential for unity and effectively coordinated actions (Stout and Dello Buono 1991: 345). To the extent that social movement activities create bona fide dilemmas for the state (in its ongoing reproduction of the political economy), they ultimately challenge the organization of capitalist production and constitute a visible manifestation of fundamental underlying contradictions. This suggests that the study of the legal limits of protest and the regulation of social movement activities can provide critical insights into social change. A critical sociology of law perspective can illuminate the interrelationships between the state and social movements as they are effectively mediated through ongoing legal processes. If examined at critical historical junctures, it can be seen that it is precisely the interplay between organized social protest and the state that can impact the strategic directions of state policy-making.

In seeking to address the dynamics of social control and popular resistance as mediated through the legal process, sociology of law theorists first turned to a critical reading of Weber. Only later did they move to incorporate Marxist and Neo-Marxist analyses. Marxist-informed theorizing within the sociology of law tended to focus more directly on the structural relations between law and society. This alternative approach transcended the Weberian and earlier pluralist models in which the legal order appeared to have real autonomy in serving to protect the fundamental principles of the Rule of Law (Chambliss and Mankoff).

Initially, Marxist informed conceptions asserted that the legal order was a direct tool or instrument of class domination. Law, therefore, always reflected the interests of the ruling class (capital) and the legal process was a little more than a direct tool of class domination (Stout 1989: 93, Beirne 1980). Increasingly, the entire legal order, including the various agencies of social control, became instrumentally viewed as part of the forces and relations of production that shape contemporary social existence.

As concerns mounted that the instrumentalist position may have oversimplified the relationship between law and society, more structuralist views began to gain ground (Chambliss 1980). Citing the many examples where new laws at least initially appeared to serve the interests of less powerful social groups, structural Marxist theorists emphasized the role of the legal order in maintaining the legitimacy of the capitalist state and its social order by mediating social conflicts in a way that on the surface appeared consistent with the Rule of Law (Calavita 1983).

The assimilation of these critical insights strengthens our approach to social problems, viewed as a multi-layered social process with built-in conflictual dynamics. State policies respond to the recurring crises of the larger political economy with an eye on reproducing an expansive accumulation of capital while struggling to maintain its legitimacy. In this regard, law can serve as an instrument of mediation that provides the state with the formal means for negotiating ongoing social conflicts with legal responses that range from cooptation of organized protest to the criminalization of dissent.

Despite providing a sound, critical basis for conceptualizing the dynamics of law and society, the sociology of law ultimately failed to incorporate the important role played by social movements in the larger dialectic of social change. Of key importance for the model currently under discussion is the inclusion of invaluable insights offered by social movement research, beginning with the resource mobilization perspective (Stout, 1989). Focusing on the developmental process characteristic of social movements, critical social movement theory formulated a vision of the interactive relationship between organized protests, social change and structurally situated social relations between groups, including the state.

Since social movements by their very nature seek to bring about social change, they embody a challenge to the status quo of existing state policies and/or the legal order. Lurking close behind this challenge is dissatisfaction with asymmetrical relations of power and the prevailing distribution of economic wealth. As state policies are challenged, their legitimacy is called into question, sooner or later drawing a state response to social protest in order to mitigate any larger political challenge. The pioneering work of Barkan (1985) first explored the conditions under which the legal system can serve as an effective deterrent to movement development, or conversely, when the legal system will actually prove to be a resource that can aid and support the goals of social protest movements.

It is clear that the nature and extent of social change resulting from the dynamic interplay between social movements and the state can vary considerably. Local efforts to address social problems can involve something as simple but important to the community as improvements in a public housing complex or increases in police patrols. On a more structural level, it is easily observable that demands for racial equality in the United States, for example, have produced a variety of legislative attempts to remedy this structured inequality. Repressive tactics by governmental agents may quash the movement, or at other times, may result in further movement growth and even full-blown social revolutions (Gamson, Fireman and Rytina 1982).

On the other hand, efforts in recent years to secure legal and human rights protections for immigrants and refugees have experienced serious set backs as economic crises and the "war on terrorism" converged to fuel nativist, anti-immigrant sentiments. The confrontations of social movement members and agents of the state, the mass media and members of existing institutions whose ideologies are compatible or oppositional to those held by the movements all form part of an unfolding power play that shapes the outcomes of social change.

As the sole legitimate entity empowered with the use of force, the state wields the power to harass, criminalize, imprison and otherwise impose constraints on social movement efforts. A focus on the processes of contention or conflict from solely an organizational perspective will probably be incapable of fully grasping the larger social dialectic that is unfolding. There is a need to move beyond the analysis of organizational and political process to capture the objective conditions and contradictory forces of the larger political economy in which these conflicts are found. While resource mobilization approaches did not generally manage to develop a coherent analysis of the state, particularly as it concretely develops in relation to the larger political economy, it did offer some important contributions to understanding the internal dynamics of social movements. In my own work, I have concluded that all of these insights are useful when folded into the larger picture.

In summary, I suggest that the structured differences in social, economic and political power between classes and groups in society becomes apparent when analyzing the socio-political struggles of those who are seeking to change the objective conditions of society and those who wish to maintain the status quo. Social movements play a key role in shaping historical development as they operate within historically situated structures of political economy and in dynamic engagement with the ongoing policies and practices of the state and its legal order. The problematic objective social conditions are frequently exacerbated by the state's policies and practices which are themselves tied to the political economy. In the U.S. capitalist system, these include, but are not limited to problems and conflicts generated by reproducing inherent structural contradictions in the political economy.

This means, for example, finding ways to legitimize the maintenance of an economic environment that promotes the continued accumulation of capital and pursuit of profit for capitalists. The failure to generate legitimacy creates conflicts between workers and owners, between consumers and suppliers of goods and services, and between other groups who are historically situated in competitive relations based on race, gender, citizenship status and the like. In the context of disaster research, it can help illuminate the struggle between survivors and the powers that be. The case of Post-Katrina Reconstruction in New Orleans serves well to illustrate the complexity of this social dialectic. At the same time, our dialectical approach can help explain the otherwise startling and incomprehensible directions taken by state authorities and the harmful decisions leading up to the disaster and especially later during recovery and reconstruction efforts.

The Katrina "Double Disaster:" Storm Aftermath and Reconstruction

In the days immediately following the devastation wreaked by Hurricane Katrina, the worst-case scenario unfolded. Every schoolchild in the area had grown up with the dread that one day, the levees would break, leaving New Orleans and the surrounding area several feet under water. On that fateful day in 2005, over eighty percent of the New Orleans area, still reeling from the effects of the hurricane, was now submerged in flood and sewer waters that ranged from depths of two to twenty feet high.

Those who were left behind had little or no shelter, food, water or medicines. They were forced to face wind damage and floodwaters contaminated with oil, industrial chemicals and other toxins. News coverage around the world showed images of bodies floating in the water running down the streets next to people wading, crowded in boats or on makeshift rafts, seeking safe haven. By now, most have heard about the overcrowded, unsanitary and unsafe conditions of those who sought refuge in the large city arena structures such as the Superdome. The vast majority of those left behind were the least powerful and poorest members of society, including the poorest racial minority members whose needs were often ignored before the devastation.

Over 800,000 people were forced to evacuate with little in the way of organizational or governmental assistance (DHS 2008). Of these displaced persons, hundreds of thousands belonged to historically disenfranchised lower classes and racial/ethnic statuses. Despite these terrible blows, even worse were the official relief plans and "reconstruction" policies that followed. Many local residents were taken by surprise at the apparent lack of care and generalized incompetence shown by rescue efforts, though in hindsight, there was little to be surprised about. This is what made Katrina a "double disaster" in every sense (Stout and Dello Buono 2008: 23).

Much has been written about the incapacity of government at all levels to protect the vulnerable populations from levee failures and flooding. There is no doubt at this time that Congress and state agencies were well aware of predictions made by environmental sociologist Shirley Laska (2004) and others who warned that a major hurricane was imminent and would result in severe devastation and loss of life if more were not done in the area of hurricane prevention and preparedness.

Consistent with the expectations of contemporary disaster research, a massive displacement of local residents formed the basis of a global media spectacle as the "underdeveloped" U.S. "south" was placed on exhibition for all to see. The first images to come out of the storm and flood ravaged areas showed a "Third World" style exodus of survivors being herded out of the area, destinations unknown, backed by a militarized police and security operation. The whole world watched as poor planning, neglect, and incompetence compounded the suffering of those left behind after the evacuations, the majority of whom were poor, African American, elderly and people with disabilities (Shapiro and Sherman 2005).

Culturally, New Orleans and the surrounding area are distinct from the rest of the United States. Primarily serving as a shipping channel and tourist attraction, New Orleans is built below sea level and is surrounded by chemical plants and oil production companies. Historically home to Native Americans, Creoles, Cajun, former slaves and free people of color, whites from Italian and Irish decent as well as others from Europe, New Orleans is characterized by an abundance of historical contradictions that can be readily seen in its contemporary social relations. In the aftermath of Katrina and the floods, these contradictions ripped open like deep wounds in the cultural fabric of society.

Various studies have concluded that key governmental agencies reaching up to the Federal executive branch failed to prevent the worst aspects of the disaster in spite of adequate warning about the probable catastrophic consequences should a major storm pass precisely through the area taken by Katrina. For decades, the Army Corps of Engineers argued that the existing antiquated levee system would not protect the area from a direct hit by a major hurricane which was thought to be inevitable. It was, however, the same Army Corps of Engineers who designed and constructed the flawed levees decades before in order to further the interests of the shipping industry.[1]

It was also apparent that the City of New Orleans clearly suffered from longstanding weaknesses in its financial base and lacked a coherent plan to evacuate the large numbers of people that were at risk from this type of disaster. A majority of those directly hit by the storm and flooding lacked adequate information and resources to escape in a timely manner, leaving them to fend for themselves in the aftermath. During the first few days after the flooding, the local police and fire personnel who did not flee were the only visible representatives of government in the area. Understaffed and otherwise ill-equipped to handle the crisis, they made numerous errors in judgment that soon

---

[1] More recently a court decision allowed lawsuits to go forth against the Army Corps of Engineers for its involvement in the plans and construction of the levees that hold back the Mississippi River. Designs for waterways and the levee system were intended to promote the needs of business, specifically shipping, over the safety of the nearby residents.

became exacerbated by corruption and theft, seriously eroding their already poor relations with the pubic, and therefore, their legitimacy. At the same time, the mass media engaged in its usual practice of creating "disaster myths." In the case of Post-Katrina New Orleans, this meant conjuring up images of widespread looting, random shootings, and general civil unrest, all of which were later debunked, but nonetheless, managed to heighten support for the militarization of the area (Tierney, Bevc and Kuligowski 2006: 57). The problem is not so much the fact that the myths are untrue, but as Tierney, et al. point out, these erroneous myths can have very real and dire consequences in terms of influencing organizational behavior, the distribution of scarce resources, and the availability of social services.

With the basic infrastructure of New Orleans destroyed, shipping from its major port came to a halt, an aging public transportation system stalled, government functions evaporated, public records floated in contaminated waters, and formerly overstretched health care facilities were rendered inoperative. The unique fury of Katrina notwithstanding, the human costs and suffering caused by the damage were made far worse by the lack of a coherent and effective response plan. The media initially focused on poorly orchestrated Federal responses symbolized by FEMA and Homeland Security, each of which struggled to define their respective jurisdictions while immediate aid was delivered at a snail's pace (Stout and Dello Buono 2008: 23–24).

For its part, the State of Louisiana quickly found that its resources were overstretched. Making matters worse, significant numbers of National Guard troops and much needed equipment had been deployed in Iraq by that time (Maass 2006). Those emergency response plans that were in place faltered because identifiable individuals failed to properly execute them. One telling example was the provision in Louisiana's emergency plan which specified that the State's Transportation Secretary Johnny B. Bradberry was responsible for evacuating all nursing homes in the area. His failure to do so contributed to 35 deaths from just one nursing home on account of the flooding that engulfed St. Bernard Parish. In testimony given before to the U.S. Senate Committee on Homeland Security, Secretary Bradberry asserted that the evacuation plan was not fully in place because this responsibility had only recently been reassigned to his office from the normal functions of the National Guard (Kiefer and Montjoy 2006: 127).

The complete inventory of criticisms of the recovery plans is out of the scope of this project. However, it is useful to bring in the voices of those most affected and organized around the reconstruction issues. Some of the most bitter public outcries focused on the farcical nature of several Town Hall meetings. These ultimately proved to be merely symbolic efforts to involve residents and displaced persons in the recovery process.

Another point of contention developed around the rapidly appearing ties of patronage surrounding recovery work contracts (US House of Representatives 2006). Indeed, the Secretary of the Federal Department of Housing and Urban Development (HUD) was placed under investigation by the US Attorney General after being tipped off by staffers that contracts were generally being awarded on the basis of political party support and affiliation. The Justice Department picked up this investigation, charging HUD Secretary Alphonso R. Jackson with steering housing contracts towards his friends and other loyal supporters of the Bush Administration, forcing Jackson's resignation in 2008 (NYT 2008).

In the aftermath of the storm, approximately 20,000 residents received federal or state support for housing, 77,000 rental units were destroyed and the more than half of the residents of New Orleans who were formerly renters made up the majority of those who became displaced. Rents in the area increased by over 50%, putting the average apartment out of reach for large numbers of low waging earning families. Two years after the disaster, only about 21% of low to mid-income rental units were being covered by government rebuilding programs (GNOCDC 2008).

HUD's eventual plan to demolish 5,000 of the city's 7100 public housing units so as to replace them with only 1,000 units designed for mixed income residents severely complicated the scenario for pre-existing African American communities. A class action lawsuit was initially required to halt the government's immediate destruction of entire neighborhoods without adequate owner notification or compensation (Filosa 2006). Most former public housing residents are still displaced, having been denied the opportunity to retrieve any remaining personal belongings even from those units that escaped flood damage. Federal agency reconstruction plans sought to impose a homogeneous, suburban configuration onto a historically diverse, multilayered urban landscape. Plans to raze public housing projects and replace them with smaller, "mixed income" neighborhoods of pastel houses simply failed to adequately address the housing needs of all those former residents who were adversely affected by the disaster.

For less than wealthy homeowners, the picture was equally bleak. The Road Home Program established to provide funds for rebuilding was soon drowning in corruption, mismanagement and faced with protests by renters who make up over half of the area's residents, but were not considered in the original plans. State funding eventually allocated billions of dollars for the Small Rental Property Program, something that inspired some hope for the speedy reconstruction of affordable housing. A percentage of that money, however, has already been reallocated to the Road Home Program designed to serve homeowners and that trend is expected to continue. By three and a half years later, very little of these funds had actually been dispersed. Congress added $3 billion to the $75 billion dollars to the Road Home Program after it was projected to run out of money in 2008 before fulfilling grants for applicants expected to number over 160,000 (GNOCDC 2007).

Widespread complaints from area residents indicated that insurance companies did not settle out pending claims in accordance with their contractual responsibilities. In defiance of state law, many major companies also decided to cancel the policies of long term customers. Official investigations of the industry were eventually conducted to establish if insurance companies colluded in fixing prices, systematically orchestrated low damage assessments, and pressured assessments to attributed damage to flooding (which is not covered), among other evasive tactics. Lower than expected payouts and rejected claims of policyholders shifts the burden from the profitable insurance companies back onto the taxpayers who provide compensation through federal flood insurance and subsidized rebuilding programs.

Meanwhile, record insurance industry profits of $48 billion in 2005 and $68 billion in 2006 have punctuated the fact that policies cover less and cost more. The post-Katrina price of homeowners insurance is expected to quadruple, signifying that an average policy will cost $8,000 a year while offering no coverage for wind or hail damage. Even still, many major insurance companies have stopped issuing policies in high risk areas, forcing the State of Louisiana to offer $100 million in incentives to entice companies back into the market. In the end, soaring insurance rates presented a major obstacle to homeowners, businesses, and non-profit groups working for affordable housing.

Toward a Critical Analysis of the Katrina Debacle

The post-Katrina legacy amounted to unscrupulous profiteering in "reconstruction plans," community disarticulation, underfunded relief and social service capacities, and the persistence of the underlying structural conditions of poverty and disempowerment that were the real social causes of the devastation. The conventional questions of "Why wasn't the city better prepared?" and "Why was the recovery effort bungled at every step of the way?" take on a new character when viewed under a critical dialectical framework. It is no longer sufficient to allege that clumsy bureaucracies, inept officials and scarce resources were responsible for the slow and highly stratified response to the problem of post-Katrina reconstruction. On the contrary, I would argue that the state response was highly patterned and could have been largely anticipated. An underlying drive for profits led the state to orchestrate a whole series of policies designed to convert recovery into a "business" and reconstruction into a reformulation of a "whiter, brighter", and more streamlined area for future capitalist expansion. Consistent with the neoliberal trends in fashion, this meant targeting public sector programs rather than rebuilding them, allowing for less regulated or totally unregulated private sector activity to move in and capture the lion's share of state and federal relief and reconstruction funds (Gotham and Greenberg 2008).

One area in which an essential continuity between pre-Katrina and post-Katrina New Orleans can be found is in public education. Before the catastrophic destruction of schools and loss of most of the teachers and staff, the New Orleans public school system was ranked among the worst in the nation on all performance measures. The storm destroyed or damaged all but eight of the city's 128 public schools. Many of the 4,000 teachers and less than half of the 60,000 public school students by 2006 had returned to the city (Flaherty 2006). By way of comparison, the city's private schools saw over 90% of their students return a year later while the public school students numbered only 25,000.

The Katrina disaster brought with it an opportunity for the system to experiment in radical right school reform. Right winged think tanks like the Heritage Foundation were already advocating for vouchers and market solutions that promoted the privatization of public education. At the time of the disaster, nearly half of the New Orleans city school students were enrolled in private or parochial schools (Flaherty 2006). Instead of building a new public school system that could provide support for students to compete in the 21st Century globalized market, the reconstruction programs that were adopted predictably favored the privatization of the public school system. A privatized system presents the risk of benefiting higher income families while leaving behind hundreds of thousands of poor and low income students.

Long before the disaster, the failure of the public school system formerly managed by local district commissions initiated a reform of the system. Charter schools were developed using public funds and run by private groups who are paid based on the number of students they admit. They are referred to as "public schools of choice" and operate outside the governance and policies of their local school districts (Childress 2008). As of Fall 2006, thirty of the fifty-three schools opened had been converted to charter schools (Flaherty 2006). By four years after Katrina, no other large school district in the United States had such a high percentage of charter schools as does New Orleans.

The school's license or Charter usually runs for five years but can be revoked if student learning assessments are low. Charter school groups can be for-profit or not for-profit. While research on the effectiveness of these schools is not yet available, early results indicate that not for-profit groups such as KIPP and Aspire demonstrate an ability to motivate and assist lower income and minority students whereas the for-profit groups such as Edison have not shown similar results. Of particular significance for this discussion is that the Charter school program presents "significant entrepreneurial opportunities" which, in turn, relieves the government of its obligations and responsibilities for providing educational opportunities to the public.

Another important aspect involves the destruction of teachers unions. Prior to the storm, teachers for the City of New Orleans comprised the third largest union. Following Katrina, virtually all of the 7,000 members had been idled and the City's contract was allowed to expire. As teachers were rehired at the charter schools, they were brought in on a non-union basis. More than just union-busting, this represented a racist attack on one of the few middle-class black professions of New Orleans. The brother of former mayor Dutch Morial said, "Elites of the city may prefer that teachers don't come back because they represent an educated class of Black New Orleans, with steady income, seniority, job protection" (Flaherty 2006).

At the university level, the Southern University at New Orleans (SUNO) stands among the nation's Historically Black Colleges and Universities (HBCUs), serving over 3,000 urban students who could not otherwise afford a college education. The campus was severely damaged and later touted as one of FEMA's premier redevelopment projects. At the time of this writing, very little progress has been made on rebuilding the original campus that was severely damaged. Bureaucratic red tape and assessments that consistently underrated the amount of damage had put SUNO's already lengthy recovery process into a very low gear. In November 2007, it was discovered that toxic mold had encroached into the temporary modules adjacent to the campus that house the university's classrooms and faculty. As a historically black public institution serving the New Orleans community, the discriminatory experience of allowing SUNO's reconstruction to flounder seems to suggest that race and class remain the primary factors guiding reconstruction efforts aimed at higher education.

A similar trend could be seen in the overall labor market in post-Katrina New Orleans. Several hundred thousand workers lost their jobs when they were displaced by the storm. The severe lack of housing and job opportunities make the road home very difficult if not impossible to travel. As workers demanded their "right to return," they discovered that little in the way of resources was being dedicated to former residents. Instead, the state and business sectors focused their efforts on luring temporary immigrant workers to the city as cheap, unorganized labor in the demolition and reconstruction industry. The Department of Labor weighed in with a temporary suspension of the Davis-Bacon Act which provides for the Federal minimum wage. This policy was implemented in the wake of other major hurricanes and served as a clear signal that immigrant labor was welcome to the area. For their part, immigrant workers were ushered into temporary, make shift housing and crowded some 10–12 people to an apartment.

In a comprehensive study conducted in 2006, over 700 workers were interviewed. The findings were reported in a document entitled "And Injustice For All: Workers' Lives in the Reconstruction of New Orleans" (Browne-Dianis et al. 2006). The workers' testimonies revealed that African Americans were being shut out of local reconstruction jobs while immigrant workers were living and working under hazardous conditions and were systematically victimized by wage theft from their employers.

Perhaps the most conflictual arena in the post-Katrina period revolved around the housing crisis. Considerable debate swirls around the issue, with governmental agencies seeking to demolish public housing projects and replace them with smaller, mixed-income residences that would accommodate about one-third of the former residents. For their part, former tenants have organized considerable resistance, fighting for the preservation of the undamaged public housing units and demanding to be allowed to return to a sense of normalcy in restoring their former communities, some of which span three or more generations. There is a clear consensus among these former tenants (which include some the area's very poorest residents) that racism and a continuing disregard for the cohesion of African American communities are the driving forces behind the "redevelopment" plans.

The African American community itself is split over the wisdom of continuing the public housing projects begun shortly after World War II. Some argue that to do so would simply perpetuate the "ghetto" mentality and lifestyle that is blamed for so many ills, particularly those falling on African American youth. Others, mentioned earlier, view the struggle to preserve public housing as vital to the maintenance of their communities and the availability of affordable housing. Organized under the name of the Coalition to Stop the Demolition, public housing residents successfully launched local protests, brought aboard the support of national organizations and made use of the media to stake their claims (CSD).

Perhaps the most combative engagement with the state occurred in 2007 during the final City Council hearings on the closures. Despite the existence of Sunshine Laws guaranteeing transparency and open meetings, many of the public housing residents were literally locked out of the meeting. Scuffles ensued between the protestors and the police resulting in arrests, the use of pepper spray, tear gas and even taser guns against the residents. Ultimately, most of the area's housing projects were slated for demolition.

Over 800,000 housing units (including apartments) were severely damaged or destroyed by Katrina. Renters make up 53% of the population, most in homes with one to four units. This sector now faces a severe shortage of affordable housing where rents have experienced an alarming fifty percent rate hike (PolicyLink 2007). The near total lack of affordable housing that resulted from the storms and extensive flooding was undeniably compounded by profit oriented development plans that failed to take into adequate consideration the needs of low to moderate-income residents many thousands of whom are still displaced. Central to the Katrina reconstruction process is expanding the availability of affordable housing for middle and low-income residents and displaced families. The city is desperate for the return of its former workers, particularly in the low wage sectors of the tourist and construction industries. A formidable obstacle exists in that the displaced workers cannot return and many residents cannot stay without the availability of affordable housing.

Independent of the redevelopment plans eventually chosen, much greater emphasis will need to be placed on diffusing racist tensions through confidence building measures of the sort successfully employed in other cities. Most white enclaves will continue to resist efforts to racially integrate their neighborhoods. An alarming indicator of the severity of this problem was seen in the City of Gretna which sits across the river from New Orleans. During the Katrina evacuation, Gretna was highlighted in the media when its police and residents formed a human chain across the access bridge, threatening to shoot anyone who crossed the bridge seeking refuge in that community (Quigley 2007). Soon after, the Gretna City Council was proposing regulations that would limit the sale of homes in the area to "blood relatives" of those already living there. Later, Gretna residents successfully blocked mixed-income housing development plans.

Government policies should strengthen and enforce existing legislation governing fair housing practices. In conjunction with private enterprise, economic disparities should be addressed by developing greater job opportunities and job training for the low-income sectors of the population who are overrepresented by African Americans. As for the housing crisis, long term solutions must include economic development programs directly aimed at the poorest sectors of the area. While immediate attention should have been given to avoiding the destruction of historically established African American communities by short-term rebuilding efforts, direct participation of the residents and the displaced is vital to developing a successful and more sustainable housing reconstruction plan.

The private sector cannot be relied on to guarantee the availability of affordable and subsidized housing for low income residents. Through ongoing consultation with local area organizations involved with housing issues, the state can support efforts to protect tenants with strong regulatory housing policies, including rent control. Previously disenfranchised groups must become the target population for economic development programs. These groups include the working poor, the unemployed, women, minorities, the elderly and those with physical challenges.

Conclusion

A critical historical juncture arises out of the ashes of disasters like Katrina that presents opportunities for positive changes that can unfold through a reconstruction process. If informed by a vision of social justice and participatory democracy, the social welfare of the most vulnerable sectors can be maximized, allowing for a more rapid transition out of the emergency and shelter stage towards recovery, reconstruction and more equitable development. But this is not possible without a dedicated effort to break with "business as usual," setting aside established practices of patronage, graft, corruption, and greed in favor of a bold approach to social planning that incorporates the principles of participatory democracy and community-based development. In the reconstruction process of historically famous New Orleans and surrounding Gulf Coast areas, significant strides toward rebuilding the region on a more just and inclusive basis would have required the organization, empowerment and very fullest participation of area residents, including the inestimable numbers of former residents who are still displaced from the area nearly four years after the storm.

In contrast, the essential thrust of government sponsored plans, policies and programs of recovery and reconstruction favored the interests of big business and the wealthy (Gotham and Greenburg 2008). Throughout the Katrina aftermath, the media highlighted, among other things, the heroism, compassion, and generosity of area residents and voluntary organizations helping to meet the needs of those most afflicted. Less talked about was the valiant struggle of such organizations to exert influence over the recovery process. Despite these organizational achievements, they have thus far proved to be no match for combined government and business decision-making bent on implementing an exclusionary and insensitive model of elite-sponsored urban redesign. As a result, the unique character of the region may well be lost in reconstruction efforts that are seemingly determined to "McDonaldize" New Orleans and convert the Gulf Coast area into one large gambling casino.

There remains a multitude of religious, civic, bi-partisan, and neighborhood groups and organizations eager to work with government and business to rebuild New Orleans and the Gulf Coast authentically, under conditions of dignity and social justice. Reconstruction policies should make local social and economic development its highest priority.

Without local development at its core, the result of the process will be to continue the historic dependency of the area on federal and state sponsored relief funds. Louisiana is ranked among the lowest in fiscal capacity, thereby limiting the state government's ability to provide direct aid to the poor. Innovative relief and job training programs can be implemented by combining federal and private money, but need to be built into a coherent planning process in the early stages.

Many major insurance companies are believed to have violated state laws by canceling long term policies and/or illegally influencing damage assessments. Demands for exhaustive Federal investigations should be energetically pursued. For its part, the State of Louisiana filed suits against major insurance agencies charging conspiracy to fix premiums, artificially low damage assessments, and below fair and equal claims payments. Louisiana State Senator Walter J. Boasso proposed the incarceration of insurance executives found to have acted in bad faith. A comprehensive review of the insurance industry is needed and stricter legal regulations including penalties must be implemented.

Meanwhile, additional Federal and State funding should be made available for studies that can shed light on how deeply rooted class, race, and gender conflicts actively manifest themselves in disaster situations and under certain conditions can lead to explosive social outcomes. Government funding should give special priority to initiatives proposed by universities located in affected and surrounding areas to help offset the drain that the recovery has put on their institutional resources.

Katrina recovery projects constitute an important case study for exploring how gaping holes in the U.S. social safety net paved the way for exacerbating the damage caused by natural disasters. An examination of the actual measures initiated following the Katrina destruction allows us to reflect upon how progress is substantially complicated by core social problems that have historically plagued the region. The lessons of Katrina suggest to us that coordinated efforts at all levels of government must develop genuine mechanisms for community and citizen participation in emergency plans. Communities at risk for disaster must be respected and involved in all preventive planning Citizens have a vested interest in working to protect their lives and property, especially in areas where significant risks have been identified (Niggs and Tierney 1993).

Federal government initiatives often excel when they carry an explicit political agenda, e.g., Cold War nuclear fallout shelters and post-9/11 anti-terrorist security measures. Yet, they fall incredulously short in confronting more imminent risks, particularly those facing historically disenfranchised populations. FEMA should be reorganized and its formerly autonomous operations restored through adding elements of the old Civil Defense Program. Once FEMA was brought under Homeland Security, it radically shifted its focus and the resulting shake-up in personnel, reduction in duties, and lack of a clear division of labor left a gaping hole in its ability to effectively respond to natural disasters. Most importantly, FEMA's organizational structure should include the active participation of local resident groups in emergency response planning. This was a characteristic of the former Civil Defense program that was lost when it was subsumed by FEMA. Special provisions should be made for the high probability that local personnel may be unavailable or out of communication with others in catastrophic conditions.

Relief and reconstruction grants should always be carefully monitored and held accountable. In the case of Katrina, rules requiring that local companies be given first choice in applying for government funded grants were suspended in the name of expediency and efficiency. This enabled grants to be awarded to large companies from other areas, many of which are known to be associated with or financially supportive of the Bush administration.

Comprehensive rebuilding must take historic injustices into account when forming reactivation plans for essential social services. The break in "business in usual" that occurs in the context of major disasters presents an unanticipated opportunity to correct stubborn patterns of structural discrimination. It is essential to seize this opportunity and take the offensive against social injustice. Failing to do so will not only perpetuate these historical patterns but heighten the risk of outbreaks of violence given the overall damage sustained by the social safety net. The needs of the least powerful social groups must be made a top priority and basic and universal human rights to housing, employment, freedom from discrimination and the right to return must be protected.

THE SOCIAL FORUM PROCESS AND THE PRAXIS OF RACE, CLASS, GENDER AND SEXUALITIES

Rose Brewer

Introduction

In assessing the 21st century social forum process, one thing is quite clear: the intellectual and political agendas of those committed to human liberation are stretched thin as humanity confronts the logic of transnational capital, white supremacy, and global patriarchy. Thus this current period requires a complex theoretical and practice understanding of the complicated intersectional and movement building energies required in this political moment. Thus, this chapter will be built upon a series of difficult questions: Has the social forum process extended its reach theoretically to think through the complicated gender, sexuality, class, race, ethnicity and national spaces the masses of humanity occupy? How much, in fact, has the still developing social forum process impacted the lives of those most caught up in the logic of neoliberalism and transnational capital? Finally, how much convergence is occurring to create a movement of movements, bringing together scholars and activists, local and global alliances? These issues and others are explored in this analysis. While I claim no final answers to these questions, I do advance the following conclusions:

1. To build a movement for social change and transformation means that social forum organizing must be located in the language and practice of praxis. This centers our struggles in the deep interconnectedness of theory and action: praxis. This is an intersectional praxis enmeshed in emerging struggles on the ground: gender, race, sexuality and class. Revolutionary practice is interlinked with theory.
2. Placing movement building at its core is fundamental to the social forum process. This means advancing the goal of building a movement of movements in the context of social forum space for connection, convergence, vision, and strategy.

Social Forum Activism in the 21st Century: The Complicated Praxis of
Race, Class, Gender, Sexualities

For those of us who are activists and scholars the relationship between
theory and practice is never easy or completely resolved. For those
of us from communities that have been historically oppressed, that
relationship is far from singular or easily theorized. It embodies a
multiplicity of oppressions. We who live in the United States reside
in a country that abandoned the poorest and most dispossessed black
people in New Orleans and the Gulf Coast. If for no other reason
than this stark moment of dispossession and travesty we must lead
with complex theorizing and practice around race, class and gender
inequalities. The opening plenary of the U.S. social forum in Atlanta,
GA, June 2007, clearly articulated that premise: the praxis of gender,
race, class, and sexualities, embodied in the New Orleans catastrophe is the terrain of struggle. Given this opening gambit, how far has
this theoretical and practice realization advanced? That Atlanta plenary represented the titillating possibilities of grassroots activists truly
uniting for social transformation in the U.S. What were the precursor
moments leading to the vision expressed in the plenary?

     Consider first a brief history of the recent social forum process.[1] It
began in Brazil in 2001 in response to the World Economic Forum
in Davos, Switzerland (Sen and Waterman 2009). The World Social
Forum from that Porte Alegre, Brazil inception has usually been held
at the same time as the World Economic Forum occurs in Davos.
The dominant economic nations and corporations gather in Davos to
discuss the transnational economic order. Many of the dispossessed
gather at the World Social Forum. The World Social Forum mantra
asserts, "Another World is Possible." Anthony Barnett captures the
process thusly:

---

[1] The use of the term social forum process draws directly from the World Social
Forum description that it is not an organization nor front of organizations but a
"space" and a "process" (cited in RUPE 2007:506). Here the idea is that a range of
formations from grassroots organizations, NGO's to political parties can gather in
a loose structure to connect and ally. In this space, the world's peoples can begin
to build movements and create movement convergence against neoliberal corporate
globalization.

The creation of the WSF as an anti-Davos ensured that the new century began with a multinational stand in the name of the peoples of the world against the presumptions of the world economic order. Since 2001, until this year, the WSFs have grown and, undoubtedly, shifted the agenda, making sure that the big battalions have not had it all their own way. It has been a remarkable achievement. (Retrieved 3/1/2007 at http://www .opendemocracy.net/globalization-protest/wsf_faces_4297.jsp)

Barnett's, "until this year," reflects the dashed hopes of the seventh World Social Forum in Nairobi, January 2007, expressed in what Barnett refers to as "a public-relations disaster". Here Barnett is referring to the heavy hand of the Kenyan state and multinational corporations on the Nairobi gathering. The stamp of corporate globalization was on the forum—from providing cell phones to bottled water. The activists on the ground, committed to an anti-neoliberal agenda in Africa, found themselves in the middle of this "disaster." Thus, the critical move to Nairobi, Kenya revealed the ugly under belly of 21st century neocolonialism and imperialism. January 2007, the Forum in Nairobi was the 7th such forum, and the first full forum on the continent. In 2006 the forum was a polycentric set held in Venezuela, Pakistan and a small gathering in Bamako Mali (about 1,000 in attendance).

The African continent is home to many of the most dispossessed people on the face of the earth, so having the event in Nairobi was important, even in the midst of its corporatization (Barnett 2007). The poor youth of the Kibera slum organized against a forum seized by commercialization. But it certainly was not easy for these rebel young. The persistence of colonialism (neocolonialism) and neo-imperialism were expressed front and center. Indeed, this forum occurred in the midst of a U.S. attack on Somalia and a U.S. backed Ethiopian military assault on the Islamic Courts, and the reality of an earlier abandonment of the Black and poor in New Orleans and the Gulf coast. This is racial formation in the context of 21st century disaster (Omi and Winant 1986).

The expropriation of human and material resources continues unabated on the African continent in this era of "New Empire" (Gilbert and Reynolds 2008). Wars and conflict, political corruption in countries such as Kenya and the global south have been hard hit by debt, privatization and the neoliberal and structural adjustment policies put into place by the World Trade Organization (WTO), World Bank, and the International Monetary fund (Moody 1997). These are the institutions

organized by global capital. The economic and political plight of Black
Africans remain harsh and structural economic exclusion continues.
So as scholars and change agents came together in Nairobi, the WSF
mantra was raised over and over again in the form of a question: Is
another world possible on the African continent? Globally? Of course
the answer is yes, but not easily and not without struggle.

The face of imperialism is still raced, gendered, white supremacist (Mills 1997), but many of the elite beneficiaries are indigenous
to the oppressed cultures. Nonetheless, this sector represents a class
integrated into the logic of transnational capital for the benefit of
the global corporations and their own wealth (Berberoglu 2005; The
Bamako Appeal 2006). Neocolonial practices, operating in conjunction
with neoliberalism and privatization, are at the crux of today's transnational inequalities on the African continent. Thus the global south
is pressed into policies which destroy the social wage and structure
the continent to operate in the interest of maximizing transnational
profits. Women are disproportionately at the center of this exploitation (Mies 1986). Structural adjustment has been the key tool of the
International Monetary Fund to accomplish this agenda. Debt is its
current face. Africa has been the poster child of these policies (The
Bamako Appeal 2006). Given this, has the forum process been able
to articulate the complex theoretical spaces in which global racialized
imperialism connects with gender and class? This leads me to question
one with an eye on Africa and the African diaspora:

> Question 1: Has the movement extended its reach theoretically to
> think through the complicated gender, sexuality, class, race, ethnicity
> and national spaces the masses of humanity occupy?: Focus on African
> peoples.

Migration is an overriding feature and recurring theme in any theoretical exegesis of gender, race, class, and sexuality in a social forum
process which centers African peoples. Beginning with the long duree
of inequality for Africa and the African diaspora, forced migration as
enslaved Africans formed the building blocks for an insipient global
economy. Africans, as slaves, provided the necessary means to transition from a purely mercantile system to pre-capitalist forms of social
and economic organization (Brewer 2006).

When in the late 19th century, the world was feeling the birth pains
of industrial capitalism and colonialism (Oyeronke 1997; McClintock
1997), African peoples too transitioned, struggling to make sense of

place in a society that had already set in motion racist, sexual, and gendered mechanisms to stifle advance. This contained the continent into an already corrupt social and economic paradigm: the entwined systems of racism, patriarchy, and capitalism (Rodney 1982; Marable 1983, and Oyeronke 1997). In the U.S. context in the era post-slavery, as Blacks moved into urban industrial centers, African American men and women were used as excess and easily expendable cheap labor in fields, factories and various service sectors (Franklin 1997). African American women's reproductive energies were nearly unchanged as they went from the homes of former owners to new ones, nursing white babies, and struggling to take care of double homes as white women fought for their own suffrage (Dill 1979). Both men and women, but especially women were demonized as negligent, as Black mothers carried on the double expectations of being mothers and laborers, not a contradiction in a capitalist social framework (Davis 1981; Hull, Scott and Smith 1982; hooks 1990).

By the time the Civil Rights and Black Power movements exploded, Black resistance was occurring globally through decolonization struggles and the fight for self determination in the African and U.S. contexts (Joseph 2006). This occurred in the vortex of the standardization of capitalism as world order imperialism. As African Americans fought for self-definition and inclusion into this society and made linkages to anti-colonial struggles globally, others around the African world fought for ending colonialism (Joseph 2006). After the Second World War and the agreements made at Bretton Woods to establish the IMF and the World Bank, structures were set in place for dispossession we have witnessed for the context of the standardization of capitalism as a world order imperialism. As African Americans fought for self-definition and inclusion into this society, others around the world fought for the same things. After the Second World War, and the agreements made at Bretton Woods to establish the IMF and the World Bank, structures were set in place for the dispossession we have witnessed for the past decades: the logic of neoliberal capitalism and multinational globalization.

In the never ending quest for cheaper labor and the easy flow of capital and goods, multinational corporations, in a perverted form of bribery transplanted skilled and unskilled labor to new shores, exploiting the economic and sexual landscapes of Asia, Africa, the Caribbean, and South America. With industry transplanted, American workers and especially African American wage laborers too often have been reduced to barely sustainable social wages. Increasingly, information technology, high technology, and the service sector have come to replace what was a highly industry-centered landscape. Given the nature of the educational system—the fact that segregation and unequal access to higher learning (much less learning on a basic level)—the working class, and especially the Black working class is increasingly left behind. This helps to create the haves and have-nots, and again fixes the Black working class in a particular place in the social economy of U.S. capital. Globally, the same processes are occurring in Africa and throughout the African diaspora in sites such as the UK (Africa All Party Parliamentary Group 2006). For Black youth and adults, both men and women, the rates of imprisonment are extremely high, rates of unemployment are too often at depression levels. Large numbers of African people globally and domestically are caught in an endless cycle of poverty and skewed social and cultural interaction: violence and predatory behavior.

As the capitalist economy shifts transnationally, migration and demographic changes are rapidly occurring, too. Transnational capital disrupts economies and social fabrics. New global south immigrants have made a striking appearance in the social and economic politics of the present moment. Either entering with high technological skills or displacing unskilled workers, they are pit (usually with racial and cultural subtexts) against an existing, alienated and exploitable class: the African American working class (Witness for Peace 2007). Or, in the case of the recent upheavals in South Africa, the Zimbabwean migrants are pitted against South Africans in the poorest areas (Bond 2007 retrieved at http://links.org.au/node/815/9693).

Given this 21st century reality, it is a fact that many sectors of the poor and the working class in the United States, the Caribbean, Europe, Africa, and the diasporas are in social, economic, and political crises. In advanced Western capitalist societies such as the U.S., the dismantling of the social wage—destruction of social welfare state supports which reach the poorest women and children, a disproportionate percentage of whom are Black—is part and parcel of global restructuring and privatization (Squires 1994). These processes in the economically dominant North are mirror imaged in the South through the policies of the WTO and World Bank. These institutions in the service of transnational corporations support systems of inequality which extract resources, wreck cultural havoc through cultural imperialism, and exploit humans for the generation of transnational profit (Moody

1997). This leads to material poverty as well as cultural genocide of societies around the world. The driving force of all of this is the search for maximum profit. Accordingly, race and class are deeply enmeshed in gender, sexuality and nation, simultaneously shaping and being constructed by political economy and ideology (Brewer 2006).

In those parts of the African Diaspora that live out the legacies of colonialism, neocolonialism and the contemporary realities of global capital, debt suffocates. For example, countries (Jamaica, Haiti, etc.) live under the policies of structural adjustment—the logic deployed by the World Bank, and globalized trade policies with deep and bloody consequences for the women, children, and men of these societies. Again, the images of New Orleans, and the Black and poor of the global north are neoliberal counterparts. Although a difficult period, the dispossessed of the world are in motion, signaling a chance for resistance and change. This is the social forum hope. For example, this kind of global resistance can be found in the tiny nation of Guadeloupe, a small island of 400,000 people located in the Caribbean. Wallerstein discusses the current upheaval in Guadeloupe in a recent piece. He notes:

> Since January 20, it has been the site of an ongoing general strike, which has managed to get 10% of its population actually marching in the streets, which must be a world record. (Wallerstein 2009)

Wallerstein goes on to point out:

> Guadeloupe may be obscure today but it has been an important locus of the capitalist world economy since 1493, when Columbus first set foot there. In the seventeenth and eighteenth centuries, it became one of the principal centers of world sugar production, one of France's prized sources of wealth along with Haiti. Of course, the sugar plantations used slave labor imported form Africa, the indigenous population having been wiped out. (Wallerstein 2009 retrieved 3/1/09 at http://hap.bloger. hr/post/-guadeloupe-obscure-key-to-world-crisis-/1269755.aspx

The strike in Guadeloupe, notes Wallerstein, is against profitization and against what is still perceived as de facto slavery.

Thus the challenge for the social forum process is to connect to struggles such as those occurring in Guadeloupe. The challenge is to build an emancipatory movement that understands a complicated global economy in the midst of articulating its interrelationality in gender, sexuality, and race. Indeed, transforming transnational heteropatriarchal white supremacist capitalism must be at the center of our theory and practice. In a movement for social transformation, we simply cannot

be race, gender and class reductionist but employ a mediated understanding of the deep interrelationality of class, gender, sexuality, race,
nation under conditions of twenty-first century transnationalism. This
is a praxis the social forum process is still trying to perfect. This is
unfinished social forum business. Indeed no real movement for deep
level social change is possible with the erasure of praxis rooted in multiple sexualities, classes, race/ethnicities, and genders (Ferguson 2004).

In this era of neoliberal capitalism the political economic crush of
profit and privatization, state realities are infused with cultural and
ideological meanings. The discourses of colorblindness stand side by
side with the discourses of inferiority, unworthiness, criminality, all
used to justify and rationalize deep levels of exploitation and inequality (Bonilla-Silva 2006). These ideologies work in tandem with political
economy to keep the current order in place as much as war, imperialism, and militarism. These ideological and material processes are at
the center of the deeply exploitative current order. Processes of political economy shape and are shaped by the exclusion, inclusion, and
fracturing of economic and civil life along racial/ethnic lines in sites
such as Kenya, Guadeloupe and the U.S. Racism, in turn, reorients
processes of economy drawing upon the most exploitable and expendable labor (the global immigrants of color of the world). Racism is
cross-cut by sexism and xenophobia.

At the same time, resistance against racism, classism, sexism and heterosexism occurs in the streets and in the social forum spaces. That is,
fight back, labor organizing, protests, rebellion, and cultural resistance
in music, art, dress, stance and attitude occurs and is being built in
social, civil, community and forum spaces (Sen and Waterman 2009).
In turn, these struggles have the potential to reshape state, economy,
cultural practices. It will not be easy. While race, class, gender struggles
in the United Sates and globally have challenged, they have never completely transformed global political economy, even as the social forums
become spaces to envision such a possibility. The forum process confronts a political reality elusive to its complete dismantling. Advanced
capitalism continues to be deeply shaped by racism and sexism where
the poorest people on the face of the earth are Black, Brown, young,
female, children. This was certainly the message of the 2007 social
forum in Nairobi, Kenya. It is certainly the lesson of New Orleans,
Katrina and the Gulf Coast. This social reality is expressed as a set of
complex social relations, requiring a complex praxis. It is within this

conceptual frame of multiplicity of oppressions that the social forum movement must be built. It is an unfinished agenda.

> Question 2: How much, in fact, has the still developing social forum process impacted the lives of those most caught in the logic of neoliberalism and transnational capital?: The case of the US Social Forum, June 2007, Atlanta, GA.

Just a few months after Nairobi, Kenya World Social Forum, the United States held it's first social forum. Other countries in the hemisphere had organized social forums, not so in the US. It had been a difficult road to Atlanta. The National Planning Committee (NPC) struggled internally but the anchor commitment of two Atlanta based grassroot organizations, Project South and SisterSong: Women of Color Reproductive Collective, as well the sharp organizing skills of the USSF National organizer Alice Lovelace, stayed the course. Very late in the process, other organizations and funding came through. Atlanta, Georgia became the site of a movement building moment as thousands of educators, activists, scholars, revolutionaries, thinkers, community, labor converged on Atlanta in June of 2007 15,000 strong. The practice and theory were this: the need to come together in the space and place to play, learn, and articulate an anti-sexist, anti-racist, anti-imperialist, anti-capitalist and anti-homophobic politics. At core was a central concern with a radical political economic critique of capitalism and its meaning for the dispossessed in the global north and south. It was a movement building space. Nonetheless, the USSF process faces the same challenges from within and without as other radical movement building moments and many of the dilemmas of all left formations in the U.S.: How does such a radical collectively cohere? What is its real connection to on the ground struggles? What is the vision of social transformation?

Thus the challenge for those grassroots activists who connected in Atlanta was not simply to embrace change but to reconnect deeply to a praxis rooted in transforming transnational capitalism with its tentacles deep in the reproduction of racism, heterosexism and sexism. This reconnect must happen in theory but most demandingly in practice. The quest is to build a movement within the U.S. and globally. The challenge is to theorize and put into practice, to understand the crisis in terms of the simultaneity of oppressions (Combahee River Collective Statement 1982). These systemic processes should be articulated through the lens of deep embeddedness and relationality with an analysis of capitalist state dynamics as expressed in ideological and cultural forms as well as state practice. The difficulties of translating intersectional movements were evident in Atlanta. Many grassroots organizations still struggle around single issues, rooted in race or class or gender or sexuality. How to build across and interconnected across multiple differences remains an unfinished agenda in the U.S. social forum process. This pushes us to consider question three.

> Question 3: How much movement building and movement convergence is occurring to create a movement of movements in the US bringing together scholars and activists, local and global alliances? are those on the ground engaged in the forum process and other movement building efforts?: Focus on the Domestic Workers United and the formation of the Alliance of Domestic Workers.

In a report released by the organization, Domestic Workers United (2006), *Home is Where the Work Is: Inside New York's Domestic Work Industry*, something is quite striking about domestic workers movement building efforts in the era of social forums. The majority of these workers are women of color. They assert that even in the 21st century, "the NLRA guarantees U.S. employees the right to organize, but specifically excludes domestic workers from its definition of "employee" (2006:3). The following are some of the selected facts highlighted in the report:

1. 200,000 domestic workers sustain New York City, its families and homes.
2. Forty-one percent (41%) earn low wages. An additional 26% make wages below the poverty line or below minimum wage. Half of workers work overtime-often more than 50–60 hours a week. Sixty-seven percent don't receive overtime pay.
3. Thirty-three percent (33%) experience verbal or physical abuse or have been made to feel uncomfortable.
4. Nine out of en domestic workers do not receive health insurance from their employers.
5. Forty-six (46%) receive stress at work.

The history of domestic work in the U.S. makes it a topic of extreme importance for understanding movement building in the era of social forums. From 1870–1970, domestic work was "black women's work." Since 1970 this work is being done by largely immigrant women of color (Domestic Workers United 2006:3). Given this history the organizing efforts of Domestic Workers United, involves working closely with the women on the ground connecting them to this history. A highly sophisticated curriculum, "rooted in popular education," is offered over a series of workshops. Core to the curriculum is this history of Black Women in the domestic industry, as well their fight back. The framework of the intersectionality of race, class, and gender in the context of a global economy is the central theory frame. Out of this organizing effort have emerged other successful efforts including: "Unity Housecleaners, a cooperative of domestic workers that sets fixed rates for services." Also worth noting is the work of "The Workplace Project." "This project involves the organizing of low-wage Latino immigrants on Long Island. Unity Housecleaners seeks to fight for better working and living conditions for domestic workers" (Domestic Workers United 2006:18).

To build a movement for social change means that the social forums process must locate itself in the language and practice of such efforts as those of Domestic Workers United. Breaking the logic of splitting theory from practice and locating within emerging struggles on the ground is key. The Domestic Workers Alliance officially formed at the USSF in Atlanta. This is an example, at its best, of the social forum process as a movement building space. Here, the forum became a public testimony and example of the work of the domestic workers in the U.S. The movement converged for the domestic workers at the United States Social Forum in Atlanta, GA. when the first national alliance was formed. This is a crucial link in the chain to advance movement convergence.

Even still a series of thorny questions remain regarding movement building and the social forum process. Despite the success of the Domestic Workers Alliance at the forum, how much, in fact, has the still developing social forum's process touched the lives of everyday women? Has this organizing space extended its reach from thinking through the theoretical positioning of women across lines of gender, race, class, ethnicity, to engagement in movement building for social change? Have its insights been deployed in transforming the lives of working class and poor women who are not organized? These questions on only partially answered, I contend, and are key to crafting a complicated 21st century agenda for social transformation. This, too, remains an unfinished agenda in the social forum process.

It is good to know, however, that the work of Zerai and Salime (2006) tracks the on the ground efforts to use race, class, and gender as an organizing framework. Zerai and Salime give several examples of how this organizing is occurring. Their analysis is relevant to the question of creating a liberatory praxis in the social forum process. Their work raises several important questions and asserts vital findings and observations including:

1. "What are the contributions of black feminism to methods of organizing to end oppression and specifically against war, racism and repression?" (Zerai and Salime 2006:503)
2. "Black feminist organizing is built from women's use of alternative resources, often necessitated by their marginal social locations. The process of embracing alternative strategies developed by women emerging out of their experiences at the margins lead to new solutions." (Zerai and Salime 2006:505).
3. "Black feminist organizers self-consciously employ integrated analysis in their organizational strategies and political discussions." (Zerai and Salime 2006:55).

Zerai and Salime interrogated several cases to make their point. These included analyses of "The Black Radical Congress AntiWar Compaign," the work of The Women of Color Resource Center, INCITE!, and other groups such as SISTER RISE UP!

What they are clear about is that we have a good deal to learn about how these principles can be applied on the ground. They signal that it is necessary for scholars and activists to connect. How scholars might work closely with grassroots women requires vision and making a break with the logic of the academy. At the theoretical center of such work on the ground is intersectionality (Anderson and Collins 1992). What it requires is the practice of movement building. As noted, this praxis is best exemplified in the organizing efforts of Domestic Workers United and the building of the Domestic Workers Alliance.

There are lessons to be learned for a social forum process committed to movement building and convergence from the work of Zerai and Salime, as well as the movement building efforts of the Domestic Workers Alliance.

Lessons Learned:

A. Study carefully the organizing successes and examples of grassroots activists employing a race, class and gender frame, rooted in the

logic of intersectionality. A good example of this work and organizing is the Domestic Workers Alliance.
B. Reclaim a tradition of study and struggle: Study theory and reflect back upon it in practice. Here scholars and activists can work in alliance and solidarity with one another.
C. Reassess leadership within the social forum process and take seriously the push for decentralized models (popular in youth organizing) that have not sought to invest a lot of leadership responsibility in a few key individuals.
D. Strengthen grassroots media and on-line innovations pioneered with internet organizing, but stepping up even more to the use of the internet to inform, publicize, mobilize, and analyze, to complement but not replace face to face organizing.
E. Build a new commitment to the arts and creative action as well as popular and political education are in order, especially in the U.S. context.
F. Give increasing visibility to the environment in political work. Indeed, a new generation of younger activists have introduced important discourses and actions on the environment and the disproportionate consequences of environmental racism for Black and Brown communities. As examples, Van Jones and the work of the Ella Baker Center in Oakland come to mind as does Majora Carter's work with Sustainable South Bronx in N.Y.

Activists must contend with and struggle around the constraints of 501–3ism (INCITE! Women of Color Against Violence 1993) for funding and the imperative to build from the bottom up. This raises, again, the issue of the relationship of scholars to grassroots activists for social change. This question of the relationship between academic insiders, the social and moral responsibilities we have as social insiders, and the implications for the communities we profess to represent must be vetted (Project South 2007). In fact, in the heady movement days of the late 1960s, there was a deep call by scholar-activists for decolonizing social research and seizing research channels to further the cause of Black liberation in this country (Ladner 1973; Project South 2007). Activists can bought into the circle of domination simply by existing within and attempting to negotiate the rules of the U.S. social order and academy. This must be critically interrogated.

In the U.S. the politics of intellectual activism is contained. Indeed, the borning seeds of scholar-activism developed most robustly outside of academia (see the Combahee River Collective Statement and narrative) and reconnecting to that heritage and practice. Breaking with the political logic of academe is, I believe, essential to movement building in this period.

More to the point, the colonization of Black women's and other women of color intellectual lives continue to be rooted in the inequalities of race, class, gender, only weakly abated within and outside the academy (Mohanty 2003 and Oyewummi 1997, Collins 1986; 1990). Our interests are by definition connected to those on the ground, to those women most exploited under the rules of racist capitalist hetereopatriarchy. Fighting back requires not only our scholarship but movement building for social change. This means working in deep relationality with women organizing to create a different social order. Yet, the need for a race, class and gender analysis which has an emancipatory political core is the too often a missing component of feminist intellectuals. We cannot simply think our way out of this. Theory and action cannot be delinked.

The discourses as well as the practice of neoliberalism mean that the language of social justice is denied. The near erasure of a tradition of radical Black thinking and practice in contemporary academic discourse is a reality of the current period (Kelley 2002; James 1997). So, the need is for rootedness in movement building for social change, placing at its center the dismantling of racism, sexism, heterosexism, and classism. Moreover, the contradictory space of US scholar activism evokes complicated questions around the roles of the academy, scholars and activists. So what does that mean for us today? Not only that we need a social forum process that gives visibility and voice to the history and experiences of scholars and activists working on the ground together in social forums, but also to the need struggle with the thorny issues of: Whose interests are served by social forums? Whose voice? Who is at the center of organizing and struggle? These are additional questions that bedevil the development of a principled movement building effort in the social forum process. So where might we begin?

Conclusion

This is a moment of rapacious transnational capital, of intense privatization and the global exploitation of human and material resources. The worlds of the dispossessed of the U.S., Africa and the African diaspora are in the vortex of these realities, facing intense economic, political, and cultural vulnerability. It is a moment in which wealth is extremely concentrated within the U.S. and globally. The rich, indeed, have gotten much richer. Nonetheless, it is a moment of extreme capitalist crisis. Financial speculation and finance capital globally has brought the system to their knees. It is also a moment of complicated racial/ethnic realities and gender divides. The immigration issue looms large in the context of the need to build alliances for movement. Nevertheless, it is also a moment of talk-speak, act up, youth in resistance—youth and not so young taking to the streets: Atlanta, GA for the first ever USSF, fighting for Katrina survivors and the right to return, confronting the murder of Sean Bell and the police face of state terrorism, facing new images of nooses. Indeed, tens of thousands demand redress, accountability. How to make common cause with the newly mobilized yet participate in deeper level movement building must be on the social forum radar.

It is a gendered moment—with women all over the world too often exploited and impoverished. The U.S. is no exception. These global realities have different gendered consequences for men and women. We've witnessed some of the most vicious attacks on Black women— our lives, our children in twenty first century United States. Again we must conjure up the vision of Katrina. The state and media attacks were especially hard—as black babies and elders died. The racist capitalist state did not respond. Even before Katrina, mortality and poverty rates in New Orleans were untenable.

Nonetheless if we lift up women, women are taking charge, claiming leadership and organizing for social change. The Domestic Workers Union is a case in point. Women across borders represent a tidewater of movement building possibilities. Thus the next decade of the social forum process requires nothing less than a reaffirmation of our radical women of color feminist roots, helping to build radical feminist sensibilities within our communities. This is an imperative but unfinished agenda in the social forum process.

Essentially, the social foro are sites of connection and struggle for a new society, a society free of racism, classism, sexism, and heterosexism. But the fight back, the social transformation must encompass a vision untried in human history: struggling against these oppressions in deep relationship to one another. Many have resisted along racial lines. Some of us have struggled along class lines. Others have struggled along race and class lines. In the final analysis our practice must be rooted in an intersectional vision which informs our vision of a new society. Indeed, this period encompassing the intense internationalization of capital represents a new moment for peoples of the world: to connect, to organize to educate, to imagine. This is the promise of the social forum process in this movement building moment.

In closing, the central challenge for the social forum process is to connect struggles of domestic workers with those of neocolonized nations such as Guadeloupe. The means building an emancipatory movement that understands a complicated global economy while articulating its interrelationality in gender, sexuality and race. Indeed, transforming transnational heteropatriarchal white supremacist capitalism must be at the center of our theory and practice. In a movement for social transformation, we simply cannot be race, gender and class reductionist but employ a mediated understanding of the deep interrelationality of class, gender, sexuality, race, nation under conditions of twenty first century transnationalism. This is a lesson the social forum process is still trying to perfect. This is unfinished social forum business.

A BUNCH OF CRIMINALS? ANALYZING POLITICAL ARMED VIOLENCE AS A SOCIAL PRODUCTION PROCESS

Simon Sottsas

Introduction

'Freedom Fighters', 'Terrorists', 'Rebels'—the list of labels for people struggling against political regimes in power is long, including different assumptions about the legitimacy of armed violent resistance. However, after the end of the East-West-conflict, peace and conflict studies seemed to have surpassed the discussion; the term freedom fighter is history, and since 9/11 the label 'terrorists' has become a broadly used term. One could guess several reason for this stronger academic uniformity to accept governments' legitimacy, so for example a liberal hegemony without global competition between political systems, or an improved knowledge on the brutal violence of revolutionary experiments.

Further arguments can be gained from the dimension conflict scientists have been concentrating on during the last years, the economical aspect of insurgency violence. Two debates structured the field: 1. the 'greed debate', focusing on motivation and possibilities of individuals to participate in violence; and 2. the 'New Wars debate', accounting for self-centric, corrupt war actors in the globalized 21st century. Both accounts base their explanations of rebels' behavior on neo-classical economic assumptions. What is the consequence? Rebel groups are either analyzed as Malthusian greedy poor who use their little value of life to enter the market of violence, or as scrupulous elites who misuse the grievances of people for their own agenda. Both accounts have seemingly unmasked the (pretending) idealistic fighters, representative for their social constituency, as a bunch of criminals—supporting the argument of the administrations crushing insurgencies in Afghanistan, Chechnya, Colombia, Palestine, Tibet, and elsewhere (Ballentine/Nitzschke 2003).

Thereby peace and conflict studies has been detached from broader studies on structural violence (Senghaas 1977), focusing strongly on direct violence (Egbert et al. 2005). This has let to a step-by-step militarization of 'problem-solving' (Cox 1981) peace and conflict studies. In consequence humanitarian interventions, for example, have become a quite unquestioned mean to stabilize conflicts. Critical positions remain voiceless in light of the astonishing brutality of war crimes conducted by rebel groups. Pictures on CNN of massacred children undermine critique on the mentioned 'humanitarian interventions' against the 'criminals' completely.[1]

My overall research objective is to contribute to a re-amalgamation of segregated research strands into a comprehensive socioeconomic analysis. The attempt of this paper is to sketch a research framework, which could function as a first bridge between the insights into dynamics of direct *and* structural violence. It is based on a historical-materialist approach, elaborated by Antonio Gramsci for the analysis of the post-World-War-I situation in Italy and adapted by international political economists for analyzing the dynamics of global orders during the last centuries.

The paper will start with two short accounts on the state-of-the art in peace and conflict studies as well as in structural violence studies and then proceed by introducing some older progressive accounts of revolutionary violence, which can inform the debate further. The next section will outline the assumptions and the basic concepts of the historical-materialist approach. In the fourth section specific aspects of the overall framework will be reworked to adapt to the needs of an analysis of violent conflicts in post/neo-colonial areas. A summary and an outlook will conclude the paper.

The Political Economy of Resistance

The end of the Soviet Union led to the expectation of a final end of challenges to a liberal world order (Fukuyama 1992). However, soon shocking massacres in the civil wars of Rwanda, Yugoslavia, and Somalia crushed the vision of a near global peace to pieces; not to forget the continuing struggles in Colombia, Afghanistan, Lebanon, and elsewhere. Conflict research has been deprived of its theory of

---

[1] Even though one should not fail to notice that these crimes are often not far from the brutality of their internationally recognized adversaries. And indeed, in terms of human suffering, there is no difference between physical violence conducted by one or the other actor.

proxy-wars and new explanations entered the scientific vacuum. It did not take long to find some people explaining the 'mediaeval violence' as the consequence of ancient hatreds between century-old ethnically constituted groups of people (Kaplan 1993). Huntington (1993; 1996) conquered the stage; the academic as well as the journalistic, and consequently the public. Scholars deconstructed the simplistic, sometimes racist, and, in a series of points, simply false accounts of conflicts (Oberschall 2000; Gilley 2004; Brubaker 2004). However, they did not answer the needs of journalism and above all politics for explanations to act upon.

What followed was a more grounded debate of the post-Cold-war-era. Jean and Rufin published an edited book named 'Économie des guerres civiles' (1996) and emphasized the key role of the economy of war in civil wars, outlining different forms of organization and requirements. A series of case studies in the volume support their argument that material constraints and possibilities matter in dynamics of violence. However, they highlighted that they just wanted to add a forgotten aspect of violent conflicts to the debate. This self-constrain has been mostly overlooked by works of a World Bank research group, who started in 1999 with a series of publications (Collier/Hoeffler 1998, 2002, 2004; Collier 1999). They reduced civil wars to a simple Malthusian individual choice of the greedy single poor to use violence as a bargaining mean, even though later they stepped back by replacing motivation by possibilities. Here, too, a series of critiques where responding, forming the 'greed vs. grievance debate' (Cramer 2002; Ballentine/Nitzschke 2003). Despite the shortcomings of this debate, it was a big step further to surpass the limited 'clash-of-civilizations-debate', emphasizing the influence of economic factors and its development on the dynamics of violence, and bringing policy-possibilities back in.

A third debate mixed both accounts into a new category, claiming the development of 'New Wars'. Its groundbreaking exponent is Mary Kaldor. She places economic motivations in a more comprehensive explanation model of a new type of organized violence which is characterized by the blurring between war, (globally connected) organized crime, and massive human rights abuses. Elites with particular interests—encompassing all actors using direct violence—cooperate by using a form of identity politics to suppress a multicultural civil society for their own egoistic gains. These new wars are embedded in a complex network of transnational relations in the context of globalization;

thus Kaldor brings the global system back into the study of local violence (Kaldor 1999).

However, as mentioned, what is striking in this scientific development is the modest critical attention, which these leading research frameworks give to neo-classical micro-economic assumptions of the rationally, self-centric deciding individual in a given global environment (see Cramer 2002). Nonetheless, contemporary studies produced helpful insights. On the one hand there are exceptions from the neo-classical trend with either a sociological focus (Fricke 2000) or a historical focus (Tilly 1990; Abbink et al. 2003) on the relation between violence and society structures. On the other hand, strongly empirically based approaches offer interesting hints. They regard war economies and business actors in conflicts (Jean/Rufin 1996; Keen 1998; Andreas 2004a+b), explore links between group violence, (in)security and ideology (Oberschall 2000; Kaufman 2001; Carmichael 2005), and analyze forms of conflict-related institutional rule outside formal state structures and its profiteers (Mehler 2003; Reno 2003; Leander 2003; Schlichte 2004; Mehlum 2006).

Explicitly progressive research meanwhile focused on the distortions of world order, pointing at globalization and neo-liberal hegemony. The most famous comprehensive theory regarding structural violence is Wallerstein's World System Theory (2000), outlining a system of concentric circles, where the center is ruling on and gaining from the periphery. However, it has been much criticized for being to simplistic and above all too static.

A more historical and dynamic approach was presented by Robert Cox, former chief of the International Labor Organization and afterwards scholar at Columbia University (NYC) as well as at York University (Toronto). Using the works of Antonio Gramsci—already present in (post/neo-)colonial and cultural studies (Hall 1986)—he elaborated a political-economy analysis of world orders over the last two-hundred years. Analyzing the rise and fall of a 'pax Britannica' before World War I, followed by the 'pax Americana' after World War II, he concluded that a new world order after the end of the Bretton Woods system has still not been established. What followed has been a broad research on the (ambiguous) new hegemony of Neo-liberalism and a possibly new Western hegemony (Gill 1993) along the development of 'transnational classes' (van der Pijl 1998) with first accounts on globalization and the implementation of this hegemony in the Global South (Sassoon 2001; Morton 2002, 2007).

However, critics pointed at a 'soft orientalism' (Pasha 2005) of these Neo-Gramscian accounts, lacking a differentiated analysis of the situation in post/neo-colonial settings, overstating the role of consent and understating or romanticizing the activity of the subaltern movements. Exceptions are few (Augelli/Murphy 1988; Morton 2002), with some authors just using parts of Gramsci's concepts (Fatton 1984, Hanifi 2004, Lecocq 2004; Borg 2001). Nonetheless, the concept seems to be fruitful in a world strongly shaped by OECD-powers and there exists a sophisticated conceptual and methodological base where to start from, discussed in the next section.[2]

What can help to combine the insights from contemporary peace and conflict studies and broader progressive accounts on world order are older approaches to revolutionary violence. Frantz Fanon highlighted the importance of violence in the revolutionary struggle against the violence of colonial suppressors. While for example the Leninist account of violence was focusing on the tactical needs of revolutionary struggle (Lenin 1905, 1916a), Fanon emphasized three arguments about the deep effect of resisting violence on the masses: "It [violence] liberates the colonialized from his inferiority complex"; it has furthermore a democratizing effect, as "the liberation [has been] the cause of all and every single one"; and finally this leads to the possibility of surpassing the colonial segregation of people in a genuine form of nation building (Fanon 1961: 76). This historical background in mind, critical peace and conflict studies in European scientific institutions of the 1960s and '70s countered the state centric view of the scholars at the beginning of the Cold War (Senghaas ed. 1977), with its most radical exponents claiming for revolutionary conflict research (Dencik 1977). It retakes the critique on the idealistic conception of harmony (of interests) (Carr 1940) and imperialism (Lenin 1916b) and claims for a more differentiated notion of violence (Dencik 1977: 256), recognizing its structural dimension (Galtung 1977), i.e. structural violence oppresses post-colonial countries even after formal independence and the withdrawal of colonialist troops.

---

[2] This paper will focus on the concepts useful for the research question. For a comprehensive introduction on this strand of historical-materialist theory in International Political Economy research, cp. Cox 1986, Gill 1993; Morton 2007.

Combining empirical and analytical insights from these strands
with caution on several theoretical shortcomings of a state-of-the art,
we can highlight that:

- Structural violence still dominates world order (Wood 1995;
  Sassoon 2001; Morton 2007)—based not just on military oppression
  but on a (crumbling) neo-liberal consent on human development
  (van Apeldoorn 2002)—which makes a world of peace impossible
  (Dencik 1977);
- Economic changes play a key role on the usage and the dynamics
  of direct violence (Fricke 2000; Collier 2002); however, they are not
  sufficient to explain them, as ideas (Kaufmann 2001) and institutions (Mehlum 2006) as well have their role;
- There are strong links between global and local developments.
  Transformation of forms of capitalism change local society structures via changing production chains and markets. They include
  social and institutional integration (Fricke 2000; Morton 2003). This
  encompasses the field of violence including foreign state interventions and (transnational) movements and ideologies of resistance,
  too (Kaldor 1999; Andreas 2004b);
- Organized direct violence needs requisites; in financial as well as in
  skill and organizational terms (Jean/Rufin 1996; Collier 2002);
- Direct violence as well as its requirements alter power structures,
  they can democratize politics as well as they can favor certain actors
  with capacities for the conduction of violence (Fanon 1961; Fricke
  2000; Mehler 2003, Reno 2003, Andreas 2004a); and
- Direct violence integrates social groups along different mechanisms,
  from the consciousness of a common struggle, the dependence of
  protection, to forced integration (Fanon 1961; Kaufmann 2001;
  Oberschall 2000)—as well as it segregates whole groups with its
  peak in genocide (Carmichael 2005).

These insights[3] should be accounted for when trying to elaborate a
research framework which can merge accounts on structural and direct
violence in the 21st century. This framework should exceed a mere

---

[3] The insights are not part of the framework but outline just questions which the
framework has to consider. In a second project they have to be reproved for the current historical situation after the framework is elaborated.

eclectic accumulation of explanations. The comprehensive attempts of critical peace and conflict studies in the 1970s (Senghaas 1977) form a good role model, even within a different historical global setting.

The next two sections will propose a heuristic framework to integrate dynamics of direct violence in a broad analysis of social conflict, following a historical-materialist ontology and consequently epistemology.

The Base of a Heuristic Framework

The concept proposed here has to go a long way, from the European struggles of the 19th and beginning 20th century over global analysis of the international political economy back down to the grounds of transnational politics in post/neo-colonial countries. Its long history is related to scholars like Machiavelli (1513) and Marx (1867, 1845, 1852). In the current debate, next to the classics, insights are taken above all from Antonio Gramsci's Prison Notebooks (1929–35), a collection of thoughts written in fascist custody. The historical circumstances of Gramsci's work are thereby the key to interpret his fragmented notes, which were never merged to a comprehensive text because of the premature death of the author. He operated in Italy in the aftermath of the Soviet Revolution. In the young, but never integrated nation, the workers in the Northern part of the country failed to overcome the bourgeois rule, which fled into a fascist coalition with the peasants of the South and smashed progressive-revolutionary attempts. Being an active agitator for the progressive cause in the Italian communist party, he fulfilled his claim for a 'theory of praxis' by researching the dynamics of revolutionary struggle, where he took part in himself—a classic instance of action research.

Historical-materialist discussions normally have to start by arguing about 'vulgar materialism', the label for the simplistic formulas 'structure determines superstructure; economics determine politics' which where heavily criticized by Gramsci (2001: Q6 §9)[4] as well as by Marx (1845: 533 ff.). These formulas incorporate the central misunderstanding

---

[4] Gramsci will mostly be quoted from the critical comprehensive edition of the 'Quaderni del Carcere' (2001) of the Roman Gramsci Institute in Italian language. To bypass the language obstacle, I will quote using the number of the single 'Quaderno' (Q—in chronological order) and the—by Gramsci numerated—Paragraph (§): "Gramsci QX §Y". This should help to find the quotes either in the Italian original as well as in the translated versions.

of a mainstream review of progressive theory, categorizing Marxism as the simple materialist opposite of an idealist liberal conception.

Meanwhile, historical-materialist approaches use dialectics as their main methodological tool. Dialectics means, that there is an underlying relation between thesis and antithesis that leads to the synthesis, which is more than just the sum of the firsts. It is therefore different from the simple continuum between two opposites, which assumes a zero-sum game, i.e. the power of one opposite would weaken the other. The two opposites *constitute* each other and just the existence of the thesis empowers the antithesis. In other words, dialectics is the method to understand the "unity within distinction" of human history (Hoffman 1984: 40).

The first application of this insight has to be on the relation between structure and agency. A historical-materialist approach is based on the understanding that structures are social constructions, which constitute, i.e. constrain and engender, human action (see Marx 1844: 115). This holds true for individuals and collective actors (see Bieler and Morton 2001) and applies as well to the relation between nature and men. To supersede the question which is first, thesis or antithesis, the way out is an understanding of social structures as the outcome of an ongoing (re)*production*[5] of social relations (see Wood 1995).

This, of course, can and has to be applied to the relation between structure and superstructure, too. Neither dominate ideas the material world in a metaphysical way; nor determines the material situation ideas, neglecting human will. However, they are not separated and autonomous, too, but from a dialectical understanding strongly interlinked. They are constantly formed by each other in the above mentioned (re)production process.

Focusing on the research objective, we will now face the link between power and resistance in society. Here, too, we can start with a vulgar approach; it would state, that in a class society there exists a hierarchy where the classes on the top are suppressing the classes at the bottom by means of physical violence, expressed by the police, and fraud, expressed by ideology. Thus, the state is regarded as the instrument of the ruling class. The subaltern classes are passive as long as they do not capture power through a revolution. This determinist concept,

---

[5] It is important not to confuse this broad notion of social (re)production with pure economic production. The first does include the second, but not vice-versa.

however, says little on the historical process of resistance and of the production of strength to conduct a revolution.

Gramsci—and previously Lenin in his "Two tactics of Social Democracy" (1905)—widened the concept of ruling by the term *supremacy*.[6] Supremacy is the ruling of man on man by two components: 1) coercion and 2) consent. While coercion is the imposition of a social system on humans against their will, consent is the conscious or unconscious approval of it by them. In political processes, both components are present and strongly interlinked in a dialectic way, i.e. they constitute each other. A ruling power then "dominates adversary groups, which tends to »liquidate« or to *overrule*, yet by armed force, and *leads* kin and allied groups" (Gramsci 2001: Q6 §24, emphasis added).

Combined with the previous discussion on the dialectical relation between material and ideal structures, we can outline the concept of a *historical bloc*. A historical bloc is defined as an *accorded* relation between a material base and ideas, which has been materialized in political institutions. Political institutions encompass the narrow state, parliament, executive authorities, etc., as well as the wider state, including churches, media, unions, etc. The historical bloc is based on a comprehensive consent between social groups with coercion as a means to protect this hegemonic system against adversaries (Cox 1981). The existence and structure of *social groups* are the reversed side of the coin of the structures of material base, ideas, and institutions. Both sides are the result of constant social (re)production, including political struggle. Therefore the approach does not think of *fixed* classes out of the economic production process, but of more or less *fluid* social groups out of the *social* (re)production process. However, their constituency can be stabilized by stabilizing the (re)production process.

This stability of society structures results out of an organic, i.e. consistently grown, system based on the ability of the ruling social groups to *universalize* their own interests, and thereby *integrating* subordinate social groups. Gramsci traces the development of social systems out of particularistic interests, starting from corporatist interests, to class interests and finally universal—i.e. in his historical setting national—concepts (Gramsci 2001: Q13 §17). Every step does alter the material, ideal, and institutional setting. Thereby, it is more than just a bargained

---

[6] As stated before, the following paragraphs will fall short on a comprehensive introduction into these concepts. Please refer to the mentioned standard literature.

compromise; to be stable it is required to be the common understanding of a *right* solution, i.e. it will be a *synthesis* of interests, embedded
in peoples' point of view.[7]

Therefore, a historical bloc can be understood as the consequence
of ongoing struggles between the subordinate and the ruling social
groups in the production of a social system, which tries to integrate as
many groups as needed to stabilize it.[8]

However, as the historical bloc is the result of an *ongoing* social production, every considered aspect keeps on *changing* over time, either
along unconscious dynamics of structures or along intended human
action. The same applies to the other side of the coin; the *reproduction* of existing structures, too, is the result of intended conservative
human action and unconscious path dependences.

Now, when progressive production is stronger than conservative
reproduction, than the formerly concerted historical bloc can dwindle
into *crisis*. The hierarchical system of social groups is no longer seen
as legitimate along a universal interest, and with it material base, ideas,
and institutions are questioned. The possibility of counter-hegemonial
struggle is at its peak (Gramsci 2001: Q13 §17), and different social
groups can try to pursuing their own hegemonial efforts while counter-
ing others, i.e. they have a twofold task: 1) to destruct rival hegemonial
projects and 2) to construct one's own on the way into a revolutionary
historical bloc.

Taking these notions as base of the framework to elaborate, and
considering the above mentioned insights and gaps of the contemporary state-of-the art, we have to expand our understanding and adapt
the approach on the following dimensions:

• the link between global and local developments
• integration *and* segregation of social groups in conflicts

---

[7] Here, the concept provides a useful link to Bourdieu's notion of 'habitus' (1970:
125), which should be traced in an own project.

[8] Therefore, the introduction of worker's rights, the establishment of public schools
and bread subsidies could be seen as fraud as they blur the ongoing hierarchies.
However, these processes are 'real', people can eat more, and benefit from
higher education. Rejecting these progresses would mean neglecting the power of the
subaltern pressure. So the consequences can be twofold: they can support the hegemonial system by obscuring the class hierarchy or they can support anti-hegemonial
struggles by highlighting the power of the subalterns.

- the link between consent and coercion in (post/neo)colonial situations
- the dynamics of a revolution regarding the (requirements of the) production of violence

Theory Transfer

The approach used has its origins in the analysis to support the struggle of Italian progressives in the Italian nation state. The International Political Economy stuck to this nation based concept, even though Cox introduces three levels of action, "social forces", "forms of states" and "world orders" (Cox 1998: 47). Every world order in Cox' historical analysis is bound to a nation state, which exports its hegemonial system to other countries and remains the center of this world order—Britain in the first phase of liberal capitalism, the United States in the Fordist post-World-War-II era. This just changes slightly with an OECD-based transnational class, which forces its will upon the rest of the world (van Apeldoorn 2002). Transferring the theory to analyze violent conflicts in post/neo-colonial countries this is not sufficient.

Now, Gramsci as well as the Neo-Gramscians recognize from different perspectives links between global and local development along the imposition of a world order. These processes of globalization are not simply a replacement of existing structures in the targeted regions. Gramsci analyses the implementation of a US-American Fordist hegemony in a specific Italian setting of the beginning 20th century and Neo-Gramscians analyze neo-colonial impositions in the Global South (Fatton 1984; Sassoon 2001; Abrahamsen 1997). Both use the term of "Passive Revolution" to describe a process, where in a historical fragile situation a social system is imposed on a nation, which is not the result of the organic development of the nation itself. Passivity characterizes a revolution from above or outside, where the leading but fading national classes adopt (with the help of outside forces) a new historical bloc—new economic structures, new ideas, new institutions—, while trying to preserve and restore their power, even though their historical role has been overcome. However, albeit this approach recognizes, that local circumstances have an influence on the local historical bloc, it remains unidirectional and thus Eurocentric. The struggle of subalterns is shaped by world order but world order is not shaped by the struggle of the subaltern. This neglects the insights from (post/neo-)colonialism research, emphasizing the key role, (post/neo-)colonialism has played in the development of the Western world (Fanon 1961; Loomba 1998).

To capture this dimension, the process of globalization has to be analyzed as the relational production process by hegemonial and counter-hegemonial *struggles*, encompassing the mutual influences of local and global developments.

The second aspect on local-global relations touches the question on territory and territorially defined concepts. Empirical accounts on transnational production processes as well as white holes of globalizations emphasize that a pure territorially defined hierarchy of levels is not feasible. Social structures span over national borders, from multinational production chains, regional resistance ideologies to globally acting NGOs. On the other hand they leave parts inside a national territory untouched as might happen for subsistence farmers or people behind the walls of slums in mega-cities.

This leads to the suggestion to talk about social spaces instead of levels. Fluid like a historical bloc, a space can be formed and stabilized as a historical entity. We can analyze how spaces integrate or segregate by changing social production relations. From an analytical perspective, for example, one could talk about the integration of isolated people when subsistence farmers switch to cash crops or the segregation to isolation when vice versa. The firing of state employees because of wrong ethnic ties would be a further example of segregation. From an ontological point of view, even micro-cosmoses already form a space by simple production processes (Cox 1981). This should not be overlooked, even if for practical reasons one starts his or her analysis on a broader range. Integration and segregation mirror new social relations, therefore forming newly defined social spaces.

So where is the difference between the integration of a historical bloc and the integration of social spaces? The difference lies in the twofold way of integration *and segregation*. Gramsci was concerned how to integrate the peasants of the South with the peasants of the North, while the bourgeoisie would fade and be merged into the new society. But little has been written about the segregation of the bourgeoisie from a proletarian hegemony during the revolutionary struggle. Furthermore, it was a struggle on roles of people; the material segregation of people has not been intended. However, in all historical and contemporary violent struggles, physical segregation of parties from one another is a key requisite to fight each other; and worse, the physical integrity of a territorially defined human collective, not doubted by the socialist Italian revolutionaries, is not an accepted given as has been shown by different forms and levels of genocide all over the world.

Consequently while a historical bloc tries to integrate all units which are merged by mutual relations, a social space can be divided into further historical blocs while keeping some form of hostile relation to other social spaces. Thus, already just the existence of the other spaces constitutes an ongoing relation which shapes the inner production process. This is crucial for the analysis of a conflict, which is constituted by the existence of *the other* and the relation between 'we' and 'them'.

Therefore additionally to processes of integration we have to analyze the relations between forms of integration inside social spaces *and* segregation processes against other social spaces during conflicts. The dynamics of the mutual relations between segregated groups have to be traced in every mentioned component of a social totality as well as their essential influence in constituting historical blocs inside the social groups. Looting, interrupted trade, war expenditures, etc. for example cover the material dimension; ethnicity, perceived threats to the group, histories of hate, etc. the dimension of ideas; and the military, martial law, war councils etc. the dimension of institutions.

But before we reach the point of analyzing the conduct of violent conflicts, we have to face the question on where to start from, regarding the usage of violence in social life. Both, Gramsci and the Neo-Gramscians—even when afterwards focusing on hegemonial crises—start with a hegemonial situation, which is based on an overall consent, stabilized by a civil society, where coercive institutions just protect the state against a minority. Gramsci analyses Italy as a Western European country, which, in contrast to Lenin's pre-revolutionary Russia, is based on a (weak) hegemony supported by liberal and conservative intellectuals and media as well as the influential Catholic Church. They form a security belt around the narrow state institutions, preventing a possible success by direct violence like the Russian Bolsheviks have had in taking power in 1917. Thus, progressive movements are forced to intensify their efforts in the *war of position*, i.e. destroying the religious-liberal hegemonial consent and creating a counter-hegemonial consent, embedded in the coalition of the farm-hands of the South and the workers of the North. The Neo-Gramscians focus on similar constellations, analyzing the consent resulting from different forms of liberal capitalism. They look for these constellations either in world order systems (Cox 1998), transnational classes (van der Pijl 1998) or the European Union (van Apeldoorn 2002) after Fordist American hegemony.

Turning the focus on colonial and post-colonial situations requires an adjustment, as the role of force is more than the deviation from the hegemonial norm; it is a key feature of colonial societies segregating a society into different social spaces and preventing a collective nation (Fanon 1961). Different from the analysis of capitalist hegemony, two phenomena seem to be central. On the one hand, overall consent and structural constraints did not replace the overwhelming usage of direct violence. On the other hand, against the liberal integration of all parts of society into a common national hegemony, 'divide et impera' has been a key feature of colonial rule.

In our analysis we have to consider the influence of this pre-war violence and the missing consensual structures on the dynamics of violence. This should not be mistaken with the blurring essentialist term of a 'culture of violence', but the influences have to be traced in all three analytical components, material base, ideas, and institutions. This can encompass slavery, violence as an accepted bargaining mean, or strong private and public military institutions.

The fourth dimension which has to be analyzed more specified is the revolutionary process itself. In progressive revolutionary theories it is mostly analyzed along fall and rise as two different categories. However, from a dialectical point of view, supported by empirical accounts, there exists a relationship between those two that exceeds a simple replacement. The revolutionary process and the means of revolution are not external to the destruction and construction of historical blocs. In consequence, revolutions do not just succeed or fail. A series of revolutions from the USSR to the Korea PDR to Democratic Kampuchea have been won in military and judicial terms. But regarding the benchmark of a more democratic progressive regime as well as a stabilized new hegemony, they mostly have failed. However, it is not of interest to discuss whether a hegemonial project wins or fails—which from a non-idealistic perspective is a sense- and useless question. Interesting is, how the dynamics of revolutions are inscribed into the development of a society, and its subjects. To address this question, it is necessary to differentiate the production process of a revolution analyzed along Gramsci as a combination of the 'war of position' (cp.

above) and the 'war of maneuver', i.e. the physical destruction of the institutions of force of the former regime; and capture the dialectical relationship between the final destruction of the old ruling system and the establishment of a new hegemony.

For example Marx and Engels (1848) as well as Gramsci (1926) suggested the necessary integration of social groups to form a powerful coalition against the ruling classes. The consequences of these alliances for the revolutionary process have to be analyzed. So Kepel (2002) emphasized that coalitions of the Iranian revolutionaries with the urban traders where the key for the Islamic ideology ruling the revolution, while socialist ideas were extorted—with the liquidation of its proponents; Schmidinger (2004) discussed the coalition policy of the Sudan workers' movement with bourgeois nationalist, which at the end was responsible for their liquidation by their allies; and Andreas (2004a) examined the integration of Sarajevo's organized crime and its influence on Bosnian resistance, however, showing that it is possible to reverse war-time power-relations by consequently replacing them with alternative structures as soon as they are available.

Therefore it is necessary to analyze, which actions have been taken by the different parties of the revolutionary conflict in the context of historical structures and how these actions shaped the future, i.e. how did they alter material base, ideas, and institutions inside the envisaged constituency?

Conclusion

The paper started with the question on the relation between political—generally regarded as idealistic—and private—generally regarded as economic—conflict factors. Unsatisfied with this categorical framework, I argued for a more integrated approach, recognizing the mutual and diverse impacts of these factors onto the dynamics of violent conflicts. At the same time an empiricist approach as well as a concentration on small scale mechanisms should be avoided. The first does not recognize horizontal similarities between conflicts around the world. The second misses to recognize the vertical relations between developments on a local, national *as well as* global level.

Therefore the aim is to analyze violent conflicts as a social phenomenon embedded in a historical process of human development. The paper proposed a historical-materialist approach to form a heuristic framework, based on a dialectical methodology, which helps to analyze social structures. This can be done by analyzing their alterations as a consequence of human actions, which again are shaped by structures.

Analytically it differentiates these structures along a material base, social ideas, and institutions, mirrored by a setting of related social groups, both of them consequence of an ongoing social production process. They can be stabilized along the universalizing of ruling interests to a hegemonic consent, creating a historical bloc. However, it might dwindle into crisis, which opens the opportunity for a struggle for a new historical bloc. Its establishment, however, is not determined by history and ruling powers might fight for the re-establishment of the former, even by agreeing on small adaptations of the social structure.

To capture the characteristics of a manifested conflict, two broad strategies can be analyzed. A war of position as well as a war of maneuver will be fought. However, both wars are not transitional and external, but intrinsic to the whole revolutionary process, thus shaped by the historical setting as well as they shape the outcome of its struggle. Thereby we have to consider the key role of violence in the specific history of (post)colonial areas. Furthermore, this revolutionary social production process does not just force the integration of people into the historical bloc, but the segregation of adversaries into diverse social spaces. Thus it is necessary to analyze these (becoming) social spaces as well as their mutual relations, which—even though hostile—they still have.

This helps furthermore to expand the territorially defined term of levels (local, national, global), that misses to account for transnational developments and white spots on the world map. Thus we can analyze the integration of these conflict production processes into the development of global hegemonial project(s).

The proposed framework supports the comment, that economic factors are *not* a new feature of contemporary struggles (Daase 2003). The resulting general hypothesis is that particular interests of rebels in a violent struggle are the necessary results of a labor division in the specific *social production process of political armed violence*. Empirically there has to be investigated which particular interests in struggles on the local level are favored by contemporary forms of production processes of violence and its relations to the production processes of global human development. Thus we should be able to analyze how sociopolitical struggles are threatened to be corrupted and how these developments can be handled.

What is necessary is further work on the operationalization to combine the mechanism-insights of contemporary violence research and broader social analysis. The result should be a better understanding of ongoing violence and possibilities to overcome structures of violence in a progressive and therefore sustainable rather than an oppressive way.

PART II

CONTRADICTIONS AND RESISTANCE IN MEXICO

FIFTEEN YEARS OF NAFTA: THE IMPACT ON RURAL MEXICO

Irma Lorena Acosta Reveles

Introduction

The evolution of Mexican society over the last fifteen years cannot be fully understood without making reference to the discourse of globalization, neoliberal politics, and the North American Free Trade Agreement (NAFTA) in particular. This agreement that governs trade relations between Mexico, the United States and Canada since January of 1994 constitutes a paradigm insofar as it is serves as a juridical-political instrument that institutionally reinforces pre-existing trade relations between developed and underdeveloped countries under extremely asymmetrical conditions. It is probably in the rural areas of Mexico where its effects have been most strongly felt given the strong ties of these regions to agriculture, one of the sectors most impacted by structural adjustment and the opening of borders.

In accordance with the demands of capitalist development and echoing the postulates of neoliberalism, it was from the early years of the 1980s that the Mexican government has assumed that the country could best advance towards economic growth and development by riding on the crest of increasing globalization. This process corresponds to the introduction of the agroexport model in Latin America that began during the decade of the 1970s (Acosta Reveles 2006). It was then that the agricultural and livestock sector began to adjust its priorities and sectoral strategies to function in the global market.

The process of economic restructuration that began back in the 1970s implied the tightening of ties with those clients and providers closest to the Mexican nation by way of multilateral trade agreements. It was through such agreements that it was hoped to: a) multiply and expand markets; b) make international transactions more orderly and regular; c) operate in a context of institutional certainty; and by implication, d) obtain notable macroeconomic and social benefits.

By the onset of 2008, Mexico had signed twelve commercial trade pacts with forty-four countries and had entered into the World Trade

Organization (WTO).[1] But without doubt, the most important move to date has been that of the NAFTA. More than fifteen years after it entered into force, no one can deny its impact on the evolution of Mexican society in many aspects of social life. Nevertheless I shall limit this discussion to demonstrate its impact on the income of the rural population and on agricultural employment. Brief mention will also be made of the crisis in food security.

Commercial Liberalization of Agriculture and Livestock

We should first remember that the content of NAFTA[2] that directly concerns the rural sector is essentially that which governs all agricultural trade between the United States, Canada and Mexico as of 1994.

As a general principle, the text of NAFTA in Part II, Chapter 7, Section A, states that "the Parties shall work together to improve access to their respective markets through the reduction or elimination of import barriers to trade between them in agricultural goods" (NAFTA 1994). In directing itself to the commitment to give preferential access to agricultural and livestock goods of the pacting parties with respect to products originating from other nations, the document specified that from the date on which the agreement entered into force, all non-tariff barriers would be immediately abolished while tariff protections would be gradually reduced.

On the other hand, it was recognized that each country offered products that were more sensitive to competition, prompting an agreement to concede specified grace periods for reducing their corresponding tariffs in accordance with a schedule spelled out over three five-year periods. From there, it can be seen that Mexico would formally retain a longer period than that of its partners in order to adapt to the conditions of free trade. Mexico would likewise have the right to fix ceiling quotas on tax-free imports on products considered strategic or extremely vulnerable to competition. Among the products that war-

---

[1] Mexico had ratified its adhesion to the General Agreement on Tariffs and Trade (GATT), a trade agreement that in 1995 had become transformed into the World Trade Organization (WTO) and which presently has 153 member countries.

[2] The complete text of this agreement is available at: www.international.gc.ca/trade -agreements-accords-commerciaux/agr-acc/nafta-alena/texte/index.aspx?lang =en&menu_id=34&menu=R (Viewed 5/5/2009).

ranted this delay to complete liberalization were corn and beans. At the end of fifteen years, the protective tariff mechanisms would end for all three countries, by which time access to their respective markets would be unrestricted.

From the Mexican perspective, this lapse seemed sufficient to provide for a transition in the rural sector. It would give time to consolidate internal political reforms, attract foreign investments in order to inject greater capital into the agrarian sphere, build greater economies of scale and establish an institutional framework for greater mobility of the principle factors of production.

It is worth pointing out that prior to NAFTA, the Mexican agrarian market had already advanced towards the dismantling of the protectionist regime that had been in place in preceding decades. With the incorporation of Mexico into the General Agreement on Tariffs and Trade (GATT), the prior system of import allowances had been replaced by a flexible tariff regime, resulting in an average level of tariffs that had declined from 24.8% in 1985 to 12.5% by the early years of the 1990s (Calva 1996: 2). By 1991, import licenses had also been eliminated except for basic products such as corn, beans, powdered milk, eggs and poultry.

In this sense, NAFTA cannot be considered strictly speaking as the watershed event in terms of commercial liberalization, even if did constitute a decisive step forward in liberalizing Mexico's trade of agricultural commodities. At the same time, it is important to understand this continuing process of dismantling tariff protections as one of the key elements in the restructuring of global capitalism and the establishment of new rules for governing the economic interaction between nations. It is in this sense that NAFTA takes on great importance.

By the end of 2008, it could be seen that the trade between the three member countries of NAFTA had grown substantially under the weight of liberalization. But in the case of Mexico, those benefits obtained in some agricultural categories were more than offset by losses in the social sphere and in domestic foodstuff availability. It can be observed, for example, that:

A) The agricultural and livestock trade balance had by 2006 registered a 261% greater deficit compared to 1993 levels (Macías and González 2007: 55).

B) The agricultural Gross Domestic Product (GNP) consolidated its historical tendency to shrink as a relative share of the global GNP.[3]

C) The gap in labor and land productivity relative to Mexico's competitors, even though diminished, remains persistent on account of technological asymmetries.

D) There was also a setback in the portion of agrarian exports relative to total exports, and in their composition such that designer fruit exports have taken the lead in sales (Coll-Hurtado and Godínez 2003: 16). It is precisely those goods that have displaced basic grains as the top crop category in the agricultural GNP.

It could be alleged in defense of the agroexport model that the objective of productive specialization across regions has been accomplished in relative terms. However, its implications for a demographic exodus from the countryside, the reconcentration of the best quality lands, and the over-exploitation of natural resources is overall an undesirable pattern.

Mexico's Agrarian Structure

To fully appreciate the effects of NAFTA on the Mexican countryside, it is essential to consider some relevant data concerning its social and productive structure. For example, one-fourth of the Mexican population resides in rural zones, amounting to around 25.6 million people. The agricultural and wildlife sector is responsible for directly maintaining one-third of the country's rural zone inhabitants, involving more than ten million people including owners, workers or direct producers.

The activity of this segment of the economically active population is concentrated in about 25 million hectares. Although Mexico has a vast national territory, the portion of its terrain that is suitable for cultivation is less than 15%. As in other Latin American countries, the majority of agricultural productive units are based in family farms or peasant agriculture, traditionally dedicated to basic grains cultivation. Corn, beans, wheat and sorghum are the predominant crops in the

---

[3] The agrarian GNP fell from 6.9% in 1993 to 3.9% for the 2006 according to data from the Instituto Nacional de Estadística, Geografía e Informática (INEGI 2008a).

countryside in terms of surface area utilized and number of persons employed.

Given the typical size of lots, 85% of Mexican peasants are considered small farmers since they have less than five hectares of cultivable land and 90% of this sector have less than 3 hectares (OECME 2004: 11). The 2007 Agricultural Census (INEGI 2008a) shows that communally farmed units have not ceased to be the most important form of land tenure in the countryside, present in 105 million hectares which is more than half of the national territory. But it also recognizes that in comparison with private property, the communally farmed lands are far less technically advanced and face major difficulties in inserting themselves in the global economy (Robles Berlanga 2008: 13).

The overall economic structure can be characterized by its diversity and polarization in various ways, including soil quality, infrastructure, technological resources, productivity and yields, labor organization, and so on, all of which reveals the coexistence of a small core of profitable and competitive capitalist enterprises, assisted in its progress by the public sector. Luis Villanueva (2005: 10) explains that this minority, essentially geared towards export activities, is comprised of 2.6% of the country's producers. In contrast, there exist millions of peasants that operate with meager surpluses and toward whom government expenditures are restricted because they are not considered a worthy investment from the microeconomic point of view.

It was therefore predictable that the larger portion of agricultural cultivators in the country were not in favorable conditions to respond to the demands of the global market. For that reason, the process of liberalizing agricultural trade via NAFTA could only take place upon the economic abandonment of the inefficient producers, a move tantamount to increasing exclusion of rural laborers and further erosion of the staple foods producing productive base.

The Effects of NAFTA on Rural Life

To understand the evolution of the average rural income, agricultural occupations and the trade of staple food goods during the period that led into NAFTA's implementation, it is necessary to discuss all three processes as part of the same problematic. One useful variable to explain these processes is the price of agricultural goods. What is hoped for in a shared regional market is an equalization of prices.

With NAFTA, guaranteed prices were effectively eliminated in Mexico for basic grains in 1993 and domestic prices for the producer accentuated its tendency to decline. From 1993 to 2004, the average price of corn, beans and wheat fell respectively by yearly averages of 5.4%, 4.2% and 4% (Serna 2005: 24). The only major exception to this tendency was experienced in 1995–1996 when a scarcity of these products was felt on the global market and Mexico attained a trade surplus in its agricultural and staple food crop exports.

The decline in agricultural prices in Mexico were not in themselves anything new but rather a common trend over the last three decades, given the increases in productivity and the expansion of intraregional markets.[4] The difference is that this time, there were no public policy actions aimed at protecting the income of the small producers, leaving the influx of imports principally of U.S. origin to mark the pattern of the evolution of prices.

This last factor has been fundamental. It is well known that U.S. agricultural products are cheaper than Mexican agricultural products. This is due not only to structural reasons and the average rate of labor productivity but also because U.S. agricultural policy is not in any way liberalized. A large part of their agricultural sector budget is used to subsidize their producers, a policy which is totally contrary to liberal economics. Meanwhile Mexican producers had to assimilate, during this same period of liberalization, an escalation in costs due to changes in public policies such as cutbacks in public spending, termination of preferential credits, cancellation of stockpiling, storage and purchasing services, increasing prices for agricultural inputs, and so on. This is summed up by the fact that state resources channeled to agricultural and lumber development over the 1981–2006 period declined from 3.2% to 0.6% of the GNP (Cabrera Adame 2008: 53). As could have been expected, the producers most harmed by this succession of events were the peasant farmers who experienced an increase in the unitary costs of their product while the market offered ever lower prices at the point of sale.

The Mexican state did not remain indifferent to the contraction of foodstuff prices but on the contrary supported it in order to help con-

---

[4] During the 2005–2008 period, this trend was broken on account of factors such as the fall in international grain stockpiles and adverse climatological events (IICA 2008).

tain inflationary prices, further tightening the domestic supply of basic grains and leaving greater space for U.S. surplus production. This aim was achieved and part of the domestic demand for grains is now being satisfied by the production of Northeastern Mexican private producers that until recently had shown little interest in raising corn. Another important segment of the domestic market for foodstuffs (42%) is thereby being met with imports at prices that are lower than their actual costs of production.[5] Consequently, the traditional small producer tends to occupy a decreasing share of a major market in which it earlier played the dominant role.

This marginal position of the peasant in meeting the national demand for foodstuffs ultimately translates into a serious decline in family income, hence increasing poverty in rural areas. The peasant producers know by experience that to produce a hector of corn or beans, it will cost increasingly more. The market price for this good will not completely compensate them while the overall opportunities for selling the product are shrinking. These producers are conscious of the fact that their efforts will not yield sufficient income with which to live, resulting in pressure to obtain income by other means. This results in forcing them into the labor market and ultimately into a migratory syndrome. Rural poverty is more accentuated in the Southern and Southeastern parts of Mexico where entire families tend to seasonally migrate to the fields of Sinaloa and Baja California.

From this crisis scenario, the income that results from peasant farming increasingly depends upon securing additional income from alternative sources in order to supplement family consumption. This confirms that:

> In the larger part of rural households, above all among the poorest sector, the income derived from the agricultural activities has ceased bring the main source of income. Rural households have sought out other kinds of income, above all in the construction and service sectors, that at times become complemented with foreign remittances from migrating family members (Rosenzweig 2005: 43).

In this manner, the restriction on traditional forms of income and precarious options for employment has had a direct bearing on the rates of poverty. The National Evaluation Council on Social Development

---

[5] The Instituto Interamericano de Cooperación para la Agricultura (IICA 2005: 40) predicted that by the year 2014, grain imports will have doubled.

Policy reported that for the year 2006, 54.7% of the rural population[6] were found to be living in conditions of "patrimonial poverty"
(CONEVAL 2008: 14), signifying that they were living with less than
1,060 Mexican pesos per month, while 24.5% of the total were found
to be living in a situation of extreme poverty and experiencing serious
difficulty in satisfying their most basic nutritional necessities.

As for the labor market, the National Work and Occupational
Survey of the INEGI (2008b) showed that the rural based population
of peasants or family farmers receiving farming income went from
3,030,629 people in 1998 to 1,554,790 in 2004, while the number of
paid rural workers that earned up to three minimum salaries grew
from 3,846,278 to 4,823,304 persons (Rosenzweig 2005: 38). From this,
it cannot be inferred that rural workers are at the same time occupied
in farming since the figures reveal a net reduction in the number of
those engaged in farming activities.

We can therefore see that neither the new rural farming activities
supported by public policies nor the agricultural export "poles" that
produce non-traditional products, such as vegetables, non-tropical
fruits and flowers, have managed to neutralize the expulsion of the
peasant labor force or contain the emigration of rural inhabitants. At
the same time, it is clear that Mexico's urban areas are at their worst
moment to absorb these surpluses of the labor force. Those jobs within
the agricultural and livestock sector continue to register the lowest
salary rates of all economic activities, despite the overall increased productivity[7] sustained in this sector over the last two decades. We can
clearly see this over the 1994–2004 period when the average agrarian
sector salary hovered at about a 40% lower rate below the national
average (Rosenzweig 2005: 39).

Satisfying Domestic Foodstuffs Needs

There is sufficient evidence on the food crisis to show that the cause
is not literally attributable to a grave deficit in the worldwide supply of basic grains. On the contrary, we believe that the phenomenon
originates in the manipulation of supply by the largest grains corporations as a strategy to advance their control over the global foodstuffs

---

[6] This agency looked at rural population centers of 15 thousand or less inhabitants.
[7] Although these productivity increases have varied significantly by product.

markets. It is in this context that a scarcity alert has been distributed worldwide, magnifying its importance so as to give rise to an extraordinary and artificial increase in grains prices.

Another sector that is obtaining great advantages from this maneuver is a segment of finance capital that has profited by way of speculation in futures markets. In 2007, this segment of non-productive capital massively entered into the international commodity market through the instrument of investment funds. This has been made possible because grains are non-perishable goods in high demand, particularly in times of crisis, thereby assuming a strategic character.

Heavily weighted investment funds in global commodity markets transferred huge sums to the international cereals markets when the housing bubble burst in the United States back in 2007. In the final nine months of this same year, the volume of capital invested in agricultural markets grew five times over in the European Union and seven times over in the United States. This speculation in basic foodstuffs pushed the prices of these commodities to new heights, essentially unreachable by a large sector of the global population of demand, principally located in Asia, Africa and Latin America (Baillard 2008). Between March, 2007 and March, 2008 the price of wheat grew by 130%, soy by 87%, rice by 74%, and corn by 53% respectively. An average increase of these cereals of 88% therefore took place even though production of these crops remained at increased levels (Dierckxsens 2008: 2).

We believe that the increase in basic grains prices cannot be accounted for either by the costs of increased productivity nor by scarcity. It is true that the increased prices for biocombustibles helped change the destination for agricultural products, that international grain reserves moderately decreased over the last several years, and that the surface volume of land dedicated to grain production has been reduced due to a reorientation of agrarian activities. Nor is it fiction that limited access to foodstuffs has been caused by the increase in poverty in many regions. The growth in Asian demand has proven to be significant as have climatological factors that have resulted in notable crop failures. Indeed, the recent commotion over supply and demand factors in the global market is better founded now than in earlier years.

What is not true is that this entire problem is attributable to a drastic increase in the price of commodities when the existing supplies could indeed respond to the demand. Prices have shot up because the lion's share of production of these goods are controlled by a group of corporations that have seized the opportunity to obtain extraordinary profits while at the same time reinforcing their monopoly over rationing the global supply.

The proof lies in the fact that the tendency towards increasing production and agricultural productivity at the global level has been uninterrupted over the last fifty years. Even with the contraction of global grain reserves, the FAO has asserted that global agricultural production capacity could potentially feed up to 12 billion persons in the future:

> World grain production during 2007–2008 are estimated at 2108 million tons: a 4.7% increase compared to that of 2006–2007. This surpasses the average 2% annual increase experience in the previous decade (Dierckxsens 2008: 3).

Ample additional evidence of the foodstuff supply exists. For example, international financial agencies such as the World Bank have rushed to support underdevelopment countries with loans to increase their capacities to import foodstuffs, arguing that this can help slow increases in their domestic prices. Others have argued that those agricultural goods most suitable for biocombustibles such as biodiesel and ethanol are crops such as soy rather than the more basic grains for direct consumption. Finally, we are left to assume that a real scarcity of foodstuffs might become a hard reality in the near future if, as we have seen up until now, countries like Mexico continue to import basic grains and continue to favor the destruction of their peasant economies. It is still not too late to change this course.

POWER AND RESISTANCE IN POST-NAFTA MEXICO: TRANSFORMATIONAL AND SYSTEM-STABILIZING NGOS

Krista M. Brumley

Introduction

In the past few decades, there have been two major restructurings in Mexico. On the one hand, the economy has undergone significant changes that have ushered in neoliberal policies focused on free trade, foreign investment, and privatization. On the other hand, the Mexican political system has experienced democratization that ultimately led to the first national party change in 71 years. Although there have been strides in Mexico's economic and political development, the restructurings have not been without difficulty. Increased political party competition by both left and right opposition parties was met with fraudulent elections in 1988. The opening of the Mexican economy in the early 1990s and the implementation of NAFTA in 1994 led to an armed uprising in the southern state of Chiapas where the indigenous protested economic globalization and the threat to their cultural heritage. Two months later, the highly favored presidential candidate was assassinated perpetuating disarray in the ruling political party. Given the political uncertainty, approximately $10 billion dollars were sent out of the country sparking a series of slow, but steady currency devaluations. By 1995 and more than a decade into the restructurings, Mexico appeared to be spiraling into a period of simultaneous economic and political unraveling that seemed unprecedented.

While this was certainly not the first time that collective action would emerge in response to economic and political crises, mobilization was framed by a context that posed different challenges. Before, participating in collective action was embedded in a semi-authoritarian political system where repression was commonplace. Acceptable forms of political participation were confined to party politics and organizations formally affiliated with the ruling party. Now, with the country embarking on a democratic transition, political participation in other forms was more acceptable and in some instances encouraged. Therefore, decisions ranging from whether or not to accept government positions, to issues of government financing, to deciding what level of cooperation to have with the newly elected democratic governments, to what types of activities should be tackled were dilemmas brought to the forefront. These issues have always plagued collective action, but the challenges have been exacerbated by the difficulties faced in an era of neoliberal economic policies coupled with democratic transition. This is intensified because much of the collective action during the late 1980s and early 1990s aided in bringing about new governments in Mexico at all levels. The primary purpose of this chapter is to analyze collective action in the post-NAFTA context in the city of Monterey, located in the northern part of the country. Because NGOs have been the primary form of visible collective action that has emerged in Monterrey since the restructurings began to take place, I ask the following question: *what role do nongovernmental organizations have within an environment of economic and political restructuring?*

NGOs have existed elsewhere in the region since the 1950s; however, they did not emerge in Mexico until the mid-1980s when these organizations gained strength in numbers and influence throughout the world (Bebbington & Thiele 1993; Gideon 1998; Landim 1987). Although NGOs vary vastly, scholars suggest one characteristic they tend to have in common is the strength in their collective voice, whereby NGOs create competition for governments and political parties by encouraging participation and activism of citizens (Lehmann and Bebbington 1998; Segarra 1997). Since these organizations have appeared on the political scene in earnest, there has been a plethora of research on NGOs that largely portrays these organizations as a positive force in making social change (Bratton 1989; Brett 1993; Courville & Piper 2004; Landim 1987). Increasingly, however, there is literature that suggests a more cautious view of NGOs (Bob 2002; Mitlin, Hickey & Bebbington 2007; Petras 1997; Veltmeyer 2005).

Despite a growing and rich body of research on NGOs, absent from this conversation is a conceptual framework to systematically analyze NGO actions. Collective action theories on political opportunities and collective identity certainly help us to understand the emergence and development of these organizations. While an important part of the puzzle, these frameworks are not sufficient for analyzing NGOs. In other words, scholars tend to claim that NGOs are either advocators or service providers, but there is no road map to get us to this conclusion. This chapter presents a conceptual framework for analyzing *what* the NGOs demand and *how* they go about enacting those demands.

Through my evaluation of the organizations' demands and strategies, I build on earlier theoretical models for examining the emergence of collective action by adding an analysis of the political behavior of NGOs. Because previous cycles of collective action shape the context within which NGOs emerged, in the following section I discuss the types of collective action in Monterrey, why, and how they attempted to enact their goals.

Cycles of Collective Action in Monterrey

Collective action in Monterrey has ebbed and flowed where there have been periods of visible and frequent mobilization and other periods where it was minimal. There are three cycles of collective action that have occurred since the end of the Mexican Revolution. Early forms of collective action in the city took the form of labor and union movements from about 1917 until 1940. The next spike began in the late 1960s until the early 1980s where collective action mostly consisted of students, women, and the poor. By 1983 the city was experiencing another downturn in mobilization until the mid-1990s when collective action peaked again, but this time in the form of NGOs. These cycles of collective action can be explained by the sociopolitical environment within which the mobilization emerged.

Cycle One: Labor Movements and Union Activity

Scholars argue that broad social processes within a given context influence the ability of collective action to emerge and develop. These large scale changes may include, for example, industrialization, urbanization, changes in demographics, war, prolonged unemployment, democratization, or changes in social policy (McAdam 1982; McAdam, McCarthy, & Zald 1996; Piven & Cloward 1977; Tarrow 1998; Tilly 1978). It is these social processes that provide the *political opportunity* for collective action to emerge and develop, such as an increase in the political leverage of the excluded, aggrieved, or oppressed population, divisions among socioeconomic and political elites, and the improved bargaining position of the excluded population raises the costs of a repressive response by the government (Schock 1999).

During the first cycle of collective action (1917–1940) in Monterrey, mobilization in Monterrey was situated in a context characterized by national political tensions over the enactment of the right to organize outlined in the 1917 Mexican Constitution and an overall yearning by those traditionally marginalized in society to reap the benefits promised by the Mexican Revolution. At the local level, the city was experiencing a high rate of industrialization that preceded other parts of the country by two decades. These factors not only provided a political opportunity, but also shaped the form that collective action took. What emerged under these conditions were labor movements whereby union activity soon became some of the strongest in the country. Workers at the *Fundidora* (Iron and Steel Works), the largest industrial park in Latin America had several strikes between 1918 and 1922 where they won some concessions, including higher wages, improved medical services, and working conditions (Snodgrass 1996).

Although workers in the city acted on the political opening brought by the revolution, the constitution, and industrialization, they experienced strong opposition by the Monterrey industrialists. To counteract unionization and labor unrest, the industrialists offered a new way of organizing for the workers in the form of savings cooperatives, the first of which was established at the Cuauhtémoc Brewery (Rojas Sandoval 1992). The acceptance of cooperatives by many workers rather than participation in the national unions was because of the welfare benefits provided by the Monterrey industrialists that were yet to be matched elsewhere in the country (Saragoza 1988; Snodgrass 2003). The cooperative developed in 1918 at the Brewery was so successful in its mission that in its more than 100 year history, it has had only one strike that was in 1924 and was quickly dispelled through the dismissal of the leaders and self-sanctioning by members of the cooperative (Snodgrass 2003). While the revolution and constitution created elite divisions at the national level thereby sparking an opportunity to mobilize, there were few elite divisions at the local level because of the pattern of industrialization in the city. Monterrey's early industrial expansion is owed to a small number of families that were organized by board membership in each other's companies, but also through marriages that united this small group, and enabled them to resist unionization (Vellinga 1979, Walton 1977).

Despite strong opposition, some labor continued to resist and was emboldened by the election of Lárzaro Cárdenas to the presidency in 1934 who sought to unite labor and incorporate them into the national political power structure. In Monterrey there was support for the new president, however, there was also much resistance by the workers to this action by Cárdenas. Therefore, when some businesses became crippled in Monterrey during the 1930s, others saw no strike activity unless organized by management. In fact, one of the major moments of labor mobilization in the city actually took place against President Cárdenas. Laborers took to the streets in 1936 to protest the arrival of the president in the city and to demonstrate their dissatisfaction with the promotion of unions linked to the official party that were viewed as "communist agitators" (Snodgrass 1996). Even the *Fundidora*, the site of the most radical strikes a few years earlier came to offer similar benefits that ensured tranquility and loyalty in the factories. The result of this tight control on labor through the use of paternalistic welfare-incentives eventually led to a decline in collective action so that from 1940 until about 1970 Monterrey did not experience mobilization. It also shaped the future collective action by establishing a sociopolitical environment not tolerant of public dissent.

Cycle Two: Students, Women, and the Poor

The next cycle of collective action (1970–1983) was characterized by a disillusionment of the Mexican political system, rapid urbanization, and systematic underdevelopment as the government could not keep pace with the increasing population in the cities. These conditions created divisions among the local elites and raised the costs of repression by the government thereby shaping another moment of political opportunity for collective action to emerge. This time, however, mobilization took the form primarily of urban popular movements and student movements, although there was sporadic collective action by urban guerilla groups and feminist activists (Bennett 1992; Pozas Garza 1995). Like the earlier labor movements, urban popular movements were largely class-based collective action. The strongest and most organized of the urban popular movements was the *Frente Popular Tierra y Libertad* (Land & Liberty). The organization's original goal was to obtain land and then through self-help initiatives build a neighborhood that had access to urban services that was not dependent on government clientelistic politics (Pozas Garza 1989; 1990). Although the government violently repressed the movement early on, divisions among economic and political elites became visible when the government began to encourage the settlements. The change in government policy was in part to capture electoral support of these newly formed neighborhoods, albeit through clientelistic measures. In addition, because the government had few resources to provide services to these neighborhoods, whereby they recognized the utility of the self-help programs. By 1979, *Tierra y Libertad* began to lose its power and in 1983 the social movement organization split due to leadership disagreements over their relationship with the government.

The other movements that developed in this cycle, however, were not embedded in class-based grievances, but illustrate grievances based on other social characteristics. Therefore, drawing on what was initially called the "new social movement" perspective offers another piece of the puzzle for this mobilization cycle. Despite different interpretations of the perspective, scholars agree that new forms of collective action were transcending class-based action by revealing an array of collective identities embedded in gender or sexuality, for example (Laraña, Johnston and Gusfield 1994; Melucci 1989; Scott 1990). Therefore, the basis for grievances in the movements is different than the economic roots of traditional class struggle. These other identities result from a multiplicity of socially constructed grievances whereby the cultural and symbolic issues of identity embedded in everyday life become visible. In this way, identity is the basis for struggle and resistance, but identity may also be the goal of the collective action (i.e., Gay and Lesbian movements, see Bernstein 1997 and Taylor & Whittier 1992; ethnic movements, see Olzak and West 1991; Starn 1992; and Stephen 1997a and on the women's movement, see Jaquette 1994; Katzenstein and Mueller 1987; Stephen 1997b; Tarrés 1998).

Collective action throughout the 1970s in Monterrey illustrated this diversity in grievances beyond a class-based analysis. Although not as large as the 1968 student movement in Mexico City, the students of the public university in Monterrey demanded autonomy and democratization that polarized the city with the Monterrey industrialists opposing the students (Bennett 1992; Pozas Garza 1989). The focus of the women's movement was on the questioning of women's roles in society and was particularly concerned with exposing the inequality between women and men in everyday life, both in the home and in the workplace. The movement was small in comparison to its counterpart in Mexico City; however, it laid the seeds for future organizing by feminists in NGOs.

The last large scale collective action in this cycle that erupted because of water shortages provides an example of the interconnectedness of the sociopolitical environment with grievances that may be embedded in class, but that interlock with other types of inequalities, such as gender. On the one hand, the water protests were comprised primarily of women because of their role in household responsibilities. On the other hand, the strategies used by the women varied according to their social class (Bennett 1989, 1995). Middle and upper class women tended to write letters, sign petitions, and make phone calls whereas poor women took their dirty laundry to wash in the fountain in front of the state governor's office, kidnapped water trucks, and set up blockades. Although the water protests did not emerge explicitly because of a collective identity, identity shaped who participated in the movement. The underdevelopment of the water system created an opportunity for the emergence of collective action. Despite a major economic crisis in the country, however, the local government developed two costly (yet necessary) water projects to combat the protests. Regaining a sense of stability and portraying to the outside world that Monterrey was the place to invest was of primary importance to the local industrialists thus illustrating that increased leverage by the participants outweighed responding with repression.

Cycle Three: NGOs

As with the two previous cycles of collective action, the third cycle (1994–2003) emerged in the city when a new set of national factors shaped opportunities. Arguably, the key factor that triggered collective action not only in Monterrey, but nationally as well was the 1994 peso devaluation. The devaluation brought on the worst economic crisis the country had seen in over two decades. Coinciding with the economic crisis, there was an indigenous uprising by the Zapatistas in the south of Mexico. Inextricably linked to this uprising is the implementation of the North Atlantic Free Trade Agreement on January 1, 1994. As a condition of NAFTA, the Mexican government was to create a national human rights commission which in turn promoted the establishment of state level human rights commissions. The opening of the Mexican economy brought the freer movement of capital and products, but it also brought the movement of knowledge and ideas. Social groups traditionally marginalized from the political process began to speak up and coalesced around collective identities embedded in sexuality, gender, and ethnicity. Adding to the confidence of these groups was an opening of the political system such that it was becoming more diversified in terms of the political party representation. Mexico was finally in the midst of a major democratic transition and voices of dissent were tolerated to an extent unprecedented in Mexican politics.

In contrast to other cycles of collective action where several movements emerged, there was only one social movement during the third period. *El Barzón*, a middle-class social movement was a clear response to the peso devaluation that was strangling the country. It began in the rural areas of the country and spread to the cities as homeowners and small business owners were at risk of losing their property because of rising interest rates. The organization emerged to collectively defend the property of its members and employed a series of strategies that ranged from visible protests in the city to quiet negotiations with the banks. However, because Monterrey has not had the same level of intensity and frequency of collective action over the past two decades as other cities in Mexico, mobilization also took a decidedly different form. What emerged in the city were NGOs, and while NGOs sprouted up all over the country, in Monterrey they were the dominant form. Certainly adding to the series of socioeconomic and political factors that spurred collective action in the first place was the increasing discourse at the United Nations and among governments globally, but particularly Western governments, towards NGOs as the "new" voice for marginalized populations and an intricate part of building democracy through strengthening civil society ties (Feldman 1997).

While their presence is now noticeable on the political scene, NGO development in Monterrey as well as elsewhere in the country has not been without difficulty. During their initial development, the government actively sought to diminish the power of the organizations by changing fiscal laws to allow the government "to treat NGOs as private profit-making corporations" (Piester 1997:486). And while there were political opportunities that shaped this cycle of collective action, there were also locally based factors that have curtailed mobilization. For example, there is not the same level of dissent in Monterrey towards the opening of the Mexican economy generally and NAFTA specifically because the city has long been connected to the U.S. markets. While there is more plurality of political parties, the city is a two party system rather than a three or four party system as in other parts of the country. The two parties are virtually similar in their embracement of neoliberalism, and although the PAN is slightly more socially conservative, the PRI rarely proposes progressive social policies. Although it has been increasing in recent years, there is no large indigenous population in the city that could identify with the ethnic struggles in the south. And, lastly, while the first cycle of mobilization in Monterrey introduced the disdain for visible collective action among not only the economic and political elites, but also among the wider citizenry, it was the second cycle that solidified a sociopolitical context intolerant of visible collective action. In this way, Monterrey provides an interesting combination of large scale processes that create opportunities and local factors that diminish the impact of those factors.

Despite these obstacles, over time NGOs began to grow in numbers in Monterrey and have now become a more acceptable form of social action. That is, social groups may not be taking to the "streets," but they are actively engaging in new ways to influence politics. In 2003, the local government began to sponsor an annual NGO conference that a decade ago would have been unheard of in the city. Even *El Barzón*, the only social movement in the city in over two decades eventually professionalized into a NGO. And, in 2008, it transformed once again by becoming a foundation oriented toward the "defense of economic and social human rights" effectively closing the chapter of the organization's "massive presence" (www.elbarzon.org). Because of the 'NGOization' of Monterrey society (i.e., the range, scope, and extent of NGOs), investigating the role of these organizations is important to advance our knowledge of how NGOs participate in the political process. However, while existing theoretical frameworks explain the latest cycle of collective action, they do not sufficiently explain what the organizations do once they have developed in the context of Monterrey. Therefore, in answering my research question in this chapter, my analysis goes beyond questions of emergence and focuses on *what* the NGOs are demanding and *how* they are going about enacting those demands.

Data and Methods

The data for this analysis are the result of qualitative fieldwork conducted between 2001 and 2003 in Monterrey, Mexico. Early in my fieldwork, I focused on gathering data through newspaper archives and informal conversations with local activists in order to identify possible NGOs for the study. My first informant proved invaluable and led me to various other organizations in the city. Selection of the organizations was based primarily on snowball sampling. This sampling technique aided me in finding organizations that were locally active. Often I read in the newspaper or "heard" of an organization, but found that the NGO was no longer active. Therefore, relying on recommendations from local activists was very important in the construction of my sample. I combined this sampling technique with another qualitative sampling method. I used quota sampling to ensure that there were a variety of NGOs included in the study. I had expected that I would find differences among the organizations based on the organization's goals. That is, I thought that those NGOs focused on women's issues would articulate their goals and use strategies to enact those goals differently than those organizations focused on urban problems, for example. Based on a list of local NGOs, I categorized the different foci of the organizations to design a sample that represented the different types of issues or conditions that the NGOs were working towards improving. In the end, the sample included NGOs from the five most common issues addressed by the Monterrey NGOs as well as only those that had been recommended by two or more other activists. Because this study includes many NGOs that focus on different social issues, I use the following notations to indicate which type of NGO I refer to in my analysis: human rights NGOs are HR, gender inequality are GE, health and sexuality are HS, education NGOs are ED, and NGOs with an urban focus are UR. After each letter abbreviation, I indicate the NGO numerically (i.e., HR1, HR2, GE1, GE2, etc.).

Formal data collection consisted of in-depth interviews with each leader from twenty NGOs. The semi-structured interviews were conducted during 2002 to 2003. I use pseudonyms when referring to the NGO leaders in this chapter. The interviews were conducted in Spanish and took place at the location of the leader's choice, such as the organization's office, the leader's home, or a coffee shop. The interviews lasted between one and two hours. All translations in this article are mine. In addition to the interviews, I collected written information from the organizations in the form of newsletters, pamphlets, or magazines. Where appropriate and feasible, I attended NGO events, such as conferences or open meetings. Although the formal and informal data collection was complete by the beginning of the summer in 2003, I continued to live in the city until the summer of 2007. My seven years living and working in Monterrey covered three election cycles which gave me a broader perspective of the political process in the city and what role NGOs can and try to play in the process.

NGO Goals and Strategies in Monterrey

The context of this cycle of collective action is characterized by major economic and political changes, but in profoundly different ways. Economic crises had occurred before, but this time the crisis was embedded in fundamental changes in economic policies. Political crises had also occurred before, but this time that crisis led to dramatic shifts in political party power. NGOs in Monterrey have responded to these restructurings, but they have also responded to the local environment. The NGOs in this study emerged because of what they identified as a specific social injustice. The NGOs focused on urban problems were formed precisely because of economic crises as well as the effects of deregulation brought on by the opening of the economy. The human rights organizations referred to the formation of the national and state-level human rights commissions and the Zapatista uprising as motives for the establishment of the organizations. The education, gender, and health-sexuality NGOs emerged because of a perceived lack of attention by local and state governments to address increasing problems. For instance, Monterrey has the second highest level of family violence in the country. The formation of all but three of the NGOs I interviewed coincided with the opening of the Mexican political system and the international discourse of the importance of NGOs for democracy (1989–1996).

NGO Goals: Advocacy and Service Provision

Although the NGOs in this study largely focus on one social issue, such as health, sexuality, human rights, education, gender inequality, and urban problems, trying to classify the organizations is difficult because they differ by activities, target group, size, funding, and their relationship to the community of interest. For example, some of the organizations focused on urban problems, such as the environment and public services, target the larger metropolitan area, whereas others address urban problems within specific subpopulations, such as the poor or the elderly. Some of the NGOs have narrowly defined activities, such as HIV/AIDS or education. Still other NGOs have a range of different activities, but they target a specific group, such as women, children, indigenous, and the gay/lesbian/bisexual/transgender community (LGBT). Some of the organizations have an all voluntary staff and others have some paid staff. The NGOs also vary in size with some organizations only run by 2 or 3 people whereas others not only have a staff, but also a membership base. Some NGOs emerged from outside the communities they represent, while other NGOs emerged from within the community. Simply put, the Monterrey NGOs illustrate a complex array of organizations.

Despite the diversity, the NGOs share a vision of improving the life of individuals in the metropolitan area of Monterrey. However, how they talk about making that change with their goals reflect *two different outcomes*. That is, regardless of the social issue, activities, the target group, size of the NGO, or whether or not it emerged from within the community, the NGOs present their organizational goals in two ways. On the one hand, their goals reflect a desire to make transformational change, either advocating for a new social organization or working towards an alternative form of social organization within a particular structure, such as the gendered social order. On the other hand, the NGO goals fulfill what they see as a gap in the current system, but they do not advocate for systemic change but rather a solution to the problem within the existing structure. In table 1 below, I present the Monterrey NGO goals in terms of these two discourses that I have conceptually categorized as either transformational or system-stabilizing. In the diagram below, I present this conceptual framework.

When NGOs present their goals as transformational they do so in two ways: (1) targeting the general citizenry or a specific social group to advocate societal change or (2) targeting specific groups to advocate specific change within that group. Those NGOs that speak broadly of *societal change,* talk about creating citizens because it is through "education that citizens learn their rights and their obligations" (Victor, HR4). Citizenship, Anna tells me, is "not an issue of age or voting, but it is the development of a level of consciousness where your personal problems are the problems of everyone, and you work towards solving your problems, but also solving the problems of others in the society" (UR1). She continues to explain that the goal of the organization is to create a "sense of belonging" and a "political consciousness" of the citizens. Although several NGOs argue that societal change requires teaching citizens about their rights and obligations, they recognize the challenges they face. As Barbara explains, "in thinking about human rights, we are in diapers in Mexico; this concept is new—the fight for the defense [of rights] has been intense because of our culture (HR1). These NGOs were some of the first in Monterrey to visibly use the language of citizenship to challenge the power structure.

Table 1. Monterrey NGO goals

TRANSFORMATIONAL	SYSTEM-STABILIZING
Challenge the order of social relations Advocate for a new or alternative form of social organization	– Do not challenge the order of social relations – Intend to resolve a particular social problem with little or no claims to systemic change
Promote and defend human rights Create citizens through education and political conscious-raising Eliminate discrimination based on sexuality and gender Form a collective identity Promote feminist conscious-raising Transform the culture of domestic violence	– Promote education and culture – Prevent HIV/AIDS; improve quality of life for those infected/affected by HIV/AIDS – Defend the consumer (i.e., consumer watch group) – Provide services to the poor and elderly – Monitor environmental violations

By framing their goals as part of citizenship rights and social justice, they are trying to reframe the conversation of who has access to goods and services—whether it is the financial system, the legal system, or the healthcare system.

Those NGOs also target specific social groups in Monterrey to promote the goal of making changes in society. Veronica's NGO focuses on LGBT youth by providing a safe house where young people have a space for meetings, workshops, socializing, and to get information on sexual health issues. The safe house, she explains "is the most important project and it is within this space we realize our goals to form leaders among a group of sexually diverse young people, educate them, and then they will take the initiative to make changes in society" (Veronica, HS1). Josie, the leader of another NGO also focused on health and sexuality, but among women, explains that an important focus of the NGO is "to create citizens" (HS4). She says that the goal "is to help women by contributing to the empowerment of gender." To do this, the organization focuses on education, particularly health education and the prevention of violence toward women. She argues that, "if women are conscious that they have control of their body, that they are autonomous, and that they have the capacity to make decisions in their lives then they can participate and make decisions towards real change in the country" (HS4).

Rather than focus on broad societal change, when some NGOs talk about creating citizens they do so by targeting a specific social group and making a change for that social group, for example women. Two organizations address the issue of family violence where one focuses on the women and children and the other focuses on men. Both organizations seek to prevent and deactivate family violence. Towards this goal, Valerie, the director of the NGO focused on women and children, explains that the organization's goal is "to transform the culture of domestic violence and to construct a healthy nation" (GE1). Similarly, Jorge, the director of the NGO focused on men, tells me that the organization's goal is to "influence the legal framework, educational public policies, and healthcare…our intention is that if we can influence these areas we can teach men to unlearn certain behaviors and relearn something else" (GE2). Carmen believes that reducing gender inequality can be done by "communicating through the media about the everyday life of women, to reflect, to make visible, to interview women about important issues, and to change the use of language in a nonsexist manner" (GE3). In this way, their goal is to make visible the everyday life of women and their problems and demands so that women can engage in changing their life.

Although an organization advocates transformation and systemic change, this does not mean that the organization continues to do so throughout its life course. When Jennifer and Ivan started working together in the late 1980s they were focused on the prevention of HIV/AIDS, but also advocacy to eliminate discrimination, particularly in the healthcare system. Over time, the organization split into two where one NGO (HS2) maintains an "activist goal and continues to fight discrimination based on HIV/AIDS" and the other NGO (HS3) seeks to "improve the quality of life of those with HIV/AIDS by focusing on providing services for those infected and affected by the virus." Jennifer emphatically explains that the NGO is "an activist organization, not a service provider organization as with many others in the community focused on HIV/AIDS." In this way, she tells me they work towards informing people of their rights because of discrimination by doctors and inadequate service for those with HIV. In contrast, Ivan admits, somewhat sheepishly, that it just became too difficult to do both, and he (along with some others) decided to focus on care and prevention and leave their activist roots behind. It is this key difference—activism versus service delivery—that distinguishes the one NGO with transformational goals and the other NGO with system-stabilizing goals. The other organizations that have goals I identify as system-stabilizing are those NGOs who seek to improve the quality of life of certain individuals, but do not strive to change the existing social order. In this way, the organizations explain their goals as trying to resolve a particular problem. Several of the NGOs focus on the urban poor in general, while others focus on a specific social group, such as disadvantaged children, the elderly, and the disabled. In all cases though, providing education is a part of their organizational goals. One NGO targets high risk children through Children and Family Services (*Desarrollo Integral de la Familia*) and offers cultural classes on music, dance, theater, and sports. Julia explains that the goal of the organization is "to provide children with activities that they would not normally have in their life" (ED2). Sara has been an activist for decades, she explains, but this time she is working with low income neighborhoods that have been left behind in education. Her organization promotes a culture of reading through a book exchange program as well as to pass down information on the history of the community (ED1). Yet, another NGO teaches about healthcare through their soup kitchen and uses that space to channel those in need to the proper governmental agency. "We want to help those that are marginalized and forgotten by the government" José tells me, and then he says, "really, we want to save people from their problems, we have limitations, but it is our desire to help that keeps us going" (UR2).

In summary, thirteen of the Monterrey NGOs in this study have transformational goals in that there is an intention of the NGO actions to strategically challenge the order of social relations in Monterrey society. The NGOs are advocating for a new or alternative form of social organization whether it is overall societal change or change for a specific group. The other seven NGOs have system-stabilizing goals. Their goals are intended to resolve a social problem and in this way the goals remain particularistic with little or no claims to systemic change. That is, they are not demanding a change to the system, but work within the existing system to resolve an issue. What the NGOs demand in Monterrey is only part of the story. The other half of the story focuses on how the organizations strategically enact the demands.

NGO Strategies: Moderate and Radical Claim Making

The second goal of the chapter is to analyze how the NGOs in Monterrey enact their goals. Similar to NGO goals, there is a wide array of strategies employed by the organizations. I identify five strategies used by the Monterrey NGOs to have their grievances heard and influence politics. These strategies include: (1) civil resistance, (2) policy action, (3) communication, (4) alliance formation, and (5) community programs. In table 2 below, I rank the strategies in terms of risk based on the Monterrey context and assign the strategy outcome as either transformational or system-stabilizing.

High risk strategies are those strategies that result in the disruption of everyday activities of all or parts of the general society and the day-to-day business of the target, such as the government, a local business, or some other institution. High risk strategies also are covered extensively in the media. Medium risk strategies refer to those strategies that do not result in the disruption of everyday activities of the general society, but does so for the targets of the demand. Media coverage occurs as well, but not on a daily basis as with high risk strategies. Low risk strategies are those that do not result in the disruption of everyday activities of the general society and have little to no effect on the day-to-day business of the targets. Low risk strategies are also typically not covered in the media. Although time and space shape the risk scale, the schema I present in this chapter provides a conceptual basis to systematically analyze NGO strategies as well as other types of collective action.

As the table below reflects, the Monterrey NGOs in this study use a variety of strategies. Three NGOs engage in strategies at all levels of risk and eleven combine low and medium risk strategies. Only six NGOs use strategies within one level—5 employ only low risk and 1 uses medium risk strategies. I had expected to find a pattern of strategy use by NGO focus, however, my results illustrate that strategy use was only partly a function of organizational focus. All the gender and education NGOs had never used nor intend to engage in high risk strategies. The education NGOs only use low risk strategies, however, the gender NGOs use both medium and low levels. The NGOs focused on human rights, urban issues, and health and sexuality primarily combine low and medium risk strategies. Notable, however, is that one NGO from each category currently engages in high risk

Table 2. Strategy Risk and Outcome

everity Level	Strategy Examples	Strategy Outcome
ow (=19)	*Communication (n=16)* - Petitions and phone calls - Workshops, Conferences, or "Talks" (*platicas*) *Alliances (n=12)* - With government , political party, or private business *Community Programs (n=7)* - Soup kitchens - Educational activities	System-Stabilizing Strategy
edium (=15)	*Policy Action (n=10)* - Lobbying - Legal mechanisms—usually in the form of a special injunction (*amparo*) *Communication (n=11)* - Mass media (T.V., radio, newspaper, or magazine) - Direct negotiation or appeal with target *Alliances (n=11)* - Within civil society only	Transformational Strategy
igh (=3)*	*Civil Resistance (n=3)* - Small or Large-scale protests - Road blockages - Marches	Transformational Strategy

2 other NGOs previously used civil resistance, but it is no longer in their repertoire of strategies.

strategies. Therefore, although the organizations varied their strategies, they tended to do so *within* a particular risk level.

High Risk Strategies: Civil Resistance

When NGOs use high risk strategies, they engage in stationary protests in front of the target or demonstrate with marches. Two patterns emerge from my data suggesting that civil resistance is not an enduring strategy over the life course of the Monterrey NGOs. First, NGOs are more likely to use civil resistance when they initially try to garner support for the social problem, but once obtained civil resistance is no longer used or only sporadically. When Patricia felt there was no response to rising rates by the newly privatized gas company, the NGO activists went on a hunger strike for 12 days in front of the governor's palace. The NGO has not since used this strategy and Patricia believes because they have gained recognition for the NGO work, they do not need to protest. The NGO led by Veronica was the first organization to draw attention to the unjust situation of the LGBT community in Monterrey by organizing a Gay Pride march. Beyond the annual march, Veronica's organization does not employ this strategy.

Second, civil resistance is used more often *before* the professionalization of the organization takes place. The two NGOs that emerged out of social movements (UR1 and UR4) were focused on economic inequalities, urban services, healthcare, and housing. They engaged in resistance to a level where there was a serious and prolonged disruption of the city and in many instances led to severe repression by the government. Since professionalizing as a NGO in the late 1980s, however, Arturo explains that the NGO does not use civil resistance, but relies on community programs. Ana's NGO (UR1) still employs civil resistance, however, large scale protesting has diminished and the small scale protests are sporadic. Victor (HR4) tells me that they participate in marches organized by Ana and sometimes organize small scale street theater. Therefore, while five NGOs indicate that they have used civil resistance as a strategy only three continue to do so albeit in a limited way.

Medium Risk Strategies: Lobbying, the Media, and Civil Society Alliances

Strategies with a medium level of severity are categorized as transformational because the strategies are more radical in the sociopolitical context of Monterrey, but to a lesser degree because of the level of disruption to the target of the demands. Lobbying is usually discussed as an institutionalized form of politics, however in the Monterrey environment lobbying has traditionally only been used by the private sector business leaders. It is a relatively new form of political participation among marginalized social groups. Likewise, the use of the mass media and the formation of civil society alliances are also newer forms of engaging in politics in Monterrey. Mexico's corporatist political system has historically structured collective organizing through official organizations affiliated with the ruling party. Organizing outside of these formal, institutionalized channels was often not tolerated. In Monterrey, for example, during the late 1960s and early 1970s when student groups aligned with other community groups to protest social conditions in the city they experienced repression by the government (Pozas Garza 1989). Public dissent has not only been repressed (to varying degrees) within collective action, but also with respect to questions of the freedom of the press. Only in the past decade has it been more acceptable and a greater degree of tolerance of public criticism towards the government or other institutions. In Monterrey, however, the media remains conservative (Smith 2008) which has made it difficult for certain social groups to be recognized by the local media.

Despite the concern of repression and the challenges to attract the attention of the media, a number of the NGOs in this study try to reach the public through the mass media. For some of them, in fact, this has been a principle strategy to disseminate information. Guillermo, the environmental NGO leader states that the media has been their main vehicle for informing the public of environmental violations. Similarly, the women's organization of journalists uses print media to disseminate information. Carmen calls this communication, "campaigns of diffusion" (GE3) where they inform the public on issues, such as abortion, HIV/AIDS, and cancer with a particular focus on how it affects women. Several of the NGOs use the radio to educate the public, but they have had varying degrees of success. Although both NGOs target health and sexuality issues with women, Josie (HS4) has been able to maintain her radio program on a private station, but Jennifer's (HS2) program on public radio was cancelled by the governor of the conservative National Action Party. Of all the media outlets, television is the least used by the NGOs and even then it is generally sporadic. Between 2002–2003, the leaders of the two family violence organizations appeared on the televised news programs only a handful of times. In contrast, Ana (UR1) regularly uses this medium and during my research hardly a week went by without hearing her on the radio or seeing her on the televised news programs.

The second most common medium risk strategy is lobbying. NGOs have lobbied for laws on domestic violence. NGOs have also lobbied to stop the passage of a proposed law that would eliminate abortion in all cases. And, NGOs have lobbied for improved policies on urban services, particularly transportation. In all the examples expressed by the NGO leaders, lobbying was the first line of action taken by the organizations to call attention to the social issue. Lobbying, however, is also almost always used in conjunction with another strategy, such as alliances. In the cases of the family violence, reproductive rights, and the urban transportation issues, the NGOs lobbied in alliances, and were relatively successful in achieving their goal. Laura, a human rights NGO leader (HR5) tells me that she continues to lobby for changes to adoption procedures, but she has yet to be successful. In this case the organization has not worked with other NGOs. This data suggest that lobbying and legal action yield positive outcomes, but when NGOs informally come together for the specific cause.

In contrast, formal NGO alliances yielded unexpected results in this study—what began as a relatively strong alliance among nine vocal NGOs became a vehicle for party politics. On the day I interviewed José he was very preoccupied with the 2003 mid-term elections. During our interview, he received various phone calls inquiring how he was going to position himself in the elections. José's NGO was part of a civil society alliance called *Grupo Nuevo León* that had formed to challenge the Monterrey power structure. The name of the alliance is a play on the name *Grupo Monterrey* that is used to refer to the Monterrey industrialists. As an alliance they have successfully challenged the government and private businesses on issues such as public transportation, economic policies, and social conditions. As the 2003 elections approached the alliance decided to try a new strategy. Initially, the alliance linked with one political party so that each NGO leader could run for local office. Seven of the nine organizations in the alliance participated in this strategy, five of which were part of this study. Because of José's membership with the alliance, he had originally committed to working with the one political party. But, as he indicated to me that day in his office, he had decided to go with the party that could offer him the best deal. He was not the only NGO leader to break ranks with the alliance and quickly the united front broke apart. In the end, José linked with the Workers' Party. Patricia (UR3) and another NGO not in this study worked with the Institutional Revolutionary Party that had ruled for 71 years in Mexico. Ana (UR1), Guillermo (UR5), Victor (HR4), and another NGO not in this study remained with *Convergencia*, the original political party in the alliance. The strategy, Victor explains was "just to get one into office," thereby signaling that there is little room in politics for civil society organizations. In fact, many of the NGO leaders I interviewed felt they had reached the limit on what they could accomplish through their organization. For them, formal politics remained the only option.

Low Risk Strategies: Government Alliances and Workshops

Civil society alliances are a medium risk strategy, but when NGOs link with political parties as in the example above or with the government as is the case with two other examples from my study, the alliance becomes a low risk strategy. In these two cases, the alliances began as loosely formed networks among NGOs focused on one social issue, but as they became more organized the organizations linked with a government department. The Inter-Institutional Committee against Violence began this way when some NGOs worked together to lobby for a law against family violence. Once successful, those NGOs focused on domestic violence formalized an alliance in conjunction with the government (GE1 and GE2 joined the network). Similarly, COESIDA is comprised of some NGOs that had been working alone or loosely with other NGOs on HIV and AIDS-related issues. All the NGOs in this study were part of the official alliance with the department of health within a few years of their emergence.

The most common of the low risk strategies are workshops. Like the media strategy, NGOs use these formats to educate the public or specific groups on a social issue. Jennifer (HS2) goes to communities to "disseminate information about sexuality" with youth, Josie (HS4) offers sexuality workshops for women to contribute to their empowerment, and Veronica (HS1) gives talks in Churches and schools on HIV/AIDS. Some NGOs also provide workshops to government agencies or political parties. Valerie (GE1) explicitly targets the police and the state judicial system in order to desensitize them towards domestic violence. Similarly, Barbara (HR1) has organized workshops on human rights and women's rights for political party members. Unlike other strategies that are used sporadically or diminish over time, workshops for the Monterrey NGOs have become the principle way to educate the public or specific groups on social issues.

Based on my analysis of the Monterrey NGO goals and strategies, I diagram the conceptual model that emerged from my data. Recall, NGO goals are conceptualized as either transformational or system-stabilizing. NGO strategies are first ranked on a risk scale and then categorized as transformational or system-stabilizing. Because NGOs use many strategies, I evaluated each NGO on the number of strategies indicated. NGOs that tend to use more medium to high risk strategies fall into the transformational category whereas NGOs that tend to use more medium to low risk strategies fall into the system-stabilizing category. My analysis of NGO goals shows that slightly half of the NGOs in this study have transformational goals (n=13) as presented in outcomes one and two. However, my analysis of the strategies of these organizations demonstrates that only a small number employ transformational strategies (n=4). This means that these four NGOs in this study participate in the political process as transformational NGOs because they have both transformational goals and use transformational strategies to obtain those goals (outcome 1). In comparison, there is a smaller number of NGOs in this study that have system-stabilizing goals (n=7) as presented in outcomes three and four. These NGOs mostly use system-stabilizing strategies (n=5). The five NGOs participate in the political process as system-stabilizing NGOs because they have both system-stabilizing goals and strategies (outcome 4).

Diagram 1. NGO Goal-Strategy Conceptual Framework

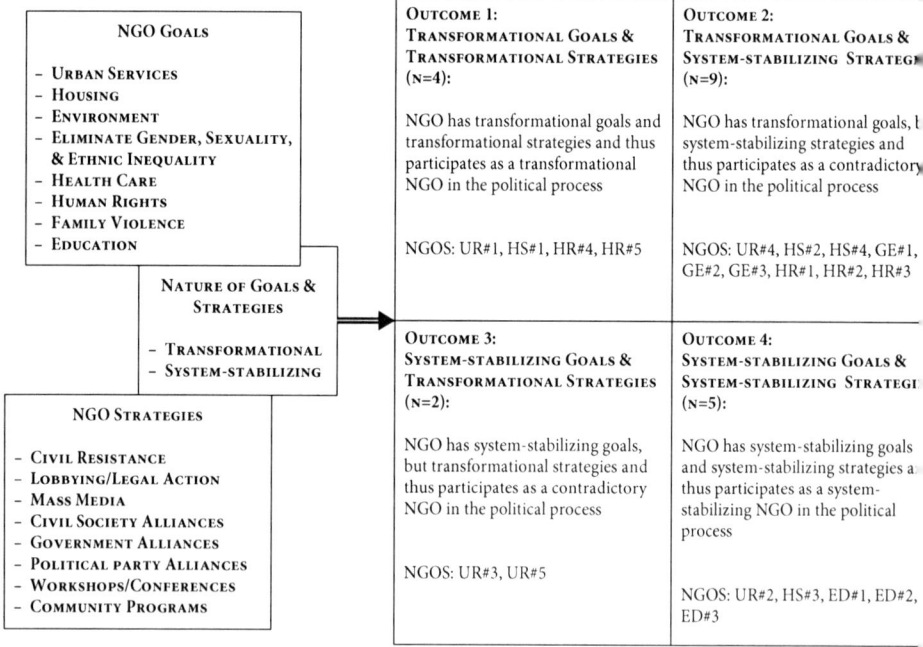

Therefore, my analysis reveals the contradictory participation of NGOs in the political process. Of the twenty NGOs in this study eleven organizations use strategies that do not match with their goals. Nine NGOs engage in system-stabilizing strategies to enact transformational goals (outcome 2) whereas two NGOs use transformational strategies to obtain system-stabilizing goals (outcome 3). As in past cycles of collective action in Monterrey, however, a political opportunity could create conditions for the system-stabilizing NGOs to (re)convert to transformational NGOs, at least temporarily.

Discussion

This chapter examines the role that NGOs play during the current cycle of collective action in post-NAFTA Monterrey, Mexico. NGOs emerge because of a set of national and international political and economic factors. Responding to these conditions, NGOs form to address urban problems, human rights, healthcare, education, and inequalities based on gender, sexuality, and ethnicity. Although there is an abundant amount of research on these organizations, absent from the literature is a conceptual framework to analyze NGO action. Political opportunity and collective identity theories are useful to explain why the NGOs emerged, but they are not sufficient to elucidate what the organizations do once they have developed. Based on my analysis of the twenty NGOs in this study, I present a conceptual framework to systematically analyze NGO actions. I argue that to understand the role of NGOs, it is important to evaluate the organizations' goals in conjunction with the strategies.

This case study illustrates two major findings. One, the majority of the NGOs in this study advocate for societal transformation, whether it is on a broad scale or for a particular social group, such as women or bisexual youth. Although NGOs have increasingly come under greater scrutiny by scholars for their role as a voice for the marginalized, aggrieved, and oppressed, my data suggest that there is a NGO narrative that seeks transformation. Two, and related to the first finding is that NGO actions are often contradictory. That is, when I examine the NGO goals, the majority presents those goals in a transformational manner and talk about the desire to make societal change. But, when I combine this analysis with the NGO strategies, more than half of the organizations use moderate or what I have called system-stabilizing

strategies rather than transformational strategies. Contradictory practices, however does not mean ineffectiveness. Rather, it might just
mean an innovative capacity by the organizations to navigate complex
sociopolitical terrain (Magazine 2003).

The implications of these findings are important for a number of
reasons. First, because the NGOs in this study play a dual role of
transformational and system-stabilizing, further analysis requires
investigating what shapes which role NGOs employ. Scholars' initial
excitement over NGOs as the new social actor of the 1990s gave way to
concern that these organizations have begun to take on a greater role
in service provision (Giddeon 1998; Landim 1987) and have moved
away from their advocacy roots. Initial contact with the NGOs in
Monterrey certainly seem to suggest that rather than an active voice
in making social change, many of the NGO actions attempt to solve
social problems though the assistance of the government or through
particularistic methods, such as community programs or workshops.
This chapter indicates that with a more nuanced analysis NGO goals
and strategies there is flexibility among the organizations. At times
NGOs attempt to resolve social problems, but with a critical stance
and in opposition to the government whereas at other times they work
as complementary organizations of the government. The dual role of
NGOs suggests we need to go beyond championing NGOs as either
negative or positive influences and examine the contextual complexities
within which they act.

Second, rather than radical strategies, NGOs are using moderate
to low risk strategies that seem to reflect the sociopolitical environment. When protests have occurred, it is not uncommon to hear people openly criticize those that are in the streets as "troublemakers" or
"irrational" or "attention-grabbers," even if the grievance of the group
is something that most agree with in private. In a setting of democratic
transition where formal politics take center stage in the process, NGOs
(as with other forms of collective action) face the dilemma of whether
or not to work within or outside institutional channels of government
in the new democracies. This study suggests that NGOs choose to do
both to achieve their goals. Whether or not collective action is more
effective if using disruptive methods or tactics that are more moderate,
however, is not agreed upon among scholars (Giugni 1998, 1999). A
future avenue of research includes systematically analyzing the specific
NGO strategy in conjunction with the outcome.

Third, the Monterrey NGOs actively engaged in alliances to enact
their demands. On the one hand, the NGOs have formed alliances

within civil society and on the other hand, they have formed alliances with political parties and specific governmental agencies. The alliances with political parties, in particular, demonstrate the concern voiced by NGOs that they have gone as far as they could in trying to make societal change. The next logical step, they argued, was to hold an elected office. The results of the election suggest that the decision by the NGOs was fruitful. Of the six NGOs in this study that formally announced their candidacy for a state congress position, three of them won. This success may suggest that rather than protest, a new generation of NGOs is embracing political party activism. But it also raises questions over the ability of civil society to provide a counterbalance to government (or even the private sector). Moreover, this action by the NGOs illustrates the tension of whether to work within institutional politics or outside the system. Because three of the new state level congress representatives were women NGO leaders, my data raises questions for how women enter the formal political arena.

Finally, the emergence of NGOs in Monterrey society is an important aspect to democratic transition (Pye 1998). This study certainly illustrates that there is a *NGOization* of civil society (Alvarez 1998) in Monterrey, however, it is not a uniform group of organizations seeking to liberalize Monterrey society, but rather is a mosaic of organizations with many different ideologies. All the NGOs emerged to address inequalities in society, but not all NGOs have the same access to the political power structure (Shefner 2007). That is, just as society is hierarchical, we can expect that NGOs as with other forms of collective action are not all equal. More analysis on how NGO ideologies influence access to the political system would contribute to recent literature that questions the role of civil society organizations.

The same large-scale processes of economic and political restructuring have taken place throughout the country, but these processes have yielded regional differences in collective action. This suggests that research on the sociopolitical context of the NGOs is an important element to gain a better understanding of the role that these organizations play in politics. The question to address now, for example, is why collective action solely takes the form of NGOs in Monterrey where in other places in the country it is just one of many different types of collective action. In this way, national (and international) factors influence the emergence of collective action, but locally-based factors shape how they develop in terms of what the goals are of the organizations and how they strategically enact those goals.

AS NEOLIBERAL CRISES PERSIST, INDIGENOUS-LED MOVEMENTS RESIST: EXAMINING THE CURRENT SOCIAL AND POLITICAL-ECONOMIC CONJUNCTURE IN SOUTHERN MEXICO[1]

Molly Talcott

When I was…nine years old, I used to go to…my grandfather's ranch…to harvest coffee beans. So, we went there to cut the coffee and we used to eat [while we were] out there. Look, we ate tortillas with salt but we [also] ate mandarins, oranges, mangos, squash, beans, fresh corn, everything that the countryside gives you. That's why I say, I don't know if we are poor or rich—neoliberalism and globalization have turned us into poor people.
—Fernando,[2] young Mixe activist of San Juan Guichicovi, Oaxaca

Mexicans living in rural areas of the Mexican South are facing ever-deepening social, political, and economic crises at the current moment. Southern Mexico is the richest region in the country in natural resources, cultural diversity, and biodiversity; yet, it is the poorest region according to standard human development indices.

Much of Latin America is experiencing a political renaissance, where social majorities are electing progressive and socialist governments and re-imagining the character of hemispheric integration. However, the case of Mexico, led by the administration of Felipe Calderón of the conservative National Action Party, remains a powerful exception to this trend. Calderón's victory in 2006 was widely contested as fraudulent by broad sectors of civil society. When appeals for recounts failed, Calderón was sworn into office at midnight on December 1, 2006. As president, he immediately pledged to continue the previous administration's policies of privatization with a renewed vigor.

The partial victories that indigenous and rural activists achieved during the Fox administration in staving off capitalist incursions in the

[1] I would like to deeply thank Kum-Kum Bhavnani, Dana Collins, Sylvanna Falcón, John Foran, and Sharmila Lodhia for the collaborative conversations, shared insights, and editorial advice that led to the final version of this essay. This research was supported by a grant from the University of California's UC MEXUS program.
[2] In this essay, I use pseudonyms to protect confidentiality.

South are, of course, temporary. Rural and indigenous communities are facing new challenges to their rights by a re-energized conservative administration. Moreover, it remains an open question whether such movements will be able to achieve gains that move beyond a defensive posture. For this reason, it is vital to examine the prospects for movement building in Southern Mexico at the moment. In this discussion, I attempt to make sense of the impasse that rural and indigenous-led[3] social movements in the South are facing in the context of the crises I will now describe.

Context of the Crisis: The Post-NAFTA Plan Puebla-Panamá and Its Discontents

Key economic, political, and social contradictions are shaping daily life, and in turn, catalyzing social struggle, in Southern Mexico at the moment. I begin with a brief mention of the *economic* dimensions of the crisis.

By the early 1980s, Mexico's policies had begun to shift from a form of state-managed capitalism that partially limited social inequalities to one dominated by liberalization. The state increasingly adopted policies favoring large-scale (and transnational) capitalist investors at the expense of social redistribution that would have benefited the majority of Mexicans. This political shift culminated in the 1994 North American Free Trade Agreement.

NAFTA was precedent setting in its focus on liberalizing agriculture, and it has most gravely impacted rural Mexicans (Stephen 2002; Barry 1995). The decline in rural credit programs for agricultural producers, the promotion of land privatization in the 1990s, as well as NAFTA's program of rural restructuring, have all contributed to the deepening crisis in the rural Mexican South, and this constellation of neoliberal policies threatens the food sovereignty of Mexico as a whole

---

[3] I purposefully employ the term, *indigenous-led*, in order to emphasize the centrality of self-identified indigenous subjectivities and resistance practices within the 'movement of movements' I discuss here, while also acknowledging the organic hybridity of such movements, whose protagonists include both indigenous and mestizo actors. By using this term, I also wish to avoid both the reinscription of mestizo nationalism (which has historically rendered indigenous peoples invisible and relics of the past) and the reinscription of indigenous communities and their movements as insular, immobile, and exclusively rural.

(Henriques and Patel 2004). Rural communities in particular that depend on subsistence farming are increasingly impelled to migrate in order to survive in a process of *descampesinización*—deruralization (Barreda Marín 2004).

The divide between the central and northern regions of Mexico and the South—which is rooted in historical relations of racism, patriarchy, and colonialism—is both material and imagined. In nationalist imaginings, the division between North/Central and South has been understood through a set of binary oppositions that characterize the Northern/Central states as modern, mestizo, upwardly mobile, urban, and part of the First World. In this formulation, the Mexican South is cast as traditional, indigenous, impoverished, rural, and part of the Third World. In her historical study of the state of Oaxaca, Francie Chassen-López argues that, like much of Southern Mexico,

> Oaxaca has been typecast in the role of the *foil*: antimodern, backward, barbarous, and reactionary. The Mexico that has wanted to be seen as modern, capitalist, and revolutionary has defined itself in opposition to traditional, indigenous southern Mexico.... As modernity's negative mirror image, Oaxaca has also doubled as *villain*, representing the backwardness that posed the major obstacle to the progress of modern Mexico (2004: 7).

The production of Indian difference as a way to legitimize minority rule in Mexico (Saldaña-Portillo 2003), has placed the Mexican South—in particular the states of Guerrero, Oaxaca, and Chiapas—as the geographical locus of cultural and economic backwardness. It is primarily the South, under this pro-modernization discursive framework, where indigenous women are cast as victims of their culture, where small farming on communally-held *campesino* lands is irredeemably inefficient by neoliberal standards, and it is from this perspective that former president Vicente Fox was able to explain away the 1994 Zapatista uprising as an indigenous demand for the fruits of capitalist modernity: 'a TV, a Volkswagen and a small business' (Gutiérrez 2001: 113).

Such discourses reflect the racial-patriarchal nationalist ideology that has equated Mexican development with capitalism, modernization, and (a Eurocentric form of) cultural assimilation throughout its history. The normative binaries reproduced in this ideological framing conceal more about the Mexican South than they reveal. And yet, it is important—from a materialist perspective—to note the economic disparities that exist between the Mexican North/Central region and the South. For example, the *Human Development Report of Mexico*

2004 highlights the gravity of regional inequalities.[4] The Executive Summary report states:

> Inequality in development is evident when considering that the Federal District [of Mexico City] registers Human Development Index (HDI) levels not very distant from those of some European countries, whereas Oaxaca and Chiapas do not surpass the index of the Occupied Territories of Palestine (2004: 8–9).

Moreover, the rate of extreme poverty (defined as living on less than one dollar per day) in Mexico as a whole is 40%, yet in the Southern states it is 66%, similar to rates in Central America. Furthermore, in the Southern Mexican states, the illiteracy rate is 17%, which is 10% higher than in the rest of the country (Bartra 2004: 29).

The human development inequalities discussed here are explained quite differently by political elites and popular classes: neoliberal institutions such as the World Bank and the Mexican state argue that Southern poverty persists because modernization and neoliberal capitalist efforts such as NAFTA simply 'have not reached the South' and therefore call for further economic integration into transnational capitalist structures of labor and trade. Scholars (Saldaña-Portillo 2003, Newdick 2005) and social movement activists such as the Zapatistas and other indigenous networks, however, point to the Mexican South's longstanding relationships with capitalist institutions and instead argue that neoliberal programs such as NAFTA, structural adjustment, and land privatization have further exploited and impoverished the indigenous peoples of the South.

Although, as Stern (1995) suggests, there are 'many Mexicos of every Mexican region,' a binary opposition has developed in nationalist imaginings, where, as Chassen-López writes, Oaxaca (and indeed the Mexican South as a whole) 'has represented the indigenous face that 'modern' Mexico has not wanted to see in the mirror' (2004: 6–7). Armando Bartra's description of this geographical/ideological divide is worth quoting at length here:

---

[4] Although averages and indices are distortions in their concealment of inequalities that exist within categories (such as, in this case, Mexican states), and in their concealment of (typically women's) reproductive labors and subsistence economies, the Human Development Index (HDI) provides a somewhat useful portrait of aggregate social conditions.

The South is a geographical concept, but it is also a symbolic one, an allegory which links abundant nature with extreme social poverty, opulent and luxurious vegetation with a humanity which is inert, lazy, incontinent, barbarous, which associates the blazing sun with a rowdy spirit, with the release of repressed impulses, with the feminine and unlaced side, with the imagination and the dream, with the unconscious, with revolution, with utopia. The South of the Americas and its broad tropical swath is the rural and campesino subcontinent, the America of the Indians and the Blacks, the periphery par excellence. Despite the fact that the Presidents of our Republics have been dreaming in English for some time, the South still begins at the Rio Grande. But tropical Mexico and Central America are the south of the South, the underdeveloped of the undeveloped (2004: 17–18).

Bartra would probably concur that in the year 2000, the Fox administration was 'dreaming in English' when it expanded neoliberal policies by unveiling with fanfare its alleged solution for 'developing' the South; this enormous proposal was the *Plan Puebla-Panamá* (henceforth, the PPP). Mexican economist Miguel Pickard has noted that:

> The PPP was born with several…problems, not the least of which was its antiquated notion that people, especially the poor, are objects of 'development,' never its subjects (Pickard 2004: 2).

The PPP, a massive, transnational infrastructural project, has waxed and waned since it was first announced almost eight years ago. At the time of its announcement, the state pledged to create transportation corridors, electrical grids, hydroelectric dams, windmills, port and airport expansions, and factory infrastructure across Southern Mexico, expand industrial forestry and agriculture, modernize petrochemical facilities, as well as to both conserve and privatize biodiversity and promote ecotourism (Carlsen 2004; Hussain 2006: 6). This massive overhaul of the South's landscape was promised, at least publicly, in the name of sustainable development and poverty alleviation.[5]

Yet despite these stated commitments, the Office of the President acknowledged on its website that at the PPP's completion, eighty percent of South Mexico's rural residents would no longer remain in that locale (Barreda Marín 2004: 193). This prediction—that *eighty percent*

---

[5] Although the Plan Puebla-Panamá is a transnational development plan that encompasses Southern Mexico, Central America, and most recently the nation-state of Colombia, my study is limited to exploring the Southern Mexican context of struggle and change, while keeping in view its transnational dimensions.

would somehow migrate or be displaced—is a profound indicator of the planned social dislocations that result from projects of 'modernization' such as the PPP.

As opposition to the PPP swelled across Southern Mexico and Central America, the Fox administration quietly removed official websites in 2003, the World Bank withdrew its overt support, and the PPP appeared, to the casual observer, to be defunct. But many in popular movements opposing the PPP asserted that corporate and political elites were, indeed, continuing to carry out the PPP quietly, project by project, but without naming them as part of the PPP.

By the time I began to attend national and international gatherings in 2005, the movement's new slogan had become, 'The PPP exists and Mesoamerica resists!' (¡El PPP Existe y Mesoamerica Resiste!). The PPP, pronounced dead in the press by 2003 (Pickard 2004), had become a powerfully concrete icon of neoliberal development on which the resistance movement had come to depend. With the inauguration of Felipe Calderón, the neoliberal projects like those included in Fox's PPP are experiencing a political revival, once again in the name of 'economic development.'

Oppositional Movements, State Repression, and Militarized Polyarchy

The current crisis facing Southern Mexico is also political, and it includes two key, interrelated dimensions. The electoral demise of the seven decades long one-party rule by the Institutional Revolutionary Party (the PRI) in 2000 fueled a wide swath of journalistic and scholarly declarations that Mexico has now entered an era of democratization. Where Mexico's democratic credentials were once in doubt, it is now widely regarded as a country with a democratic, if somewhat corrupt, political system. William I. Robinson, however, more convincingly argues that Mexico—like many capitalist countries in the Americas, including the USA—is more accurately described as a *polyarchy*. In a polyarchic system, elites compete in tightly controlled electoral contests, but popular democratic power is suppressed through a variety of political-economic mechanisms that lead to the exclusion of a wider set of social and political possibilities. This distinction between a political democracy and a political polyarchy is critical, given the slippery and near-omnipresent equation of 'democracy' with capitalism (Robinson [1996] 1998).

The second and related crisis, which has already produced devastating social effects, is that a dirty war against dissidents, journalists, and activists is clearly underway. Italian social theorist Antonio Gramsci has famously argued (1971) that when popular consent erodes, the state invokes force in order to maintain its hegemony, and the ongoing erosion of popular consent defines the contemporary Southern Mexican political moment. Mexico has been called a 'militarized democracy' (North American Congress on Latin America [NACLA] 1998, cited in Norget 2005: 116) that relies on both the appearance of the 'rule of law' alongside a combination of state-led and paramilitary forms of political violence.[6] Militarization is intensifying in Mexico under the government of Felipe Calderón to an even greater degree than existed during the Fox administration, with the assistance of US government funding via the Mérida Initiative, also known as Plan Mexico. The Mexican State's response—at both the federal and state levels—to popular withdrawals of neoliberal consent has been a bloody one involving detentions, disappearances, torture, rape, and murder and has drawn condemnation from the United Nations, and from prominent human rights organizations such as Human Rights Watch and Amnesty International.

As neoliberal capitalist policies devastate the social conditions of poor, rural, and indigenous Mexicans and promote staggering levels of migration and displacement (Vandergeest et al. 2007), several key oppositional currents are struggling to build alternative futures in the South—even in spite of the mix of official State and paramilitary repression and violence they face. These key social movement forces, which I discuss briefly, include the Zapatistas in Chiapas, the *campesino*-led movement in San Salvador Atenco, the Popular Assembly of the Peoples of Oaxaca, and the Mexican Alliance for the People's Self-Determination, which stretches across the Mexican South. In the current political moment, this 'movement of movements' faces renewed forms of political violence despite the federal government's official commitments to a neoliberal version of human rights. In what follows, I briefly map this landscape of indigenous-led resistance struggles:

---

[6] Drawing on Robinson's argument ([1996] 1998), I find it more theoretically accurate to describe the Mexican state as a militarized polyarchy.

Chiapas. The most well-known of resistance movements within Southern Mexico is the Zapatista movement, which has been an inspiration and a model for many currents within the global justice movement since 1994. Zapatismo has taken hold across the country, including in urban areas like Mexico City (Zugman 2001). 'The Other Campaign,' launched by the Zapatistas in an effort to build links of solidarity among 'from below, and to the left' social struggles, has further spread Zapatismo across Mexico. However, autonomous communities within Chiapas are facing renewed invasions by Mexican military convoys. On June 4, 2008, over 200 military and state agents led convoys into several Chiapan towns populated by Zapatista communities. The state justified these attacks by accusing these communities of growing marijuana on plantations. Girls, boys, men, and women reportedly used machetes, shovels, rocks, and whatever was at hand to repel these invasions. The Zapatistas issued an international appeal after these attacks took place, where they stated:

> Comrades of the Other Campaign in Mexico and other countries, we ask you to be on the alert because the soldiers said they'll be back in two weeks. We don't want war. We want peace with justice and dignity. But we have no other choice than to defend ourselves, resist them, and eject them when they come looking for a confrontation with us in the towns of the Zapatista support bases (http://chiapas.mediosindependientes.org).

The Zapatista movement is the most well-known movement facing ongoing forms of militarized repression. Yet, many civil society groups have also been targeted as police activities are increasingly converging with military operations (Hardt and Negri 2004; Norget 2005). Atenco is one such example.

Atenco. The struggles being waged by *campesinos* and *campesinas* in San Salvador Atenco (located in the State of Mexico) have also become inspirations for many Mexican activists. In 2002, residents of Atenco successfully resisted attempts by the state and federal governments to expropriate agricultural lands in order to build an airport. Local farmers who opposed the plan were able to halt it. With machetes in hand, they seized control of the area and took 15 police officers hostage (Weinberg, October 10, 2006); as a result, the state's plans were withdrawn. Many indigenous activists cite 'Atenco' as an example of how popular struggles waged by local communities to retain land and stave off top-down development can be successful.

Four years later in May of 2006, local authorities attempted to evict unlicensed flower vendors (informal laborers) from a local market in Atenco. Two youths, Javier Cortes Santiago and Ollin Alexis Benhumea, were killed as a result of police brutality (gunfire and beatings, respectively). The National Human Rights Commission (CNDH), known for its rather weak stances on human rights, has confirmed that at least 26 women were sexually abused upon being taken into police custody. Many more detainees, both women and men, were tortured and held in *incommunicado* detention. Atenco continues to be a site of rural oppositional forces in an area not too far from the expanding Mexico City metropolitan area.

More recently, the Calderón administration has pledged to revive the plan to build the airport that Fox was unable to carry out. In reference to it, Calderón has said, 'Let the experts, not the machetes, decide where it should be' (*El Universal*, October 9, 2006, cited in Weinberg, October 10, 2006). Calderón's reliance on the discourse of development as an endeavor of experts (Escobar 1995a) directly challenges the popular idiom that, 'The land belongs to those who work it' ('*La tierra pertenece a los que la cultivan.*'). That is to say, it is 'the machetes,' not the experts who have the right to the land, and to deciding upon its uses.

APPO. During the same month of the struggle of flower vendors in Atenco, May 2006, the Oaxacan teachers of Section 22 set up an encampment in the center (*zócalo*) of Oaxaca City in order to demand that more public resources be invested in education, especially in rural areas. After just over a month, the state's governor, Ulises Ruiz, ordered a brutal repression of the teachers; municipal and state police attacked the encampment, injuring about 100 people. After this initial episode of repression, Oaxacan civil society[7] converged in a broad-based popular movement of over 350 organizations, and named it the Popular Assembly of the Peoples of Oaxaca (Asamblea Popular de los Pueblos de Oaxaca, or, APPO). Nevertheless, militarized repression against APPO adherents has continued, and the Oaxacan state government has continued to refuse to negotiate with civil society actors. As Electa Arenal has noted:

---

[7] I follow Douglas Lummis's use of the term *civil society*, as 'a multiplicity of diverse groups and organizations, formal and informal, of people acting together for a variety of purposes' (1996: 31).

Police, secret service, local PRI office-holders, and military forces have spread terror everywhere, among schoolchildren and adults, in villages and schools, and throughout a good part of Oaxaca, in addition to the capital city (2007: 114).

As police violence against APPO adherents in Oaxaca City continued during the latter part of 2006, indigenous-led organizations in the rural regions of the state continued to monitor the events in the city, and to act in solidarity with their allies struggling against the despotic state government of Ulises Ruiz. However, the APPO, and Oaxacan movements more generally, are at an impasse. Their demand that governor Ulises Ruiz step down or be removed from power has not been successful, despite massive demonstrations that have taken place in cities and towns across Oaxaca.

AMAP. The Mexican Alliance for the Peoples' Self-Determination (*Alianza Mexicana por la Autonomía de los Pueblos*) is a coalition of over fifty organizations (henceforth, I will call it by its acronym, AMAP). AMAP formed in order to oppose the Plan Puebla-Panamá and neoliberal policies within Mexico more generally, with a focus on the rural South. AMAP's members include groups with long histories of movement building (of twenty-plus years), as well as groups that formed recently, at AMAP gatherings. AMAP is populated by an amalgam of anarchists, adherents to Zapatismo, social democrats with links to the center-left Party of the Democratic Revolution (*Partido de la Revolución Democrática*, or PRD), liberation theology Catholics, and socialists. It is led by an indigenous and rural majority, and the struggles it wages are squarely centered in the Southern part of Mexico, although the network has recently built solidarities with groups waging struggles in Central and Northern Mexico as well.

AMAP has declared itself to be anticapitalist and to be concerned with advancing 'indigenous rights' in the South; its members largely identify with the Zapatista movement and endorse its goals, if not always the *means* by which the Zapatista National Liberation Army (EZLN) has challenged the state. For instance, one key organizer within AMAP explained it to me this way, he said, 'My grandparents were Zapatistas, *I'm* a Zapatista. But I'm not a *Marquista*,' as in, a follower of Subcomandante Marcos. AMAP is also an active supporter of the APPO and of the campesino struggles in Atenco.

The AMAP coalition, and the social organizations that belong to it, form a lesser-known yet equally vital sector of the anticapitalist indigenous rights movement. I collected ethnographic data on AMAP activism between 2005 and 2007. Based on my analyses of AMAP's attempts to build an effective oppositional coalition that advances alternatives to neoliberal capitalism, especially for rural, indigenous, and poor peoples of the South,[8] I offer the following observations about the prospects for movement building at this grave period in Mexican history.

Indigenous-Led Political Cultures of Opposition

The prospects for achieving meaningful gains in this bleak—and downright deadly—political climate, I argue, hinge on the ability of indigenous and rural movements to generate effective 'political cultures of opposition' (Foran 1997; 2009).[9] My ethnographic research suggests such political cultures of opposition, if they are to become transformational forces, will likely embody following five vital dimensions. These include: (1) building gender equity into indigenous movements; (2) harnessing the cultural-political power of human rights discourses; (3) centering the experiences and subjectivities of youth; (4) continuing the foster international solidarities; and finally, (5) working to

---

[8] In my use, 'indigenous and rural peoples' include urban mestizos, rural mestizos, rural indigenous peoples, and indigenous peoples with histories of migration between rural and urban locales. I use the word 'poor' with a deep ambivalence, guided by my attention to the poststructuralist development critiques of Arturo Escobar (1995a), and by the Marxist and materialist analyses that assert poverty as a grave global social problem. Based on my ethnographic fieldwork, I am quite certain that the majority of those I interviewed would (and many, in fact, explicitly did) identify themselves as being one among the collective group of *gente pobre*, or, *gente humilde* (poor people). By United Nations standards (using a Human Development Index), the vast majority of those with whom I hung out, interacted, and conducted interviews are living in poverty. However, I remain uneasy with the word 'poor' due to its misuse by institutions, such as the major international development banks, that equate poverty with noncapitalist subsistence activities and other forms of subaltern cooperative economic development (Gordon Nembhard 2008). When I do use the term 'poor,' I do so with the words of Comandanta Ana Maria of the Zapatista movement in mind, who said, 'As for the power, known worldwide as 'neoliberalism,' we do not count, we do not produce, we do not buy, we do not sell. We are useless in the accounts of big capital' (cited in Nash 2006: 112).

[9] John Foran (1997; 2009) has argued that 'political cultures of opposition' articulate "the process by which both ordinary citizens and revolutionary leaderships [come] to perceive the economic and political realities of their societies, and to fashion a set of understandings that simultaneously [make] sense of those conditions, [give] voice to their grievances, and [find] a discourse capable of enjoining others to act with them in the attempt to remake their societies" (Foran 2009: 145).

articulate the 'yeses.' Below, I discuss each of these five dimensions as they are unfolding within the Southern Mexican context of struggle.

Integrating Gender Equity and Women's Struggles

Indigenous and rural movements continue to struggle to fully institutionalize gender equity (*equidad de género*), and women within these coalitions persist in striving to foreground their gendered problems and experiences within the movement of movements occurring within the Mexican South. While the Zapatistas have made progress in this regard, Josefina Saldaña-Portillo (2003) and Karen Kampwirth (2002; 2004) have argued that the EZLN is not a feminist institution, even though at times, it tries to depart from patriarchal logics. Nevertheless, the efforts of the Zapatistas to build a gender-inclusive movement that respects women, men, transgendered persons, and that destabilizes patriarchal systems of control are noteworthy.[10] These ongoing efforts by the Zapatistas through the Other Campaign, are critical to building social alternatives, especially in light of Margaret Randall's (1992) argument that the failures of the Cuban revolution were linked to its overall failure to embrace feminism and women's rights. I am using the term 'gender equity' rather than feminism, as it is this concept and wording that is gaining currency within indigenous movements like AMAP. My research indicates that centering women's lives (and the lives of queer and transpeople who are 'gender-Others') will require that movements address violence against women within communities, as well as the institutionalized reproductive violence that indigenous and poor women are facing within government programs like *Oportunidades*, which is, in many cases reported to me, nonconsensually sterilizing women and attempting to contain women's resistances by enlisting them in a small cash assistance program, which in these times, is badly needed (Talcott 2008).

As long as indigenous women are reeling from the structural and personal violence of racism, patriarchy, and class exploitation (as both

---

[10] Notably, the Zapatistas have reached out to queer, transgender, and sex worker communities across Mexico in an effort to build solidarity towards a 'world where many worlds fit.' See the journalistic accounts of Mark Swier (http://www.narconews.com/Issue40/article1691.html) and Raúl Zibechi (http://americas.irc-online.org/am/4822) for detailed accounts of these alliance building projects; see also Lind and Share (2003).

productive and reproductive laborers) in their daily lives, they are less able to become effective agents of change. Organizations like the Association of Indigenous Communities of the Northern Zone of the Isthmus (UCIZONI), in Oaxaca, have begun to institute gender quotas within their leadership structures as well as broaden the scope of their struggles to address the forms of oppression indigenous women are facing. This trend is promising, and a coordinated strategy for nurturing the political subjectivities and participation of women is key to movement expansion.

Harnessing the Cultural-Political Power of Human Rights Discourses

Second, I argue that indigenous movements can gain momentum by continuing to harness and expand globally circulating discourses of human rights. This process, which contests neoliberal and individualist interpretations of human rights, is underway within indigenous-led Mexican movements. Radhika Coomaraswamy has argued that:

> [E]ssentialist discourses like human rights are socially constructed and…are rooted in political, economic, and cultural power relations…. [T]omorrow there may be a better discourse that helps us move the world in the direction we choose and…we should never stop working for that alternative. However…in today's context and in the world we currently live in, this discourse is one of the best available to fight against social oppression and exploitation and that we should use it creatively and imaginatively (2002: 13).

In this conception, human rights discourse is a self-conscious cultural-political expression and framework for social action. This formulation of human rights discourse as a *self-conscious form of oppositional cultural politics* is promising for grassroots social movements. While institutions such as the World Bank and International Monetary Fund are incorporating human rights, including women's human rights, 'as a top down managerial concern thus robbing it of its radical potential' (Coomaraswamy 2005: 13), local grassroots movements are making human rights-based arguments for social transformation, including popular democratization, redistribution, and cultural recognition (Coomaraswamy 2002: 13).

What, then, is the 'radical potential' of human rights discourse, of which Coomarswamy writes? Audre Lorde, in her cultural-political interruption of the racism and homophobia of the mainstream, white, U.S. women's movement wrote that, 'There is no such thing as a single-issue struggle because we do not live single-issue lives.' The radical potential of human rights discourse, then, is that it can embody Lorde's assertion and can express a discourse of dignity (Foran 2009). Struggling for dignified lives for all peoples—lives where human rights are respected and actualized—requires going beyond 'single issues.' Thus, the radical potential of human rights discourse is that it is able to link seemingly disparate struggles. Blau and Moncada (2005) discuss this 'bundling of rights' as a major strength of human rights discourse:

> Human rights come in bundles because prioritizing humans over political and economic interests leads quite inevitably to encompassing all of the rights humans must have to live lives of dignity' (171).

AMAP activists I interviewed tend to confirm this notion that human rights, although it is invoked by imperial institutions, is *not* a doctrine containing a set of foregone definitions and conclusions, but rather, is *a social process*, which—if used strategically, can contribute to arguments for indigenous self-determination and social justice. Moreover, in the dangerous political climate of the moment, activists find themselves relying on human rights discourses in order to survive state repression and harassment. These 'negative' uses of human rights (in the sense of freedom from state violence, repression, detention, etc.), however, are being situated alongside a 'positive' set of arguments for collective rights to self-determination, and increasingly, to 'human dignity.'

Centering Youth Movement Praxes

Part of the cultural-political work that indigenous-led movements are engaging in has to do with dismantling hierarchies of leadership with respect not only to gender, but also to age. Indigenous youth are organizing to reshape the social landscape of opposition. The material conditions they face today are distinct from those of prior generations; they form the 'post-NAFTA generation,' whose transitions into becoming adult economic actors have occurred entirely within the neoliberal political-economic moment. The rural character of their futures is gravely uncertain, as they witness their parents' livelihoods as small farmers transformed by rural economic crisis, state neglect, economically-motivated migration, and development projects that threaten physical displacement. Moreover, it is youth who are forming new political praxes and forms of popular education within their communities, principally through the use of media. In particular, I cite the organizing work of the Network of Indigenous Community Radios of Southeastern Mexico (*La Red de Radios Comunitarias Indígenas del Sureste de Mexico*, henceforth the RRCI), which is entirely youth-run. This network is best described by one of its key organizers:

> On [community radio], we play the music that everyone is listening to, what they're listening to these days, whatever they want, Mexican music, you know? But the commercial radios, what do they do? A song ends and they offer you Sabritas [potato chips], the best food for your health, right (joking)? We said: No, we're not going to advertise Sabritas. We're going to say, 'Take care of yourself, because you're very valuable; you have rights; you are an indigenous person that has the right to justice;' and things like that. So, we began that way and saw that it works for us. The people listen to it.

This organizing praxis is vital as media consolidation, coupled with the advance of militarized polyarchy, continues its attempts to limit voices of dissent. In April of 2006, outgoing president Vicente Fox signed into law the Federal Law of Radio and Television (commonly known as the *Televisa Law*), which ends the presidential system of granting media licenses and replacing it with an auction, where new licenses will be granted to the highest bidders. Two media conglomerates—Televisa and TV Azteca—control more than 95 percent of the national television viewing audience. Moreover, indigenous, rural, and poor communities are disproportionately impacted by this lack of media democracy, as they tend to rely more heavily on television and radio, than on print media, as news sources. It is indigenous youth who are involved in efforts to reclaim the airwaves as both an example of, and a tool for, realizing a politics of self-determination.

Continuing to Build Transnational Solidarities

As the crisis of the political dirty war continues, and will likely deepen with the adoption of the Plan Colombia-like Plan Mexico, indigenous movements will need to continue to build cross-border solidarities and rely on international human rights observers. The Zapatistas, whom I quoted earlier, sent out just such an appeal with respect to the June 2008 attacks, and many have argued that their ability to generate transnational support has enabled them to survive state repression for fourteen years.

Most recently, two young Triqui women, Teresa Bautista Merino and Felicitas Martinez Sanchez, ages 20 and 24, were killed on April

7, 2008. They were journalists with the radio station, The Voice that Breaks the Silence (*La Voz Que Rompe el Silencio*), a member station of the network of indigenous community radios mentioned above (the RRCI). The women were traveling en route to Oaxaca City, where they were to conduct a workshop on community media as a tool for human rights struggles within indigenous communities.

Twenty bullet shells were found at the site of the murders, along with an AK47. These killings illustrate the ongoing nature of the political crisis in rural Oaxaca, where indigenous-led movements are disproportionately targeted by the state. In this deadly climate for journalists and activists of all genders and ages, transnational solidarity is vital for the movement's ability to move beyond a defensive politics of mere survival and into a strengthened position of waging proactive struggles for change, which brings me to my fifth and concluding point.

Working to Articulate the 'Yeses'

The Zapatistas and the global justice movements in general have embraced the idea that this 'movement of movements' should be a coordinated effort to articulate 'one no and many yeses.' If the first four conditions I discussed become centrally integrated within the movement—and to varying degrees, these new cultural-political formations are being enacted—indigenous-led movements of the Mexican South will be better able to imagine and articulate a program of 'yeses.' That is to say, indigenous-led struggles might move '*de protesta a propuesta*' (from protesting against the incursions of elites to making alternative proposals).

To close, I return to the example of community radios being run by indigenous youth across the South. As I mentioned earlier in the chapter, the activities of AMAP and its member groups, of which the Network of Indigenous Community Radios of Southeastern Mexico (RRCI) is one, are lesser known than the Zapatista and APPO movements that are celebrated by leftists worldwide. Yet the APPO (famous for its bold media activism), in particular, owes some of its strength to the solidarity activities of rural youth, who are using media to build—person by person—a rural base of support for the more visible, popular struggles that took place (and will again surely erupt) in the center of Oaxaca City.

As police violence against APPO adherents in Oaxaca City continued during the latter part of 2006, indigenous-led organizations in the rural regions of the state continued to monitor the events in the city, and to act in solidarity with their comrades struggling against the despotic state government of Ulises Ruiz. The RRCI was instrumental in facilitating information flows between Oaxaca City and rural areas of the South. For example, Fernando spent weeks camping with the APPO adherents and calling in live radio reports that were broadcast on Radio Ayuuk in San Juan Guichicovi, Oaxaca. These reports contrasted starkly with the misinformation most residents of San Juan Guichicovi were receiving via their television sets. Fernando explained Radio Ayuuk's growing influence in the community to me this way:

> When the problems with the APPO began, that's when we earned our presence, our credibility. The people began to know us and trust us, and the APPO movement. Why? Because…the elders used to not believe that the government is killing people, that the government is doing this or that…because they have been members of the PRI [political party] for many years, and it hurts them to know that the PRI has long since changed and become just a manipulative government.…So it's very difficult for them to understand this, but we started—as youth—to get moving, to investigate. There they [members of the APPO] were [in Oaxaca City], doing a blockade, so we went to investigate, do interviews, and bring them to the radio, and tell the people [in our community], 'look, this is what is happening in Oaxaca [City] right now.' And the people began to see it, and they started to believe in us.

Thus, not only has the work of the RRCI been vital to raising the consciousness of indigenous and rural communities by providing accurate news and information that corporate media outlets will not provide, but it also has bolstered the participation of youth and women (as the RRCI is a gender-balanced network run in large part by young women and teens), thus broadening the possibilities for movement growth in multiple ways.

This cultural-political formation demonstrates an instance of how youth are creating new cultural-political tools of popular education in defiance of the State's neoliberal *Televisa Law*, but also in an act of creation of new social landscapes which center rights, dignity, and justice. This act of media creation exemplifies one such community-controlled 'yes' (*propuesta*), which is not only a means for movement-building, but also a creative end in itself.

As the crises of capitalism, state and paramilitary repression, and accelerating inequalities continue to devastate indigenous and rural communities across the Mexican South in spite of the existence of popular networks of resistance, the immediate future appears grim. Although indigenous-led movements remain at an impasse in terms of achieving deeply transformational changes, their continued creative organizing—of the sort which integrates the experiences and leadership of women and youth, which takes strategic advantage of the radical possibilities of human rights discourses, and which builds transnational relationships of solidarity—seems the most promising avenue for building incremental change in the contemporary moment. Just as the land belongs to those who work it, the future of Mexico, perhaps, belongs to those who defiantly and imaginatively rebuild it.

PART III

MIGRANTS AS SOCIAL CHANGE AGENTS

THE PRODUCTION OF THE "ILLEGAL SUBJECT"

Nicole Trujillo-Pagan

Dominant theories of international migration contend that social capital motivates human movements across national borders. For instance, Douglas Massey explains that migration expands social networks that lower the costs of subsequent waves migration (Massey et al. 2003). These theories remain focused on the migrant. Applied to the study of labor migration, this perspective emphasizes supply and reproduces a "downstream" approach that misses broader institutional mecha nisms stimulating migrant streams (Sassen 1999; Krissman 2005). An emphasis on social networks' influence in lowering the costs of migration, for instance, occludes the role of institutional actors that increase these costs. When we focus on migrant's actions, we often underemphasize the political context that facilitate U.S. corporate influence in economic dislocation, consumption patterns, and sustain inequality. Similarly, institutions within receiving societies influence demand for specific types of immigrants, particularly undocumented migrants. These institutions include immigration policy, a changing economic structure, and the new international division of labor (Frobel et al. 1978; Piore 1979). As a result, dominant theories of internal migration cannot account for the context that sustains demand for undocumented migrant labor.

Migration from Mexico to the United States is heavily influenced by the institutional contexts in which labor demand is embedded. Some scholars view migrant labor supply and demand as interdependent but, disrupted by increased militarization of the U.S.-Mexican border (Fernandez-Kelley and Massey 2007). Other scholars view the border as more than mere gatekeeper. In their analyses, the border is a place of creativity, entrepreneurship, and opposition to hegemony. Although this scholarship begins to conceptualize the productive capacities of the border and institutional dynamics within receiving societies that propel migratory flows, this literature similarly ignores institutional actors beyond the border that shape its meaning and profitability. For instance, federal immigration policies undoubtedly influence the definition of illegality and stimulate economic expansion at the border.

This chapter argues neoliberal policies are selectively enforced by social actors embedded in what is often considered a circular migratory flow between Mexico and the United States. In essence, it finds that the production of the "illegal subject" is profitable and that state policy expands formal and informal markets through its management of migrant flows. The undocumented migration economy is sustained not only by employer demand, but also by neoliberal policies that promote a variety of interrelated phenomena including: the privatization of state functions, the expansion of U.S. capital on the border, and the proliferation of informal economic activities (Sassen 1997). In this way, policymakers' concern to "protect our borders" is not only a political strategy to control the border and colonize Mexican migrants, but also a struggle to promote economic expansion by consolidating U.S. control over the informal economy at the border (Gonzalez 2006; Coleman 2008).

A host of actors misunderstand the critical aspect of demand for undocumented workers. Workers decry undocumented immigrants' negative influence on their wages and job availability. Citizens resent undocumented immigrants as parasites who tax public resources. Nativists denounce the "invasion of illegal aliens." What these perspectives share is a negative, but almost exclusive, emphasis on the undocumented immigrant. This emphasis is consequential. For instance, Fred Krissman argues "a myopic and largely self-serving focus on supply-side factors will continue to waste public resources, increase the death toll along a highly militarized international border, and stimulate periodic efforts by political opportunists to blame the victims of this system of indentured servitude" (Krissman 2000). An exclusive emphasis on the migrant also obscures "a long-established and deeply-entrenched cross-border labor market that is an integral (even if clandestine) dimension of U.S.-Mexican interdependence" (Andreas 1998: 593). Finally, overemphasizing the migrant ignores ways institutional actors, such as Customs and Border Protection (CBP) and Immigration and Customs Enforcement (ICE), shape the future class and ethnic landscape of the United States.

Scholars have criticized the ways undocumented migration is conceptualized. With important exceptions, however, this scholarship tends to undertheorize the relationship between the state and capital. For instance, Krissman assumes the state is increasingly unable to enforce workplace violations and favors employers (Krissman 2000).

This reading reinforces the perspective that neoliberalism weakens states, assumes immigration policy operates somewhat autonomously from corporate influence, and asserts enforcement is misdirected. An alternate interpretation suggests corporations influence immigration policy, which includes public spending on detention and deportation efforts, and the state's interest is limited to promoting the illusion and profitability of control. This chapter argues U.S. corporations benefit directly from undocumented labor and indirectly from undocumented migration. Politicians implementing detention and deportation initiatives are rewarded with both corporate and public favor for their "cracking down on illegal immigrant" campaigns. The relationship between the state (policies, politics, expenditures), capital (employers, entrepreneurs, and businesses), and the public (voters, persons who use or benefit from undocumented labor) reveals a migration industrial complex that profits from manufacturing difference and exclusion of a specific type of worker. The costs of this complex are paid by all workers.

The following discussion of the migration industrial complex and the migration industry is developed in four sections. The first provides a context for understanding the impact of neoliberal policies on migration by historicizing the immigration and labor policies that shaped early Mexican labor in the United States. It is followed by a discussion of how immigration policy invented "illegal aliens" to produce a temporary labor force and labor policy codified their exclusion from legal protections afforded other groups of workers. Both groups of policies expanded U.S. employers' control over legal and illegal Mexican workers. Understood in this way, the Bracero Program, an early guestworker program, was only one side of a coin that paid to develop a "disposable" workforce.

The third section outlines neoliberal policies affecting the Mexican workforce, which promoted labor migration both within Mexico and north across the U.S.-Mexico border. Anticipated outcomes of the North American Free Trade Agreement (NAFTA) included increases in both legal and undocumented migration. Politicians used undocumented migration, to generate political capital and opportunities for corporate contributors (Philp 2008). In essence, neoliberal policies stimulated increased concerns over border "security" and the immigration policies that resulted promoted increased public spending on policing and deporting undocumented immigrants.

The final section begins to outline the influence of neoliberal policies in expanding economic activity at the border. Public spending toward increasingly privatized government functions, including policing the border and detention and deportation of undocumented immigrants, inform a different type of demand for undocumented immigrants. This demand implicates new relationships between employers and migration intermediaries, such as federal subcontractors. In turn, the proliferation of public and private, formal and informal, legal and illicit activities at the border demonstrate that employers have become more sophisticated in their use of immigration policy such that they obscure their complicity in undocumented migration and labor control. Neoliberal policies expand markets of undocumented migrant labor to groups as diverse as middle-class homeowners and informal service entrepreneurs, i.e. landscaping and housecleaning.

The shift in employer demand implies an apparent contradiction: a greater reliance on immigration policy to produce "illegal subjects" also sustains undocumented migration. This reliance is mediated by institutional actors, such as the private prison industry, that promote the illusion of control over undocumented labor. The relationship between growing demand and greater reliance on policy suggest an alternate framework for understanding current immigration debates. The chapter concludes that the nature of demand for undocumented labor is inextricably tied to the reproduction of the "illegal subject."

The Historical Origins of Mexican Labor in the United States

The popular sense that "illegal aliens" have invaded the United States is a projection of a historical relationship in which the United States expanded its investment in, and control over, Mexico's politics, its economy, and its workers. Generations of Mexicans indirectly refer to their subordination in viewing Mexico as "so close to the United States…and so far from God." This view reflects a sense of being lost and subordinate to the U.S. political economy, which dates back to the mid-nineteenth century. Undocumented Mexican migrants fit within this historical context. On the U.S. side of the border, migrations were shaped by Mexican subordination to political, economic, immigration and labor policies. The enduring significance of this relationship is embedded in Mexican and Southwestern U.S. culture. For instance, migration to the United States is recognized as a cultural right of passage for poor and working-class Mexican men (Reichert 1982). When we ignore the historical context and call for broad removal of "illegal aliens," we perhaps unwittingly reinforce well-established social conduits that produced a disposable and subordinated workforce. The terms upon which Mexicans migrate to the United States, and the institutions that shape their experiences, are informed by a history that originates before the 1848 Mexican-American War. This history locates Anglo settlers in Mexican territory as the initiators and benefactors of the post-war dislocations, which included dispossession and the industrialization of the Southwestern United States in ways that disadvantaged and undermined Mejicanos' control over land-based industries, like mining and cattle ranching. Anglos' reliance on Mexican resources were not limited to minerals, gold, copper, silver, sheep, and cattle. Their wealth also grew by acquiring cultural capital, such as learning Mejicanos' methods for cattle ranching and mining to support prospecting during the California Gold Rush. Anglos appropriated many symbols we associate with "cowboy culture" from Mejicanos in Texas, such as cowboy boots and hats. U.S. agricultural and mining interests in Mexico proletarianized Mejicanos as a subordinate class of labor. Their interests were effected in the United States through labor recruiters who attempted to manufacture a flexible, but controlled, labor force that would meet employer demand.

During the 1920s and beyond, employers maintained control through both coercion and cultural stereotypes that obscured their role in emmiserating Mexican workers. This period is important because it both produced and institutionalized Mexican workers' subordination to the U.S. economy. In this period, "employers had integrated Mexicans into the region's [Southwestern United States] economy under their terms...Growers argued that the economy of the Southwest greatly depended upon Mexicans to do the difficult, unpleasant work refused by Anglo workers as a matter of course" (Vargas 2005: 46). By manufacturing Mexican workers' racial difference, Anglos defined a supply of a "specific type of migrant" that could be sustained. Employers sometimes resorted to outright coercion to control their Mexican workers, but they also promoted workers' dependence and broader exclusion from the mainstream labor force. Historians demonstrate that agricultural industries resorted to a variety of tactics to maintain this workforce, including withholding pay and not providing return passage so workers wouldn't have the

ability to leave. Ultimately, however, the press largely ignored deplor-
able working conditions and popularized the "Mexican problem,"
which tied "delinquency, poor housing, low wages, illiteracy, and rates
of disease" to Mexican migration and Mexican culture (Schein 2006:
119). Employers benefited from their workers' isolation.

As agricultural employers in the United States expanded production,
their demands for subordinated Mexican workers were increasingly
supported by U.S. immigration policy. In this way, immigration policies served similar purposes in controlling labor as Jim Crow policies
in the neighboring South. Mae Ngai demonstrates the Immigration
Acts of 1921 and 1924 expanded Border Patrol's jurisdiction and
invented both "illegal" status and Mexicans as iconic "illegal aliens"
(Ngai 2004). DeGenova argues "illegality" is a political/legal construction designed "not to physically exclude them [migrants] but instead,
to socially include them under imposed conditions of enforced and
protracted vulnerability" (DeGenova 2002). Mexican migrants were
desired as workers, but despised and segregated as residents. The Act
reconciled these tensions by facilitating the policing, invisibility, and
control of Mexican workers. As a transnational workforce, the 1924
Act ensured "Mexican Americans, legal immigrants, undocumented
migrants, and imported contract workers (braceros)...remained
external to conventional definitions of the American working class"
(Ngai 2004: 129).

Mexican workers attempted to increase their economic incorporation but government policy evolved to reproduce their exclusion. In
the case of Mexican and Mexican-American labor organizers and radi-
cals, Zargosa Vargas finds they were characterized as foreigners and
targeted for deportation. "Those suspected of having communist ties
were especially singled out for immediate arrest and expulsion. At the
same time, the U.S. Border Patrol colluded with ranchers and growers
by allowing the latter to fetch Mexican workers during strike situations and labor shortages" (Vargas 2005: 50). Acuña also demonstrates
that, despite confirmed evidence of employer abuse, agencies like the
U.S. Justice Department sided with employers and raided union locals
(Acuna 2007).

The Makings of the "Illegal Subject"

The Great Depression underscored Mexican workers' vulnerability
regardless of their legal status. Immigration policies had far-reaching

consequences throughout Mexican communities and worked to bolster control over Mexican workers who were increasingly blamed for the lack of jobs. Instead of receiving relief, Mexican workers were repatriated, sometime involuntarily. Mexicans' exclusion from consideration as workers was solidified by the American Federation of Labor (AFL) who "lent its support to drive the Mexican worker across the border" (Vargas 2005: 62). The repatriations promoted distrust and secrecy within Mexican communities and disrupted their intensifying struggle for labor rights. The Depression intensified employers' ability to expand "a labor surplus so they could obtain workers on demand, at low wages, and in plentiful supply to pick their crops early and quickly" (Ngai 2004). This objective was supported by New Deal farm policy, which excluded agricultural workers from social and labor legislation, reinforced Mexicans' exclusion from the legal definition of worker, and facilitated employers' control over the agricultural workforce.

Rather than a coherent government effort to promote Mexican labor's exclusion from political protections, the Bracero Program (1942–1964) emerged despite "concern" and "warnings" from both the Immigration and Naturalization Service (INS) and the U.S. Labor Department. Despite internal dissent, the Labor Department extended its political control over Mexican labor in the interests of U.S. employers. Ngai demonstrates that both INS and the Labor Department ultimately collaborated in admitting workers and administrating the program, which meant "the federal government [formerly] assumed the role of labor contractor." The Bracero Program institutionalized practices developed in smaller proto-guestworker programs initiated during and after World War I and expanded government control over what ultimately remained subordinated labor. Even the Labor Department official in charge of the program, Lee Williams, called it "legalized slavery." About 4.6 million Mexican contract laborers were brought into the United States for jobs in agriculture and railroads. Although "only 2 percent of American farm operators employed braceros…they were the wealthiest ones" (Ngai 2004: 139).

The program fits within a broader trajectory of public investment in labor control, which sponsored employers' ability to extract greater profits from their workforce. It reproduced Mexican workers' lack of legal standing in the United States and did not enforce contractual guarantees involving housing and working conditions. Braceros endured contract violations that spanned from underpayment to inadequate housing to threats and mistreatment. Despite the program's apparent failure, it was extended beyond its explicitly-stated mission to meet wartime labor shortages. The Labor Department rarely terminated employer's contracts. Integrated in the agricultural economy, the fortunes of Braceros and undocumented farm workers affected the industry overall. For instance, farm wages declined relative to manufacturing wages in the postwar era.

The Bracero Program elucidates the unique relationship between state policy and employer control over Mexican labor. Mexican labor was only policed when it could not be controlled by employers. Tichenor writes the INS unevenly enforced immigration laws toward undocumented Mexican migrants. It "avoided search and deportation procedures... during crop seasons" (Tichenor 2002: 174). Similarly, the Bracero Program designed to meet a high demand agricultural workers, coexisted with other policy initiatives to deport "illegal aliens," such as Operation Wetback in 1954. Philip Martin et al. (2007) noted detention rates of undocumented Mexicans increased after the Bracero Program was implemented. The apparent contradictions of immigration policies surrounding the recruitment and deportation of Mexican workers demonstrate how immigration policy became embedded in formally regulating labor supply in the interests of U.S. employers. Deportation efforts magnified government control over Mexican workers and uneven enforcement shaped and directed undocumented migration streams. Tichenor confirms "Mexican labor inflows would be sustained for decades by an iron triangle of Southwestern growers, Immigration Bureau officials, and powerful congressional committees dominated by Southern and Western conservatives" (Tichenor 2002: 152).

Mexican workers' subordination to U.S. policy has always been limited by their ability to destabilize U.S. efforts to police and control the border. The history of the Mexican-American War begins with a disputed border that Mexicans crossed to win the Alamo. It was followed by resistance that made liberal use of the border. For instance, Juan Nepomuceno Cortina characterized Anglo domination after the war in terms of dispossession: "Flocks of vampires, in the guise of men... [robbed Mexicans]... of their property, incarcerated, chased, murdered, and hunted [them] like wild beasts" (Thompson 2007). Cortina challenged the eviction of Tejano ranchers and defended a Mexican farmhand against an Anglo sheriff. He also raided Brownsville, proclaimed Rio Grande a Republic, and raised the Mexican flag. He was chased back over the Mexican border repeatedly by the Texas

Rangers who were not able to capture him. Similarly, the Mexican Revolution is remembered for border transgressions within the United States, in particular for Pancho Villa's apparent disregard for the border. Despite significant obstacles posed by groups like the U.S. Immigration Bureau and the Texas Rangers, Mexican and Mexican-Americans alike organized and used the border to build labor solidarity. For instance, Emma Tenayuca was trained as a union organizer in Mexico and joined the labor movement when she returned to Texas (Vargas 2005: 119). Powerful unions like the Mexican CTM and the U.S.-based Unemployed Councils, Workers' Alliance of America, Confederation of Mexican American and Mexican workers, AFL Agricultural Workers Union No. 20212 (AWU) and "the International Mine, Mill and Smelter Workers Union of nonferrous metals workers in the Southwest" established significant cross-border links (Vargas 2005: 159).

In important ways, U.S. immigration and labor policies have shaped undocumented Mexican workers' subordination to U.S. employers. These policies produced the "illegal subject" and sponsored employers' control over Mexican workers as a subordinated and disposable workforce. In particular, the Immigration Acts of the early 1920s, the Repatriation Campaigns, New Deal farm policy, the Bracero Program, and Operation Wetback all worked to compliment and expand employers' control over Mexican workers. Although they differed in form, they shared a critical role in producing Mexican workers as iconic "illegal subjects" who were simultaneously integrated in U.S. economic growth and excluded from consideration as members of an American working class. These policies, for instance, undermined Mexicans' ability to organize and improve their work conditions.

Over the second half of the twentieth century, immigration and labor policies continued to reflect an economic philosophy that required exceptional concessions in controlling undocumented Mexican labor. For instance, Mexican workers were recruited as contracted braceros and many deserted abusive employers. The number of apprehensions also increased in this period, from in the 1940s through the first half of the 1950s. At the same time, the Immigration Act of 1952 exempted Texan agriculture from penalties for "harboring illegal aliens" (Espenshade 1995).

Despite important structural parallels with the first half of the twentieth century, the state's relationship to employers has shifted. The state benefits from its persistent collusion with employers but in ways that are more directly tied to acquiring capital. In particular, the "iron triangle" has been supplanted by a larger group of institutional actors that embed corporate interest in policy making. Employers' influence expands beyond direct congressional representation to include, for instance, lobbyists and significant contributions that finance modern campaigns.

In particular, selective enforcement magnifies state influence over undocumented migrant streams and its sponsorship of labor control. Detention practices similarly manage migrant labor supply and their "success" remain firmly tied to a changing economic structure within the United States. Hillman and Weiss consider undocumented migration somewhat "permissible" and argue "once a population of illegal immigrants is present, illegal immigration need no longer be an unintended consequence of laxity in enforcement. Illegal immigration may rather be a concertedly chosen policy that combines de jure illegality with de facto selective illegality as a discipline that permits sectoral containment of immigrants" (Hillman and Weiss 1999). The implication is that a demand exists for "a specific type of worker" and that undocumented workers are both directly and indirectly produced by policy.

Changes in statecraft seem to challenge current neoliberal philosophies that treat states and borders as obstacles to free trade. The border has historically represented a crossroads between controlling undocumented Mexican workers and structuring Mexico to accommodate U.S. capital. Beginning in the 1960s, however, neoliberal policies and large migrant labor flows have become coterminous. These policies have recreated the border as a stage for neoliberal development where "free trade zones" and maquilas indirectly recruit and generate new migrant streams (Bandy 2000). The next section discusses how neoliberal policies have encouraged undocumented migration from Mexico and how the state (policymakers and policy) have created new opportunities to benefit from "illegality."

Labor Migration and the North American
Free Trade Agreement (NAFTA)

The North American Free Trade Agreement, or NAFTA, was passed in January 1994. Supporters of the trade-liberalizing agreement argued the expected increase in migration would be temporary, representing something akin to a "shock treatment" during which wages in Mexico and the United States would adjust and eventually reduce the incentive to migrate. Although predictions seemed to materialize amidst increased migration, immigration policies did not adjust for this increase. Specifically, U.S. Department of Homeland Security (DHS) numbers show that the number of persons obtaining legal permanent resident status declined after 1994 and, despite increasing after 2000, never reached the levels of 1990 and 1991 (MPI 2007). At the same time, and number of undocumented Mexicans entering in the United States after 1994 rose 1.88 million to 3.47 million in 1999 (Hoefer 2008).

Increased trade with the United States undermined Mexico's agricultural sectors, displaced many farmers and promoted domestic inequality. "The value of the Mexican minimum wage dropped 23 percent in NAFTA's first decade; 19 million more Mexicans are living in poverty than 20 years ago, and today, one quarter of Mexico's population cannot afford basic foods" (Lewis 2008). National trends were also reflected at regional levels as sharp increases in income disparity within Mexico have disproportionately "shocked" subsistence farmers displaced by the "privatization of Mexico's collective farms...", the elimination of agricultural subsidies," and competition with U.S.-agricultural imports (Fernandez-Kelley and Massey 2007).

Wage differentials also increased within Mexico because access to foreign trade and investment varies regionally (Hanson 2003). The growth of maquilas in northern Mexico and inequality in southern Mexico motivated internal and external migration. Although U.S. policymakers emphasized complementary development and maquilas' expected role in creating jobs in Mexico, NAFTA essentially reproduced Mexican subordination south of the border. The primary Mexican export became its labor. In Mexico's "labor export-led model" of development, the workforce is exported to maquilas before it crossed the U.S.-Mexican border (Wise and Cypher 2007).

Once in the United States, undocumented Mexican migrants support demand for low-skilled labor at rates that promote U.S. industries' global competitiveness. For instance, scholars like Edna Bonacich (2000) and Roger Waldinger (1999) demonstrate that low-skilled migrants bolstered declining industries and kept more manufacturing jobs from being exported outside the United States. Others like Hondagneu-Sotelo (2007) suggest migrants accommodate increased middle-class consumption patterns, particularly in relation to domestic work, and "subsidize the careers and social opportunities of their employers." Larger corporate interests that depend on migrant labor, particularly agribusiness, lobby against liberalizing trade policies that would undermine their control over domestic markets. They argue their competitiveness relative to other industrializing countries requires more competitive wage rates and less restrictive labor regulations.

U.S. immigration policy since the mid-1990s has not explicitly mediated the effects of NAFTA. Instead, it has promoted the further subordination of Mexican migrant labor by promoting federal and local spending on surveillance of "unauthorized aliens," which are most frequently assumed to be Mexican. The period since the mid-1990s has also been marked by a perception that new threats to national security, such as international crime organizations and terrorism, are centered on the U.S.-Mexico border (Andreas 1998). As policing efforts expanded to include an ever greater number of public and private actors, domestic unemployment rates declined and our economy expanded. Given our own domestic economic growth in the period from the mid-1990s to 2000, what explains the emergence of punitive anti-immigrant legislation?

Although scholars recognize the role that neoliberalism has played on reinforcing anxieties about territorial authority, they do not explain how these anxieties tie public expenditures on security to political outcomes that move beyond the illusion of controlling the border. For instance, in debates of the 1986 Immigration and Reform Control Act (IRCA), the Republican Governor of California, Peter Wilson, sponsored an amendment that made agricultural workplace raids virtually impossible. In his reelection campaign, after polls showed Wilson trailing behind his Democratic opponent by 17 percentage points, Wilson drafted the "Save Our State" Initiative, otherwise known as Proposition 187. Wilson's reelection was tied to passing a piece of legislation that was ultimately deemed unconstitutional in federal court. In other words, Wilson's political fortunes were tied to not only ignoring the practices of employers who rely on a predominantly-Mexican agricultural workforce, but also denying these workers and their families access to basic services, including emergency health care and public education.

President Clinton similarly seized immigration as part of his 1997 reelection campaign platform, a year after having suggested that the Border Patrol's workforce should be reduced. He legitimized the perception that migrants derived significant benefits from public assistance. In 1996, under his administration, the Personal Responsibility and Work Opportunity Reconciliation Act (PRWORA) was passed and scholars like Fix and Tumlin (1997) warned it would have "far-reaching effects on immigrants, on the nation's immigrant policy, or on the new role state and local governments will play in shaping the policies that govern immigrant integration" (1997: 1). Also known as the "Welfare Reform Act," the PRWORA reduced immigrants' access to public assistance programs.

Clinton also refashioned the discourse of illegality to promote local development through policing. Specifically, the 1996 Illegal Immigration Reform and Immigrant Responsibility Act reinvented "illegal aliens" as "unlawfully present" persons who paid penalties in the form of bans to reentry to the United States. Limits range from three years to permanent bans, which clearly expand the social boundaries of exclusion and atomize undocumented persons by disregarding social relationships that tie migrants to the United States, including having a spouse or child that is a U.S. citizen. The Act represented part of a broader effort to "beef up" border patrol (Andreas 2002). The Act expanded detention policing in a variety of ways that have been tied to decreasing oversight and human and civil rights violations, including deputizing state and local law enforcement personnel to enforce immigration matters (Hernandez 2008).

Neoliberal policies clearly had an impact on undocumented migration. The state's relationship to employers, and the boundaries between policy makers and entrepreneurs, has shifted in the late twentieth century. Policymakers market illegality to their public, the media, and increasingly, to private contractors. Policies expand state apparatus to both control undocumented Mexican labor and generate new sources of revenue. In essence, the state has come to rely on migrants for more than their labor. The state now requires undocumented immigrants as subjects for new economic markets built around border "security." The next section turns to the new migration industrial complex and maps the diversification of demand for undocumented Mexican migrants.

The Undocumented Migration Industry

The section above argued the presumed inevitability of increased migration was "managed" by policies and politics that benefited from subordinating undocumented Mexican labor. Neoliberalism facilitated the expansion of U.S. corporate interests in Mexico (particularly agribusiness), stimulated intra-regional inequality, and encouraged migration toward the border. Internal migration facilitated economic opportunities for a different group of U.S. capitalists profiting from free trade zones. Crossing the border mobilized an entirely new set of entrepreneurs which included U.S. employers and the prison/detention industry.

Despite broad interests in keeping migrants mobile, interested actors often overtly oppose undocumented migration. For instance, media hides itself as an interested actor that profits from undocumented migration both directly, because it provides information for news stories, and indirectly by legitimizing this migration industrial complex. "Widely publicized threats and news coverage of deportations serve to germinate a climate of fear among undocumented immigrants and their legal immigrant relatives. This fear makes the undocumented super-exploitable as they feel they have no recourse in the case of crimes committed against them or in the case of mistreatment (including breaches of contract, lack of safety precautions, under-payment or non-payment) by employers" (Wilson 2000: 202). Media reproduces the illusion that undocumented Mexican migrants are not workers in a traditional sense, which undermines solidarity around, for instance, labor rights violations.

What distinguishes the migration industrial complex is that it is promoted through opposition to undocumented workers. As a result, it enjoys broader public support and participation (Welch 2000). In this way, citizens become complicit in bolstering public spending on "security" and making undocumented migration and its management profitable.

The apparent contradiction between an expected outcome (increased undocumented migration) and an increasingly restrictive immigration framework suggest an important shift in neoliberal frameworks. Free trade policies effect a migration industry that is both formal and informal. The recognition of a socially disadvantageous outcome, i.e. increased migration, is likened to "collateral damage" as a result of economic development. On the one hand, neoliberal policies have a dialectical effect of producing and solidifying profitable borders (De Giorgi 2006). These borders are erected protectively, in the name of "security," and generate significant political and financial capital. On the other hand, free trade policies expand a migration industry and its both formal and informal economic activities. These policies do not apologize for the excesses of the industry. It cannot, for instance, implement remedial strategies that would undermine the privatization of state security, such as an open border.

Immigration policy's emphasis on policing and deportation should be understood as an outgrowth of neoliberalism and the state's shifting alignments with the economy. In terms of regulating migration, the state's actions should be understood less as a response to anxieties about globalization and more as a creative response to expanding its own economic relationships within a dynamic global economy. The state regulates migration not because it seeks to assert sovereign control over territory, but rather because it seeks to "set up…chains of enrolment [sic], 'responsibilization' and 'empowerment' to sectors and agencies distant from the centre, yet tied to it through a complex of alignments and translations" (Barry et al. 1996: 12). In this way, the state can be seen as transferring resources to businesses within the migration industry. The state's alignment with a greater number of economic actors promotes its influence and objectives. "Of key importance to neo-liberalism, for example, is the development of techniques of auditing, accounting and management that enable a 'market' for public services to be established autonomous from central control. Neo-liberalism, in these terms, involves less a retreat from governmental 'intervention' than a re-inscription of the techniques and forms of expertise required for the exercise of government" (ibid.: 14).

New institutional actors within the migration industry render illegality increasingly profitable for U.S. businesses. This section does not claim to establish a comprehensive survey of the migration industry. Instead, its more modest goal is to demonstrate how the state, the economy, and the public sustain the migration industry's markets. Demand for undocumented migrants falls into three general groups: i) those who assist in the logistics of undocumented migration, particularly transportation, ii) those who hire undocumented workers, and iii) private capital and state agencies. The following section provides examples of actors falling within each category.

Demand for undocumented migrants begins with a chain of profiteers whose lifeline starts at the U.S.-Mexican border. Small entrepreneurs, including hotel owners, food vendors, convenience stores, polleros and coyotes facilitate an uneasy entry into the United States. They are relatively vulnerable and unstable group. Nonetheless, the cost and importance of these intermediaries increase along with the risks of unauthorized entry and employment. For instance, Wayne Cornelius suggests that these costs have more than quadrupled since 1993 (Cornelius 2005). Within the group, polleros take greatest physical risk as they guide people crossing through the desert, across fences and rivers, and help migrants avoid dehydration, snake bites, and ICE officers. Polleros also ferry undocumented migrants within the United States for hefty fees.

Polleros are contracted by coyotes whose average rates vary and increase depending on enforcement efforts that must be circumvented. For instance, a coyote charges an average of $4,000 for facilitating undocumented migration from Guatemala but only about half this amount for migrants in Mexico because the Guatemalan migrant must pass through a greater number of checkpoints. Coyotes are known for being involved in the underground economy and they may present unique challenges for the migrant, such as including drugs or collaborating with thieves on the journey. Migrants experience the journey as threatening and justify high fees based on not only reputation, but also security and presumed distance from the illicit economy.

Once in the United States, the labor migrant is most likely to secure work through a labor recruiter. A friend or family member acts as a recruiter that directs migrants toward specific employers and jobs. Sometimes referred to as a form of "negative social capital," friends and family members also exercise control over migrants' labor more intimately than traditional employer-employee relationships and replace the paternalistic relations characterizing, for instance, low-skilled agricultural and domestic work. In essence, labor recruiters are the social lubricant that helps these industries to thrive.

The boundaries between the formal and informal economy are destabilized by profit-making opportunities arising from workers' illegality. For instance, entrepreneurs fabricate the illusion of legal formality by creating and selling fraudulent work and identity documents. The most explicit examples of employers operating on the boundaries of formality, or at least the illusion of formality, involve larger employers within the United States. The recent example of the largest workplace raid in U.S. history, in Postville, Iowa, shows us that labor recruiters can also pick up another job within the industry and fabricate fraudulent work documents. In this case, although intermediaries expanded their involvement in the industry, greater profits were secured by formal employers who enjoy legitimate participation in the formal economy. Agriprocessors, Inc. was under investigation at the time of the raid for wage and labor law violations but workers were the main targets of the raid. After a five-month delay, the company's CEO was also arrested and Agriprocessors declared bankruptcy. The case demonstrates two interrelated phenomena. First, the migrant worker is emphasized in state regulation over workplaces. Second, when predominantly undocumented workers gained attention for illegal work conditions, they are excluded from traditional remedies enjoyed by legitimate workers. In this case, an undocumented workforce demonstrated its salience within a local economy when Postville residents also lost their jobs and wages after the raid.

Cases like those in Postville, Iowa demonstrate that legal representatives and state agents are embedded within the migration industry. Immigration lawyers certainly promote the industry insofar as they justify the continued employment of immigration judges and court clerks. To the extent these lawyers can secure legal documents for their clients, they expand their business. Legal representatives also include many fraudulent groups who compete with immigrant advocates for legitimacy. The legal system is not the only, or even the most influential, group interpreting policy that guides enforcement. Instead, it works at the margins of legislative reforms encouraged by well-paid corporate lobbyists.

At the top of the profit chain are two types of big money-making businesses. The first group is private employers. Scholars simultaneously contemplating legal admissions and economic growth ask "how has the supply of immigrant labor to the United States been so carefully calibrated to demand?" and many agree that immigration policy and enforcement have been driven by the needs of the U.S. economy. In other words, because undocumented workers' labor is "illegal," employers can turn a greater profit. They can pay less and worry less about the treatment of their workers in terms of benefits, safety on the job and worker complaints. These U.S. employers include agribusiness, "the largest economic sector in the United States" (Krissman 2000). Agribusiness claims to need a large and seasonal migrant workforce that they can work in the most difficult of circumstances, like a hot sun that can kill from dehydration, and pay less while doing it. In the end, their political influence has simultaneously created "the world's most profitable agricultural sector and the most disadvantaged class fraction of America's working poor" (ibid.: 280). The profits flow to a few employers and meager rewards are allocated to their overworked and drastically underpaid employees.

The detention and deportation sector of the migration industry, inhabiting that nether realm between private firm and state agency, ensures their interests vis a vis circular migration. They are a large and growing sector and benefit directly from policing the border and facilitating the deportation of undocumented persons. In 1995, Josiah Heyman argued that the Immigration and Naturalization Service (INS) used "unstated policies" to guide selective enforcement. He discussed the "voluntary departure complex" in which enforcement efforts target Mexicans who are released directly on the southern side of the U.S.-Mexico border. Ultimately, INS deportation practices are largely ineffective at deterring subsequent attempts at unauthorized entry. The INS "arrests many persons, thereby reinforcing the state idea of bounded citizenship (emphasizing symbols of "border control") for media sale and consumption, and negates the effectiveness of these arrests, thus permitting labor migration in numbers well beyond those permitted by law" (Heyman 1995: 267). INS was restructured and placed under the new DHS. Despite the shift, scholars recognize that border policing still "has less to do with actual deterrence and more to do with managing the image of the border and coping with the deepening contradictions of economic integration" (Andreas 2002: 593). ICE is currently the federal government's second largest investigative agency after the Federal Bureau of Investigations (FBI).

The migration industry is predicated on enabling undocumented migration. For instance, border patrol agents are employed in large part because there are undocumented migrants. At one end, policymakers can make voters happy that they're creating jobs along the U.S.-Mexican border by policing illegal immigration. At the other end, policymakers privatize security and stimulate businesses who profit directly from the detaining and deporting undocumented immigrants. The variety of businesses that benefit from major contracts include, for instance, auto that produce vehicles for agents to monitor the border and companies that produce agents' uniforms. These contracts are quite small in comparison to those that secure the most sophisticated and expensive surveillance technology available today.

In November 2005, DHS created the Secure Border Initiative (SBI), a multiyear, multibillion dollar program to "secure" U.S. borders. One example of spending under this initiative is SBInet, a technology-building program that includes developing policing capacity through the use of radars, sensors, cameras, and satellite phones. To get a sense of the size of this program, in January 2008, the Senate Committee on Homeland Security & Governmental Affairs reported that DHS would need $7.6 billion through 2011 to "acquire and deploy the necessary technology and fencing along the Southwest border" (SCHSGA 2008). This amount represents a revised estimates based on earlier contracts with companies like Boeing who, in 2006, was awarded a three-year contract valued at $2 to $8 billion dollars.

What happened to all that spending and Boeing's work with SBInet? A 2008 Government Accounting Office report confirmed the work had been subcontracted and there was insufficient capacity for over-seeing these contracts. These problems were compounded by delays in meeting timelines for pilot systems to go into effect. The Department of Defense was responsible for overseeing the contract under David Norquist. Norquist was questioned in 2006 for leading a team of offi-cials that concealed KBR, a Halliburton subsidiary, had overcharged Iraq in its contract. The 2007 GAO report on SBInet predicted that Boeing's contract costs would increase because CBP would be using commercial labor, rather than its own officers, to build the projected 370 miles of pedestrian fence and 200 miles of vehicle barriers.

What is important to understand about this spending is that it is strategic but not effective. It is strategic in that it is located predomi-nantly near urbanized areas where voters can see their hard-earned tax dollars at work and feel proud of the growth in their local economy. It is not effective for the same reasons that undocumented migration has historically destabilized control at the border. Native American lands in states like California and Texas predate territorial divisions between the United States and Mexico. These lands interrupt the border and reflect the interconnectedness of American peoples.

Boeing shares affinity with other corporations that benefit directly from policing beyond the border. A brief look at the 2007 and 2008 budgets of ICE's budget reveal increased spending on detention beds, which represent the most expensive single line item detailed in its report. In a 2008 broadcast of NOW on PBS, the focus was on "Prisons for Profit." In her investigation of private prisons, Maria Hinojosa called detention a "gold rush" because undocumented persons repre-sent the fastest growing population behind bars (Hinojosa 2008).

Detention contracts are offered to private prison companies like Corrections Corporation of America (CCA), the largest private prison company in the country. CCA had been struggling to repopulate their prisons and even considered closing in 2004. It positioned itself to benefit from Congressional legislation authorizing ICE to triple the number of immigrant detention beds. In 2004, CCA's lobbying expenditures reached $3 million. Since then, it has spent an additional $7 million on lobbyists. These lobbyists include "Philip Perry, Vice President Dick Cheney's son-in-law, who later became general counsel at the Department of Homeland Security" (Mencimer 2008). CCA's business continues to grow. In its second quarter announcement last month, CCA posted a total revenue increase of more than 10 percent to almost 400 million (Gupta 2008). It's revenue results not only from detaining undocumented persons, but also from subordinated work- ers. After reviewing CCA's personnel files, ICE arrested 10 undocu- mented workers.

Other private detention companies like the GEO Group built on their important relationships in Washington, cultivated through their lobbyists and through campaign contributions. The GEO Group's director, George Zoley, was a major contributor to President George W. Bush's 2004 reelection campaign. As a Bush "Pioneer," he raised at least $100,000 for the campaign. His biography credits Zoley for devel- oping "opportunities in the privatization of government services" (The GEO Group 2009). In 2007, the GEO Group earned more than $100 million through their immigration detention centers and, of course, these private detention facilities ensure business for a host of feeder industries like food and health providers, airline carriers...and the list goes on.

Private detention facilities charge the government about $100 per person, per day. Despite the profit (or perhaps cynically because of it), immigrants complain that they're treated inhumanely. Often, human rights monitors are denied access to these facilities. The American Civil Liberties Union's (ACLU) case against these private detention centers show violations of standards on children in custody. According to the ACLU, children were kept in cells 11 or 12 hours a day, forced to wear prison garb, fed "unrecognizable substances, mostly starches," and denied toys, bathroom privacy, and access to medical care (ACLU 2008). Hinojosa interviewed one of these center's guards who also reported that detainees aren't always fed, they're given dirty blankets, put in leaking and/or freezing cells, get sick, and catch foot funguses. Many activists blame the lack of oversight over these facilities, and inad- equate access to medical care, for deaths that occur while immigrants are detained. In a report it just published in June, the Department of Homeland Security itself concurs that oversight could be improved at ICE Detention Facilities (Inspector General 2008).

When one of its primary incentives is profit, the function of security becomes more important than form. In the mutated structure of the migration industry, ensuring beds are filled is the primary concern. The undocumented migration industry thrives on the backs of subordinated workers. As in other industries, exploitation generates profits in the migration industry. Unlike other industries, however, profiteers risk not only the livelihoods, but indeed the lives of those who are forced to consume its services. The pollero, the ICE officer, the large farm owner, and the GEO all reproduce a more devastating way of generating revenue that requires a willingness to risk someone else's life and a lack of responsibility over the lives of others.

Conclusion

Despite broader demand and growth in the number of persons who use undocumented labor, public policy seems poised to expand its definition of "illegality" in ways that reproduce the migration industrial complex. For instance, immigration reform proposals debated in 2006 redefined "alien smuggling" to include "family members, neighbors, co-workers, and relief organizations who provide nonemergency aid to undocumented migrants" (Hernández 2008). The expansion of this category demonstrates the ways in which the political fate of "a special kind of migrant" may alter the fortunes of both the U.S. economy and those who depend on it for their livelihood. This chapter argued demand for undocumented labor was, and remains, part and parcel of our collective race to the bottom. The number of entrepreneurs and intermediaries within the migration industry expands along with the reach of central institutions reproducing demand for undocumented labor. We experience this demand as workers, and residents of a country that expands its global effort to subordinate and control an ever expanding population of migrants.

The task before us now is to better understand this migration industrial complex and work to promote a more humane and rational system that does not exploit workers, whatever their country of origin. Much like the unheeded warning by Eisenhower anticipating the military industrial complex arguably creating a defense industry that perpetuates itself to the detriment of people in this country and abroad, the growing migration industrial complex feeds on the fears and xeno-phobia of people in this country while it builds the foundation for the long term immiseration of our neighbors to the south.

MIGRATION, TRANSNATIONALISM AND POST-MODERNITY

Alejandro I. Canales and Israel Montiel Armas

Introduction

In the United States, the Spring of 2006 will be distinctly remembered for demonstrations by millions of Latin American immigrants
who opposed US immigration policies and for the official attempts to
approve reforms leading to criminalization of undocumented migration. In several U.S. cities, immigrants literally took over the streets.
The protests were not confined to the largest cities such as New York,
Chicago and Los Angeles but also spread to dozens of cities of varied
sizes. The peace and quiet of such places as Salt Lake City, Utah and
Arlington, Texas was suddenly shattered by the voices of young Latin
American people protesting anti-immigrant policies.

While American society recognizes the mobilization and struggle
in defense of the human rights of Mexican immigrants and Latin
Americans in general (Delgado 2008), the Spring demonstrations of
2006 differed in several ways. On the one hand, these demonstrations
were not supported by a strong leadership, but were instead articulated from the bottom-up, based on a complex system of social and
communal networks that migrants have been constructing for decades
(Zlolniski 2008). The organization of marches and mobilizations were
made possible by the strength of social networks that for the first time
had acquired a sociopolitical connotation that went beyond the community itself.

On the other hand, the participation of young migrants was notable
as was the presence of the children of migrants, people who were born
in the United States. This was very revealing since not only does it
indicate a high degree of intergenerational solidarity, but also the configuration of a protagonist social subject, the youths, who were claiming their own rights and were no longer relegated to the defense of the
labor or migratory rights of their parents. A third and related point
was the character of the demonstrations. Even if the catalyst for the
protests was the attempt to approve immigration reforms aimed at
the criminalization of undocumented migration, there were demands

and claims being made in the heat of the mobilizations that went well beyond the margins or frames that traditionally revolve around migratory policy. The stated demands of the protests were in fact oriented not so much toward the defense of immigrant rights but rather for broad civil and citizen rights. Young people took to the streets to demand their own rights and spaces in a society which has increasingly come to marginalize and exclude them.

"Here we are, here we stay" read one of the numerous protest banners. Perhaps this text best reflected the demands of hundreds of thousands of Latin American youths. Not only did they demand better labor conditions, access to social security, and access to education, but they also demanded a space in society where they could be recognized for what they are, namely, Latino citizens of the United States. They were claiming their social insertion without renouncing their cultural roots. As children of Latin American immigrants, many of them already are American citizens, but have yet to be recognized as such.

For their entire lives, society has demanded that they renounce their cultural, ethnic, and social origin.[1] What the demonstrations brought to light for all to see was not only the injustice of US migratory policy, but also the quantitative importance and, above all, the qualitative importance of a new social subject emerging from American society. This new social subject springs from the social, demographic, cultural and ethnic roots that form part of the social crucible of a changing American society. The demonstrations left no doubt that Latinos or Hispanics are not simply just another migrant group. In short, we have witnessed the appearance of a new vector from the ethnic-cultural matrix of American society. Confronted with the binomial of preserving their marginalized identity and cultural roots or risk being diluted and absorbed by the larger American matrix, the Spring 2006 protests put forth a third opinion: integration without assimilation. The vision was one of becoming integrated into the larger society as an active component, and contributing to it with their own cultural, social and demographic roots that in so doing could enrich and transform that society.

---

[1] Several analysts have compared these demonstrations of Spring 2006 with those of the 1960's that developed in the struggle for Black civil rights.

If we consider that the migration of Mexican people to the United States goes back more than a century and a half, characterized by conditions of economic exclusion, social vulnerability, and precarious labor conditions (Bustamante 2007), then why was it that this new social movement suddenly appeared in 2006? Indeed, Latin people's protests in the United States have been longstanding. The real novelty is to be found in two aspects of these mobilizations that transformed them into a new phenomenon, giving new social meaning to immigration originating from Latin America. The first was related to the new factor of the magnitude of the mobilizations. This could be seen both in terms of the number of people involved and its territorial expansion. There is no question that the demonstrations were massive, totaling millions of people, and no longer remaining confined to the traditional Latino population centers. This made the movement's capacity for articulation, organization and mobilization self-evident as it created a nationwide movement out of a new correlation of social and political forces.

The second aspect so noteworthy was the distinctive character of these mobilizations. Latin people as an emergent social subject in American society now ceased to be a mere category referring to a group of immigrants. In its place was a social group category emerging out of a demand to stop being considered immigrants, foreigners, and aliens. It was not a demand for pure and simple legal citizenship, but rather an assertion of social citizenship with all its concomitant cultural, demographic and political implications.

In order to understand the reach, character, dimensions and consequences of this movement, it is necessary to start from a broader conceptual framework that grasps the dynamics of international migration and the conformation of transnational communities.

International Migrations in Contemporary Society

International migration is not a recent phenomenon. Almost all of the Western countries and Japan up to the mid-Twentieth Century expelled considerable numbers of people, thus far making them the largest countries of origin for international emigration (Portes and Rumbaut 1990). If anything distinguishes the current situation in relation to prior epochs, it is that international migration has become diverse and more complex, both in terms of the routes of origin and destination as well as the modalities of displacement and the diversity of people involved (Castles and Miller 1993). All of this has now become inserted into the framework of structural transformations derived from the globalization process. The redesign of the world's geography has opened new spaces for displacement, not only of material and symbolic goods, but also of people and their labor.

While the structural conditions that shape and unleash the movements may change from time to time, the displacement of people is an inevitable phenomenon. Rephrasing Marx and his Law of Population (Marx 1967), we can affirm that each stage of capitalism's development corresponds to a particular migratory system, with its own specific and historically determined tendencies, dynamics and problems. In this sense, what is acutely relevant is not simply the question of whether international migration has increased or decreased. Nor should we be solely concerned with identifying the most efficacious mechanisms for exerting control over the phenomenon. Rather, there is a need to critically understand the specificities of its dynamics and how this becomes problematic in contemporary society. In particular, we consider that the complexity of migration issues in the present era forces us to reconstruct those traditional approaches that are no longer in synch with the new historical moment. To this end, we suggest that the experience provided by Mexican migration toward the United States points to several complex aspects of the present era.

A first aspect refers to the character assumed by the population's spatial mobility in this global and postmodern world. International migration has become a diverse and complex process that not only involves a flow of people and their labor, but also an equally important flow of material and symbolic goods. It is by means of migration that social, familial and cultural networks become solidified and active. It is through these networks that a complex system of interchange and circulation of people, money, goods and information has developed that articulates and integrates the settlements of migrants on both sides of the border into a single, large and configured community. Various authors refer to this process in terms of the configuration of "transnational" communities (Smith 1995; Pries, 1997). This signifies that through migration, diverse factors and articulation processes in the cultural, social and economic spheres become active between distant and geographically separated communities and social institutions. This suggests a dislocation and de-structuring of the traditional concept of "community," especially in terms of its spatial and territorial dimensions (Kearney and Nagengast 1989). The virtual de-territorialization of communities occurs due to the continuous flow and interchange of people, goods and information which appear with and from migration, and make the reproduction of the origin communities directly and intrinsically linked to the different migrants' settlements in urban neighborhoods and rural towns in the United States (Canales and Zlolniski 2001; Alarcón 1995; Hondagneu-Zotelo 1994).

Hence, one of the principal manifestations of mass migrations in contemporary society is the ethnic-cultural diversity that increasingly characterizes receptor societies, something which rests on international integration between migrant communities that directly link origin and destination communities free of the mediations of national-states. Migration in this context does not necessarily imply a severance of community and family. On the contrary, migration becomes a way to broaden and extend familial and communal relations. In this sense, the immigrant is not alone since they carry their community along with them, no longer in a metaphoric sense but in a real and literal sense. Emigration is no longer a synonym for "leaving behind" but "for bringing along" since the emigrant does not leave their community but now carries it with them.

Another consequence of this phenomenon of migration is that the social dynamics in the origin countries turn into relevant factors of development for the social dynamics in the destination countries. In practice, these dynamics become endogenous factors. All of this implies that the socioeconomic and socio-demographic structures of the recipient countries become more open to the exterior, not only because the migratory flow contributes to their evolution, but also because, through emigration, the social dynamics of the origin countries directly echo the dynamics proper to the destination countries. With this, we refer not only to emergency situations such as the devastation produced by Hurricane Mitch in Central America in 1998, the civil wars in the same region during the 1980's, or the Mexican Economy's collapses in 1984 and 1994, which in each case caused a notable increment in migration toward the United States, but also and perhaps principally to processes of the structural kind.

One of the processes that display this kind of structural interdependence is that of the historic demographic dynamics of the recipient countries. In this case, we can observe through analysis of the population's evolution that immigration is not a merely a complement of relative growth but, for a large part of these countries, an intrinsic part of their population's reproduction system. It becomes essential to consider the subsequent contribution the immigrants and their descendants make to the population's natural growth. This fact is evident not only in the so called "settlement countries" (chiefly, the United States, Canada, Argentina, Australia, and New Zealand), but also in others such as France, which are historically characterized by having low fertility rates. In those cases, population growth is explained in large part by the continual arrival of migrants and their double contribution: as they immigrate, they reproduce as well as their descendants.[2] Therefore, we see demographic complementarities between expulsion and recipient countries of a structural nature, the historical shifting of the actors notwithstanding. The developing countries of today now hold the position previously held by others, e.g., Mediterranean and Slavic European countries. The ageing demographic profile in occidental countries is a contemporary factor that will undoubtedly further accentuate this complementarity.

In reference to the other part of the binomial, emigration also fulfills a fundamental role as a population regulation mechanism. It allows for assuaging the social effects produced by stagnation in peripheral countries in the world's economic system. It is evident that a situation of stagnation and underdevelopment can cause emigration just as the processes of change can also have the same effect.[3] The processes of modernization and integration of the productive system of developing countries into the international economic circuit is a case in point. Previously, it was believed that such processes promoted development and improved the standard of living in the developing countries that could act as a brake on emigration. For this reason, development assistance, foreign direct investment and free trade were stated as possible instruments to help stop those flows. An example of this can be seen in the 1986 Immigration and Control Act which hardened the management

---

[2] The demographer Anna Cabré (1999) develops this thesis from the case of Catalonia, which for a century received immigrants from the rest of Spain and currently receives them from other parts of the world. The author shows that women, out of those who were born between 1856 and 1960, and only those who were born between 1936 and 1950 reached a net reproduction rate above 1. From her calculations, the author concludes that, in the absence of immigration, the current Catalonian population would be 2,400,000 inhabitants instead of more than 6 million people. Gabriel Estrella, Alejandro I. Canales and María Eugenia Zavala (1999) present a similar analysis for the case of the Mexican northern border.

[3] Paul Singer (1975) developed an in-depth thesis, although referred to the countryside-city migrations inside the same country.

of immigration in the United States. It also provided for the creation of a Congressional Commission for the Study of International Migration and Cooperative Economic Development whose mission was to recommend measures of economic cooperation and development assistance in order to alleviate the negative effects of greater border control on the countries where emigration originates and, at the time, allow for reducing those flows. In reality, it has been observed (and was also one of this commission's conclusions) that the alleged linkage of development and emigration was extremely simplistic. The insertion of these countries into the international economic circuit has provoked the destructuring of traditional local communities and reduced the means of subsistence for broad segments of the population, something which clearly causes an increment of the migratory flows toward other countries.[4] It is enough to remember how the industrialization of European countries and Japan was accompanied by massive emigrations from the countryside to the city and then also overseas.

Migration and Transnationalism

In classical approaches to migration, there is a distinction between temporary and definitive migration. By the latter, it was considered that in spite of the close ties immigrants have with their countries of origin, their drive to settle and integrate into their country of adoption was such that former ties would gradually disappear in time, eventually resulting in the group's complete assimilation. This "Americanization" does not imply that the linkage with the origin country necessarily disappears nor that the immigrants give up all their customs, but rather that immigration has effects on the idiosyncrasy of the recipient society. Let us remember that despite the United States' origin as a refuge for several protestant sects being persecuted in England,[5]

---

[4] The thesis that capital's mobility generates international migration is found in Sassen (1988). An instance of this process is to be found in the entrance of foreign investment into the industrial corridor of El Salto (Jalisco, Mexico). This industrial zone was one of the main sources of employment for the metropolitan area of Guadalajara and contributed to maintaining low levels of emigration toward the United States. When the exporting assembly industry was introduced, the preference for feminine workforce created a lack of labor opportunities for men and a significant increment in emigration toward the United States.

[5] Curiously, the State of Maryland was founded by Catholic refugees who were also persecuted in England around that time.

(something that helped form the model of the United States' collective self-image), that country now has a significant Catholic population as a result of Irish, Italian, Polish and other immigration from other largely Catholic countries. Another instance is U.S. policy with respect to the Ulster conflict, marked by its substantial population of Irish origin. The maintenance of these links does not suppose a questioning of integration or the American Dream, but they often contribute to the cultural milieu of the United States (parades on Saint Patrick's Day, pizza, popular Jewish artists, and so on).

On the contrary, Mexican migration had been traditionally considered more typical of "temporary" migration. Many Mexican migrants settled in the United States during the Twentieth Century and most of them did not intend on establishing themselves there. In reality, it can be said that these migrants lived more in the migratory circuits mentioned earlier rather than in a concrete localization. Nonetheless, they preserved their Mexican national identity. In the 1980s, there was a significant change in that many of these migratory circuits became transnational communities. The density of movements and social bonds extended the origin community to encompass all those places where its migrants arrived.

The reproduction of the origin communities from Mexico is directly and intrinsically linked to the different settlements of their migrants in urban neighborhoods and rural towns in the United States. This is to say, it is the same community now dispersed across several localizations. The new social and spatial form of community being created by this migratory nexus requires a reformulation of traditional concepts of migration that we are exploring. At first glance, these cases do not seem to imply any radical change of socioeconomic context. The migrant simply lives in their community in a different setting, with all the previous forms of social reproduction. While both settlements are separated by thousands of kilometers and an international border, they are the same community and this allows residents not only to preserve their original national identity but their local one as well. Thus, it now frequently occurs that a neighborhood of immigrants maintains a closer interrelation with its community of origin than with those communities that physically surround it.[6]

---

[6] For a general view on transnational communities, see the collective works by Glick Schiller, Basch and Blanc-Szanton (1992), Mummert (1999) and Smith and

The consequences of all this for the origin communities are quite important. Nevertheless, there is debate over whether the net effects are negative or positive. Up to the 1980s, the negative effects were usually emphasized, adducing that emigration cut down the available workforce, exacerbated social inequalities and generated dependence (the famous "migration syndrome" coined in 1981 by Reichert), which impeded the possibilities of local endogenous development. Since that time, the positive impacts have been more commonly stressed, especially the potential of the remittances sent by migrants if they can manage to become destined towards productive investment. It is a point of view shared by the international development agencies that have tried to foster it as a development strategy for countries with substantial emigration.[7]

Within the framework of the new productive and occupational structure of the occidental countries, we are interested in highlighting the fact that transnational communities acquire a special meaning. Social networks of reciprocity, trust and solidarity that provide a communal base also work as a mechanism to confront social vulnerability derived from their condition as immigrants. Immigrant workers, marginalized in a context of inequality and precariousness generated by the globalization process, develop ways of responding to (but not leaving) these processes by retreating into their own communities. In this sense, their articulation by means of transnational communities provides them with defense mechanisms to survive situations of vulnerability such as displacement risks, settling expenditures, job searching, and social insertion into the destination communities as well as familial reproduction in the origin communities. All of these needs are met by the resources provided by the system of social networks and relations that transnational communities manage to configure.

Transnationalization is thus the result of behaviors adopted by migrant workers in order to ensure the adequacy of their subordinate insertion into the process of labor globalization. This process is

---

Guarnizo (1997). Two other works on transnational communities from an anthropological perspective are Kearney and Nagengast (1989) and Smith (1995). A summary of these works is found in Canales and Zlolniski (2001).

[7] An excellent critical revision on this topic's literature can be found in Durand and Massey (1992), with a positive overview on the role of migration in the development of the origin communities, and in Binford (2002) from a more skeptical perspective. For a discussion on the role of the economic role of remittances in the case of Mexico, see Canales (2008).

marked by a reinforcement of the transnational borders between states and even more by the existence of interior borders that limit their labor and living possibilities. In spite of being a mechanism to confront the existence of internal borders, it also has the effect of blurring the borders between states. As for the migrants' social identity, transnational communities are based upon a sense of "belonging" that is a very different condition from that of citizenship. It is the configuration of an identity that is both prior and beyond citizenship, i.e., a transnationalization of the sense of community above national borders. For this reason, Mexican migrants abiding in the United States preserve and increase ties with their origin communities even after their legal, stable and definitive establishment. For them, a possible integration in the destination country does not imply renouncing their origin communities, especially since belonging to them is more vital and essential than the politically constructed belonging of residence. In many cases, integration is nothing but a way for defending and preserving the communal bonds with greater guarantees.

All in all, social networks and transnational communities constitute the social capital of migrants and they exhibit two faces. In the "have to" category as for response strategies rather than for "exit," they are also a form of reproduction of the conditions of social subordination generated by globalization. This is to say, they help make possible the social reproduction of the immigrants in a hostile environment. They do not, however, question the system of social stratification that generates vulnerability in migrants and permits the perpetuation of the system. As a mechanism that guarantees its social reproduction, it moreover turns out to be functional for a system based on the overexploitation of migrants.

With respect to the "having" as an alternative action field, transnational communities can also build social environments where the migrants (who generally have a subaltern position, both in their origin countries as well as in the destination ones) can transcend the reduced frameworks of negotiation imposed by globalization and the existence of borders. An example of this is the so-called Home Town Associations, popularly known as "migrant's clubs." These associations originally gathered as organizations of compatriots to celebrate festivities and preserve traditions from their hometowns, while helping to sustain mechanisms of mutual support and solidarity. These institutions extended their activities toward their origin communities through the channeling of financial and material resources to their hometowns and the improvement of migrant living conditions. These activities have raised immigrants to the category of political actors with a capacity to negotiate vis-à-vis dialogue with Mexican authorities, especially at the state and local level. On the other hand, some of these associations have also adopted a political profile in the destination country, actively defending the economic, labor, human and political rights of their compatriots in the United States. Often times, this activity is carried out by means of establishing coalitions with communal organizations, trade unions, non-governmental organizations and other civic organizations that defend the rights of the general population living in the United States, constituting an active form of insertion in the destination country. In the final analysis, the relations established between those migrant communities and the receptor communities are not predetermined, but they will depend, to a certain extent, on the decisions made by the different actors and the integration models developed in each particular case.

From the Demand for Assimilation to the Challenge of Tolerance

One of the most far reaching implications of our approach to transnationalism and migration is its critical vision towards the classical hypothesis of integration and assimilation of immigrants into destination societies. Indeed, one of the most analyzed and elaborated upon aspects of contemporary international migration by transnationalism rests in its contribution to understanding ethnic, cultural and linguistic diversity of the receptor countries where it is shown how countries internally integrate characteristics of the countries where emigration originates from. Such is the case, for example, in Eastern Los Angeles where the largest concentration of Mexican and Hispanic populations in the United States can be found. As a matter of fact, its population is almost exclusively of Mexican origin and Spanish is virtually the only language spoken.

This part of Los Angeles not only constitutes a piece of Mexico inserted in the United States, but also constitutes a sort of neighborhood pattern that is reproduced with similar composition and characteristics in many other cities of the United States. In other words, not only is East Los Angles a Mexican *barrio*, but it is also a typical American neighborhood, autochthonous and as representative of what Los Angeles is today as any other. In the era of globalization, this kind of *barrio* as defined by its migratory origin does not constitute an ethnic enclave, a picturesque singularity perhaps useful to promote tourism, but rather an intrinsic characteristic of global cities.

It could be argued that in reality, what these cases produced is a phenomenon of juxtaposition without greater consequences. In other words, immigrant communities create autochthonous subcultures with epidermal contacts with the rest of society, a situation that gradually fades until the complete assimilation of that group, or until it forms a cyst and becomes a ghetto, isolated from the rest of society. In fact, the United States experience with immigration had traditionally been one with constant assimilation of successive waves of immigrants after two or three generations, something that would seem to endorse this imagery.[8] However, an example can help us illustrate the importance of a critical mass of immigrants from the same origin which we have made reference to as a change factor on the receptor society.

After several decades of increasingly receiving immigrants from Latin America, the United States has become one of the countries with the largest number of Spanish-language speakers in the world.[9] Even if it is true that most Americans do not understand or speak Spanish, it is probable that in the near future, being bilingual will become a rather indispensable qualification in order to be elected to political office in many states, something that will extend to state judges, local police chiefs and other political positions. It is therefore not so far-fetched to foresee that in the short term, this tacit obligation will likewise extend to any executive or technical position, such that Spanish will share with English the condition of a language proper to the United States, even if it does not become an official language.

In this case, we are not up against any alteration of the traditional logic of assimilation. Immigration is integrated into the recipient society while at the time it deeply transforms its social structure. Indeed, it was in facing the growing presence and opposition to Hispanics that appeared from broad segments of American society that ultimately found their intellectual expression in the work by Samuel Huntington

---

[8] For an exposition of American immigration history, see Portes and Rumbaut (1990).

[9] According to data from the 2000 census, slightly more than 28 million people older than five years of age speak Spanish at home (*U.S. Census Bureau, Population Division, Education & Social Stratification Branch*), a number which is on the rise. This will soon make the United States the second largest country in number of Spanish speakers after Mexico.

entitled "Who are we? The Challenges to America's National Identity" (2004). Here, the scenario was explained as an imminent threat that can be summed up as follows: Mexicans and Latin Americans in general, are not the kind of necessary and desirable immigrants that the United States can count on as evidenced by their lack of assimilation and Americanization, i.e., their failure to adopt the American way of life.

Even though the subheading of Huntington's work is unfortunate (after all Latin Americans and Hispanics are also Americans), it shows that what is sought and defended is a determinate conception of national identity, defined by common values incarnated in a nation settled upon a territory which belongs to it exclusively.[10] Even if this community had ever really existed, it is an increasingly challenged conception due to the increasing diversity in occidental societies. We should consider this reaction as nothing more and nothing less than the ideological project of an elite represented by Huntington with many followers who are influential in decision-making spheres.

Conversely, our vision is based on a radical critique of these kinds of statements. In the first place, Huntington's position is not essentially a defense of what is "American" but what a particular group (the White-Anglo-Saxon-Protestants) has idealized as "American." Secondly, it is indeed worth wondering why migrants must be assimilated into this hegemonic way of life. Why is it that this society cannot be based upon a principle of ethnic and cultural tolerance? In this sense, we would reassess the discourse on transnationalism as it brings to light the issue of integration without assimilation, i.e., the combination of mechanisms of economic and labor integration, with diverse forms of social and cultural exclusion. The focus becomes the configuration of social exclusion spaces which is a necessary condition for a subordinate and vulnerable economic inclusion.

From the approach of transnationalism, it can likewise be stated that the relations established between these communities and the receptor society are not predetermined. Rather, they will to a certain extent depend on the decisions made by the different actors and integration models developed in each particular case. In this sense, we can

---

[10] In this framework, the reaction of a group of ranchers from Arizona is understood, as well as the anti-immigrant stance which Arnold Schwarzenegger, Governor of California, has held.

anticipate that the different integration scenarios will not be free from tensions and conflicts.

On the one side, transnational communities could be melted like ice in water, thus increasing the amount of water without making any changes in the content. We can also think of a behavior similar to that of sugar, i.e., that transnational communities can end up becoming dissolved in the recipient society, however, adding a "taste" of their culture and identity (thereby "sweetening" American society in this case). In other words, it is an integration model where the receptor society not only integrates immigrants, but also their culture, hence becoming transformed in the process.

Another possible scenario is more similar to a rock placed in the same bucket with water, such that in the long run, there would always be a strict and evident separation between both elements. While erosion progressively wears down parts of the rock and eventually may even pull it apart, it would never be absorbed or assimilated by the destination society. Quite improbably, we could even find an integration similar to that of a sponge, such as Huntington seems to foresee, where the inverse relation occurs, i.e., the transnational community would absorb and take the place of the cultural community that first received it.

Conclusion: Challenges and Proposals from Transnationalism

In spite of the measures taken against immigration such as the construction of physical and cultural walls, attempts to criminalize migrants, and so on, migrants have become one of the main protagonists of globalization. In contrast with the past, one of the peculiar aspects of migration in contemporary society is that it does not necessarily imply a severance from the origin community and family. On the contrary, migration becomes a way to broaden and extend familial and communal relations. In this sense, the immigrant is not alone but rather they take their community with them. Emigration is no longer about leaving behind but about bringing along, and in such movement, they create a transnational community.

This reference to transnational communities is not only a concept but also part of an analytical perspective on migratory phenomenon based in a particular mode of thinking. In some cases, it is even understood as a political stance before challenges and affairs stated by international migration in the framework of global societies (Portes, Guarnizo and Landolt 2003). The framework of transnationalism provides a paradigm that enables us to interpret the peculiarities of international migration in the era of globalization. It allows us to comprehend contemporary migration without a singular focus on cyclical unbalances in the labor markets of Western countries or the need to colonize new territories. It also allows us to transcend an integration and assimilation type of approach in observing the adoption of the destination society's national identity.

In considering the new modalities and meanings of international migration from the approach of transnationalism, theoretical emphasis is drawn towards inter-local connections which are constructed through migration and articulate the origin communities with the immigrants' settlements in the destination societies. On the conceptual level, we need to be able to capture the growing diversity, complexity and dynamism currently being displayed in this phenomenon. Traditional discourses on international migration are out of phase with contemporary realities, especially those rooted in national frameworks and thus limited both in their attempt to understand the phenomenon and in their definition of policies and programs directed towards migrants.

The colonial model which prevailed in several countries until well into the Twentieth Century was not only based upon a regressive vision, but was abandoned early by the very countries that fostered it (Spain, France, among others). On the other side of the classic models of immigration, assimilation (used so extensively in the United States and other countries in need of being populated, such as Australia, Argentina, New Zealand and Canada) has been historically superseded by the transnational character of contemporary migration. In the context of globalization, people do not migrate alone but instead do it all together with their local and national identities as well as with all of their cultural baggage. It seems clear that the proposals of integration-assimilation are in reality an ideological project aimed to justify a specific immigration policy (assimilation) rather than comprehending the complexity of a social phenomenon.

The contemporary models of "temporary workers" or "hosted workers" (such as that supported by the Bracero Program) have also been overcome by the very dynamics of international migration, which makes these programs mere insufficient palliatives and requires that they be continually reviewed and restated. This emphasis also implies a severance of the methodological nationalism that underlies such concepts and models. Migration cannot any longer be seen as a process of simple displacement between nations but rather as a social field of local-local articulations that transcends borders and overcomes geographies. In this sense, transnationalism is an approach that allows us to understand and approach those practices and behaviors that transcend the territorial borders of nation-states. In this regard, the concepts of social and cultural capital networks become fundamental since it is a way to provide an account of and to analyze these spaces and configured social fields that continuously transgress the political and territorial limits of nations.

At a political level, this approach also implies important ruptures, or at least, critical positions with respect to the prevailing discourses. Indeed, from this approach it becomes naïve to cling to the delusion of national governments struggling to control and stop migratory flows. Not only are migratory modalities and patterns diverse, they are no longer circumscribed to a mere displacement of people. Instead, they imply a system of social networks by which migration is constructed, material and symbolic goods are exchanged, and cultural identities, information and social capital migrate as well. These flows may well be impossible to control.

It is clearly ludicrous to think that a migratory law (such as restricted or total amnesty) will be sufficient to resolve major problems posed by migration. These policies are nothing but conjunctural responses that arise from already obsolete and ideologically charged paradigms. They do not consider that the bases and causes of migration are the very processes of globalization that are being fiercely defended by other means. In contemporary society, the attempt to halt migration turns out to be as absurd and ineffective as trying to stop globalization. As opposed to proposals for migratory controls, restrictive immigration policies, the construction of border walls, and calls for the militarization of borders, only a proposal of liberalizing migration can make sense. While we are clearly aware that the opening of national borders does not solve the problems of segregation, vulnerability and exclusion experienced by the migrants, we simply want to point out the dysfunctional nature of all those policies that seek to control and restrain migration.

THE GLOBAL STRUCTURING OF GENDER, RACE, AND CLASS: CONCEPTUAL SITES OF ITS DYNAMICS AND RESISTANCE IN THE PHILIPPINE EXPERIENCE

Ligaya Lindio-McGovern

An important question to ask in understanding the global structuring of gender-race-class interlock is: How and where do we locate "conceptual sites" in which to examine the dynamics of its social construction in the context of neoliberal globalization as well as its contestation from those whose lives get enmeshed in it? I argue that one of the ways to gain insight into the global structuring of the intersections of gender, race, and class is to examine the globalization of reproductive labor, particularly as propelled by some developing country governments subjected to the negative impact of neoliberal globalization.

Neoliberal globalization is conceived here as the global expansion of capitalism through the implementation of neoliberal policies of deregulation (limiting government regulation of the market), liberalization (lifting restrictions on the mobility of capital and goods on the global scale), privatization (dismantling state-owned, or state-subsidized enterprises and services), and labor flexibilization (limiting protective regulations on labor and full employment to create abundant supply of cheap labor). The structural adjustment policies of the International Monetary Fund, the World Bank, and the World Trade Organization have been instrumental in supporting the neoliberal strategy of globalization. Reproductive labor, as referred to in this chapter, is defined as the work necessary to maintain the household: care for the young, the elderly, household chores such as doing laundry, cleaning, and cooking meals for other members of the family. Marxist-Feminists argue that reproductive labor is necessary to maintain the capitalist system as it provides the services needed for the daily maintenance of the labor force and the reproduction of the next generation of workers (Glenn 1967).

The export of reproductive labor has become a development response by some non-core governments in order to mitigate the massive unemployment and other negative impacts of structural adjustment that place a stranglehold on their political economies. In this instance, reproductive labor—which was generally an unpaid labor done mostly by women in the confines of their homes—becomes a waged commodity for exchange in the global labor market, bringing forth the interplay of various actors and processes. The Philippines is one such country. Therefore, the Philippine experience offers conceptual sites to examine the dynamics of the global structuring of gender, race, and class and its contestation.

In this chapter, I will show how the Philippine labor export that concentrates women in domestic service work creates sites enabling the global structuring of gender, race, and class interlock. In so doing, we can see how Filipino migrant domestic workers turn these sites into spaces of resistance. My work is drawn from a larger project that I have completed on the globalization of reproductive labor through the Philippine labor export program. My fieldwork has been conducted at multiple sites where there is a considerable number of Filipino migrant domestic workers, specifically, Hong Kong, Taiwan, Rome, Vancouver (British Columbia, Canada), and Chicago (Illinois, USA).

Labor export is when the government and other non-governmental entities take an active role in facilitating labor migration as part of its development strategy. The Philippine government embarked on labor export during the mid-1970s in order to deal with unemployment and a debt crisis that resulted from the implementation of structural adjustment policies imposed by the International Monetary Fund (IMF) and the World Bank, typically by way of conditional development loans. Currently, it is estimated that export labor comprises about 8,000,000 Filipino overseas workers spread out over more than 160 countries, with an annual deployment of approximately one million and a daily deployment of approximately 3,000. A growing portion of export labor is made up of women, comprising more than 70% of it. The majority of these women are placed in domestic service work in other countries in Asia, Europe, North America, and the Middle East. This process has created structures of power that interplay in the export of reproductive labor, creating "conceptual sites" to examine the intersections of gender, race/ethnicity, and class along with its contestation within a micro-macro level of analysis. I argue that these "conceptual sites" include the (a) nation state, (b) the impact of neoliberal structural adjustment policies, (c) non-state actors that profit from labor export, (d) and the transnationalization of the household.

The Nation State

In the current debate on globalization and the nation state, one argument contends that the nation state has a diminished influence over the dynamics of the neoliberal agenda (Held, et al. 1999). However, the nation state plays a significant role in the global structuring of gender, race, and class in the context of globalization. This is demonstrated in the policies of labor-sending and labor-receiving states that shape the globalization of reproductive labor. A clear example is the active role that the Philippine government plays in promoting labor export that relegates Filipino women to work in the domestic service sector. This reinforces the stratification of the labor market in the labor-receiving countries, creating an expendable supply of "underclass-ed" women who provide chcap reproductive labor that is often unregulated and vulnerable to sexual and other forms of abuse. Many of these women experience downward occupational mobility since a large number of them have college degrees, possess work experience as teachers, nurses, and other white collar professions, while their cheap migrant reproductive labor frees up productive labor for the formal labor market in the labor-receiving countries.

Marxist-feminists would argue that social reproduction must be subsidized by the state and economy since it is essential to the daily maintenance and the generational reproduction of the labor force. But as labor-receiving countries increasingly privatize child care and elder care, migrant women from the global South (including the migrant Filipino domestic workers considered in my study) are the ones who partially subsidize this service through their cheap reproductive work. The labor-sending society is also made to partly subsidize reproductive labor in the labor-receiving countries since it is the former that had invested their human capital in these migrant domestic workers through educational spending. The consequent brain drain has an important social cost on the long term development of the Philippines. It siphons out human talents that could otherwise spur its internal development even if it may bring in remittances that can help the country pay its foreign debt.

The role of the nation-state in the global structuring of gender, race, and class is also seen in the labor-receiving countries' immigration laws and migrant labor policies that shape the status of migrant domestic workers in their societies. For instance, Canada's Live-In Caregivers Program (LCP), the EU's (European Union) migration policy for migrants who come from non-EU member countries, and Taiwan's and Hong Kong's labor migration policies for domestic workers, all shape the social construction of a "steady" but cheap and expendable migrant reproductive labor force. Taiwan and Hong Kong require that these women not engage in any other kind of work if they come into the country as domestic service workers. Canada's Live-in Caregivers Program, which has historically imported Third World women into domestic service work, requires that these women do continuous domestic work for twenty-four months before they can apply for a change in their status from temporary contract workers to immigrant. Italy, which follows EU's immigration policy, relegates migrants who are coming from non-EU member countries to perform mainly domestic service which includes what they define as *"laboro subordinato,"* i.e., work that most Italians shun.

Thus, both the labor-sending and labor-receiving nation states have become targets of resistance on the part of organized Filipino migrant domestic workers. One example of this are the contentious politics of UNIFIL (United Filipinos in Hong Kong) that have been consistently critical of the labor export policies of the Philippine government. UNIFIL has been able to organize an inter-ethnic alliance of domestic workers to counter the Hong Kong government's attempts to lower their minimum wage. In Vancouver (in Canada), a group of Filipino nurses (FNSG—Filipino Nurses Support Group) employed as domestic workers are advocating to abolish LCP and to allow these women to work as nurses without having to work long months as domestic workers that results in their de-skilling.

While labor-receiving governments see the importance of reproductive labor to maintaining their societies, something evidenced by their participation in the import of temporary migrant domestic workers, they tend to make reproductive labor as cheap as possible. In Hong Kong, for example, the government attempted to lower the minimum wage for foreign domestic workers by 30% during the financial crisis of the latter 1990s. But the Filipino migrant domestic workers of Hong Kong joined forces with other migrant domestic workers from Indonesia, Sri Lanka, Malaysia, India, and Bangladesh to collectively resist this state action. After massive street protests and intense lobbying, the Hong Kong government eventually compromised by reducing the minimum wage by 5% instead of 30%. Although migrant workers deemed it a partial success resulting from their collective resistance, it implied state participation and power in cheapening reproductive labor. Nevertheless, the compromise also indicated the potential power of the collective action of migrants in challenging labor-receiving governments so as to protect their interests.

Neo-liberal Structural Adjustment Policies

Neo-liberal structural adjustment policies have had a devastating impact on the economies of poor countries and they also contribute to the global structuring of the gender-race-class interlock. In the Philippine experience, structural adjustment policies have exacerbated poverty and unemployment along with the debacle of debt crisis (Bello 2004; Lindio-McGovern 2007). Such impact produces the pre-conditions for labor migration which labor export feeds on.

Labor export has become the major source of remittances to pay the debt of the Philippines. Since the bulk of export labor is made up of Filipino women who are relegated to domestic service work, it is precisely these women who largely bear the brunt of foreign debt while transnational capital continues to benefit from it. Structural adjustment policies mainly serve the global expansion of capitalism via corporate globalization (Harvey 2007; Sklair 2002). As the Philippine foreign debt continues to escalate, labor export is becoming a long-term development policy—thus creating a source country for cheap migrant reproductive labor in richer destination countries. This scenario reinforces global inequalities, creating a transnational division of female labor where Filipino migrant domestic workers are placed in a subordinate position. This has arguably cemented the gendered division of labor on an international scale.

Reproductive labor in the labor-receiving countries that was once unpaid female labor has been transformed into low wage labor (often disposable and exploited) for migrant women from poor countries. The gendered division of reproductive labor in the labor-receiving countries has not been transformed. The entry of migrant women from the Third World or Global South racializes and ethnicizes the gendering of the division of reproductive labor. This makes it even more complex to challenge since women in the labor-receiving countries may tend to believe that this is beneficial for them, thus creating class divisions among women as well. This class divide can undermine a united women's movement in the labor-receiving countries where feminist solidarity with migrant domestic workers could otherwise be forged. Thus, the dynamics of inequalities based on gender, race/ethnicity, and class becomes reinforced by this disunity.

A critical stance on structural adjustment policies promoted by the International Monetary Fund (IMF) and the World Trade Organization (WTO) had formed part of the collective action agenda of the United Filipinos in Hong Kong, comprised mostly of domestic workers. This is also part of the agenda of the Philippine Women Center in Vancouver, British Columbia, Canada which organizes Filipino migrant domestic workers in the area. Gabriela, an organization that is leading the progressive and more militant women's movement in the Philippines and currently in the process of organizing the GABRIELA Women's Party List among migrant women, also promotes a critical stance on structural adjustment policies and its impact on Filipino women. While a radical political stance on the part of the Philippine government against the imposition of these structural adjustment policies has never been endorsed, this critical stance advanced by these organizations forms part of a discursive resistance to the ideological project of globalization so deeply embodied in structural adjustment policies. Discursive forms of resistance contribute to consciousness-raising towards envisioning alternative development policies that can alter the structures of power that subordinate Third World women.

Non-State Actors

The role of non-state actors such as employment agencies who benefit from export labor also offers a conceptual site for examining the global structuring of gender, race and class. These employment agencies have become a new class of entrepreneurs who profit from the trade in migrant reproductive labor. As earlier mentioned, the Marxist-Feminist view on class would include reproductive labor as essential to the reproduction of workers for the maintenance of capitalism. The emergence of profiteering employment agencies/traders in the export/import of reproductive labor further reinforces global capitalism, consistent with the ultimate ideological and policy goal of neo-liberal globalization. By turning once-unpaid women's reproductive labor into wage labor in the global labor market, employment agencies and traders are able to extract large profits with very little capital, with migrant women serving as their commodities for exchange. It is therefore in their interests to maintain a steady supply of migrant women workers who will provide cheap reproductive labor. So, some of these traders facilitate illegal termination of domestic workers before their contract expires, as I have observed in Taiwan.

Sometimes these traders charge exorbitant fees that put these women in debt. Being in debt has a powerful domesticating effect on domestic workers as they would tend to suffer harsh conditions until such time that conditions become so unbearable that they escape from their employers. But if they escape from their employers, employment agencies will gain because this opens up a new demand for recruitment. For these and other reasons, non-state actors, such as employment agencies, have also become targets of the resistance activities being waged by organized Filipino migrant domestic workers. For example, United Filipinos in Hong Kong (UNIFIL) have campaigned against the exploitative practices of employment agencies and traders. In framing their issues, they have linked the nation-state to the existence of these employment agencies. UNIFIL made explicit the primary role of the Philippine government in the proliferation of employment agencies, in privatizing labor export by giving these employment agencies greater role in the recruitment and in the deployment of export labor and in passing on to them the provision of services that should otherwise be a state responsibility. UNIFIL sees the interconnections of these power structures. Thus, they have advocated for the Philippine government to exert greater responsibility and social control over the exploitative and abusive practices of these employment agencies.

In Taiwan, the Ifugao Association, made up mostly of domestic workers, has also campaigned against the power of traders who charged exorbitant fees almost equivalent to the domestic workers' one year salary. Some of these traders in the labor-receiving countries also make profit from the abusive conditions of the women who ask them for a transfer when they cannot any longer endure their harsh working conditions, especially when facing sexual abuse or physical violence. The trader is able to garner higher profits from the migrant women by charging them fees once more and they profit still further by charging fees on the new employer. Many traders are men who earn a living from brokering the services of migrant domestic workers. This trade is quite profitable since there is so little investment involved. The emergence of this class in the globalization of reproductive labor complicates and nuances the global structuring of gender, race/ethnicity, and class.

As this class commodifies migrant women in the reproductive trade, they play a role in the stratification of the reproductive labor market where they benefit from the waged reproductive labor of migrant women while they help entrench the gendered, classed, and racialized/ethnicized division of reproductive labor. Taiwanese traders have gained political power as there is minimal state regulation on their enterprise and they usually align with the interest of Taiwanese employers. Since it is generally female employers who deal directly with the migrant domestic workers, there is a blurring of gender between these two classes in the management of migrant domestic workers' reproductive labor. It is precisely this blurring, however, that reinforces the dynamics of class, ethnicity, and gender in the trading of cheap, controllable migrant domestic workers. When Filipino migrant workers challenge the power of reproductive labor traders, it represents an attempt to break this matrix. When they resisted the Philippine government's ban on direct hiring (Arkibong Bayan 2009), it was an attempt to break the state-employment agencies-trader alliance over the control of reproductive labor that would strengthen the power of this new class of reproductive traders.

The Transnationalized Household

Labor export has transnationalized the household as mothers migrate to do paid domestic work in the global labor market. Economic pressures created by neoliberal policies in the labor-sending country complicate the economic hardships and unemployment among both men and women. The transnationalization of the household offers another conceptual site for examining the global structuring of gender, race, and class. The macro-structures of neoliberal globalization require micro-structures to entrench and fortify itself. The presence of foreign migrant domestic workers in labor-receiving countries creates a microcosm of the global dimensions of this interlock. While the migrant woman may be experiencing familial alienation and estrangement (Lindio-McGovern 2004) while bearing the social costs of migration and depriving her own children of direct parental personal care (especially for migrant mothers), the labor-receiving households are maintained without feeling the impact of these social costs. In most cases, the migrant domestic worker deals more frequently with wives who assign their tasks, freeing the husband to deal with such matters. The working and living conditions of these migrant domestic workers, the lack of respect afforded them, their vulnerable and marginalized position in the labor-receiving countries, and doing the invisible, low-prestige, low paid work that local citizens in their host societies would shun—all emerge from the proletarianization of migrant women in domestic service work.

Resistance of migrant domestic workers within the household site sometimes takes the form of "hidden transcripts" (Scott 1990) just as it can likewise result in publicly and verbally expressed conflict. According to James Scott, hidden transcripts are covert forms of resistance that the oppressed engage in to undermine the power of their oppressor when they deem that open public defiance is too costly and risks losing their jobs. Filipino migrant domestic workers who migrate into a foreign household as domestic workers are often powerless, especially when they are deprived of social networks outside the household. Their economic survival in the foreign country depends on maintaining their job even while they deal with loneliness, homesickness, and long work-hours.

In some instances, hidden transcripts become a strategic response to employers who attempt to control or degrade them and this works to put some degree of limits on their power over them. While they may appear non-defiant on the face of things, they may therefore be defying their oppressors "backstage." A Filipino domestic worker in Rome with whom I closely associated with exemplified the utilization of hidden transcript when she threw away the spoiled food that her employer offered her for supper. She later answered her employer affirmatively when asked if she had eaten the food given to her. She told me that she was insulted when her employer offered her spoiled food and felt degraded. But rather than confront her employer openly to express her disgust, she instead threw the food behind her back into the garbage. Here we see a hidden transcript of defiance on an affront to her human dignity.

Often I heard the statement, *"Tao ako!"* ("I am a human being!") when the domestic workers tell stories about the lack of respect and maltreatment they receive from their employers. This indicates that they highly value their human dignity while paradoxically receiving little respect for their work from the larger society. Other forms of hidden transcript involve the domestic workers attempt to control their labor. One example of this, usually among those on "live-in" arrangements, is leaving very early in the morning during their days-off and coming back late at night so that their employers will not have the opportunity to ask them to do errands. Some employers would ask their domestic workers to do some errands or tasks for them when they stay in during their days off. So they would leave the house all day, stay in the park, on church premises, and other public places to spend their time with other domestic workers who are also having their day-off. Domestic workers who are on live-in arrangement usually cannot afford to have an apartment of their own to go home to when they have their day-off. Sunday is a typical day-off, but there are others whose day-off falls on a weekday. Hidden transcripts apparently are convenient means of recourse when the domestic workers do not want to engage in direct, face to face conflict with their employers. They are "weapons" not "of the weak" (Scott 1985) but perhaps of those who have the potential for collective power gained through collective resistance as publicly articulated.

Resistance in the transnationalized household—where migrant domestic workers embody the micro-macrocosmic intersection of gender, ethnicity/race and class—sometimes go well beyond hidden transcripts. Some domestic workers engage in open defiance and conflict with their employers to defend their dignity as persons and rights as workers. They may answer their employers back assertively when their actions become intolerable. Some may engage in direct negotiation with their employers for the benefits and entitlements denied them as workers. Sometimes employers turn sour when their domestic workers begin to assert what they are legally entitled to, constituting a form of control. Some may eventually decide to terminate the assertive domestic worker.

When domestic workers in this situation understand the rights that they are legally entitled to, the law becomes their weapon to make their defiance public. When they have a social network or access to a migrant rights support organization, they become even more empowered to bring their case before legal institutions such as labor tribunals. This scenario links the household and the state, making the invisible, often unreported transgressions in the household, wholly public. With the presence of non-governmental organizations who can publicize and support the struggle of domestic workers, the transnational household ceases to be a private sphere where violations of human/ workers' rights and of women's dignity can be shielded from public scrutiny. This wields the potential of limiting the power of household employers to exploit migrant domestic workers.

Employers also want to make reproductive labor as cheap as possible so they want domestic workers to be docile. Giving gifts such as old clothes to the migrant women tends to create gratitude among domestic workers that sometimes preclude them from confronting their employers. When domestic workers use open conflict to resolve their intolerable or unjust working conditions, even when domestic workers' claims are within the law, some employers consider such action as "ingratitude." The transnationalized household then becomes a site where women of different class positions in the hierarchy of reproductive labor create dynamics of subordination and resistance. Sometimes female employers who have not challenged the gendered division in their households become dependent on the reproductive labor of the migrant domestic worker. There are cases, for example, during the domestic workers' day-off where they will pile up their dishes and used clothes without washing them themselves. When the domestic worker comes back from her day-off, the workload for that day has doubled, thereby effectively extending her work hours. For live-ins, this is especially difficult to deal with. Some domestic workers opt to live-out if they can afford to do so and where there is the absence of a law that requires them to live-in so they can better control their working hours.

With the globalization of reproductive labor, households in labor receiving countries increasingly become public spheres that blur the private/public dichotomy. This has implications both for the women's movement in the labor-receiving countries and for public policy. For the women's movement, two critical questions pose a challenge: Can the transnationalized household be a locus for forging "sisterhood" (Gimenez 2009) that will address public policy to promote the rights of migrant domestic workers? Can this sisterhood promote, advocate, and create alternative policies and new social arrangements that will alter the gendered, racialized, ethnicized, and classed nature of globalization where both women of the Global South and the Global North can create alliances to bring about a more just social order?

Conclusion

The globalization of reproductive labor, facilitated by the labor export practices of poor countries like the Philippines that have been negatively affected by structural adjustment policies, has brought about a complex interplay of various structures of power. These power structures include the nation-state (labor-sending and labor-receiving governments), structural adjustment policies promoted by the IMF/World Bank and WTO, non-state actors (such as employment agencies and traders), and the transnationalized household of labor-receiving societies. These structures of power offer conceptual sites to examine and understand the global dynamics of gender, race, ethnicity and class as they become sites of the structuring of global inequalities and resistance.

The periphery nation-state, as exemplified by the Philippines, plays an active role in the globalization of reproductive labor when it promotes labor export. It results in the placement of migrating women into domestic service work, many of whom are educated. The labor-receiving state also plays an active role in this process by formulating labor import policies tied to immigration policies that restrict the potential mobility of migrant domestic workers to other professions or occupations, thereby creating and maintaining a low-wage reproductive labor force while increasingly privatizing social services such as child care and elder care. It is the peripheral labor-exporting state, however, that subsidizes the human capital development of the migrant domestic workers. Their education is both underutilized and drained-out of the country of origin, thus losing talents that are needed for long-term internal development. The role of nation-states (labor-exporting states and labor-importing states) in the globalization of reproductive labor therefore offers a conceptual site to understand the global structuring of gender, race/ethnicity, and class inequalities.

The IMF and the WTO has promoted structural adjustment policies that help to destroy the local economies of periphery nation-states. It has resulted in increased unemployment and debt crises that are also implicated in the globalization of reproductive labor, relegating many Third World women including those from the Philippines to work in this highly exploitable, unprotected, disposable, and disrespected occupational sector. The concurrent implementation of labor flexibilization along with the neoliberal policies of liberalization and privatization create a massive supply of exportable labor that offer the potential to bring in foreign remittances to help pay foreign debt. With the feminization of labor export, it is largely women who migrate and it is they who are segregated into low-wage domestic work. It can ultimately be argued that it is Third World women who are made to bear the greater brunt of structural adjustment policies which in a myriad of ways create the conditions conducive for the global expansion of capital. The complex structural consequences of neoliberal policies in the context of globalization offer another conceptual site to understand the seemingly invisible power structures that interplay in the global structuring of gender, race/ethnicity, and class interlock.

The export-import of domestic workers led to the emergence of a new class of entrepreneurs who profit by exacting exorbitant fees from migrant domestic workers. This has linked the nation-state and non-state actors in the commodification of reproductive labor. The migrant domestic worker becomes their "commodity" for exchange as they profit from the trade with minimal investment. Labor export becomes increasingly a long-term development policy of the labor-sending county as it continues to be detrimentally affected by structural adjustment policies in the context of globalization. As labor-sending and labor-receiving nation-states allow the proliferation of private employment agencies and traders in the export-import of domestic workers who profit from the trade, an interplay of state and non-state actors occurs in the globalization of reproductive labor. How employment agencies/traders exploit migrant domestic workers both in the labor-exporting and labor-receiving countries offers another conceptual site in examining the complex dynamics of gender, race/ethnicity, and class interlock.

Finally, we have seen how the consequent transnationalization of the household in the globalization of reproductive labor comes into play. This happens when the presence of low-paid foreign domestic workers has allowed middle class men and women in the labor-receiving countries to participate in the formal labor force that is better paid and more protected. Meanwhile, the educated migrant domestic workers experience downward occupational mobility and face restrictions that put them in a subordinate position in the stratified labor market. The presence of the migrant domestic worker has reinforced the gendered division of labor since reproductive labor continues to be relegated to women, with the foreign domestic worker doing the manual reproductive work, while her female employer does the supervising of reproductive labor. The presence of foreign domestic workers has also allowed the efficient maintenance of the labor-receiving households while the labor-sending households are paying the social costs of migration. The children of migrant mothers are deprived of direct, personal care.

The transnationalized household, nation-states, structural adjustment policies, and non-state actors, such as employment agencies and traders, have become sites of resistance by migrant domestic workers, articulated both collectively and individually, publicly and in more covert ways. As migrant domestic workers make their resistance more collective and public, the interplay of these centers/structures of power in the globalization of reproductive labor become more visible as a micro-macro embodiment of the global structuring of gender-race/ethnicity-class interlock. These dynamics have implications for theorizing about, analyzing, and ultimately transforming the diverse and interlocking forms of inequalities in play within the context of globalization.

DISMANTLING THE DEFENSIVE WALL OF THE COLONIZED: THE VEIL AND THE FRENCH LAW ON SECULARITY AND CONSPICUOUS RELIGIOUS SYMBOLS IN SCHOOLS

Mohammad A. Chaichian

On October 22, 1989 thousands of French Muslims staged a demonstration in Paris in support of three Muslim students who were expelled from the Gabriel-Havez secondary school in the Creil municipality. The students' only crime was that they wore headscarves while attending school, in defiance of the French Education Minister's decree that banned wearing any "ostentatious religious insignia" (Seljuq, 1997; Kaitlin, 2007). Two political events make the year 1989 particularly significant related to the headscarf controversy: The Iranian leader Ayatollah Khomeini's religious decree (fatwa) that was in fact a death sentence for the British writer Salman Rushdie on the occasion of publishing his novel *Satanic Verses*; and the Algerian Muslim militants' killing of several French residents that rekindled a debate on Islam's alleged violent nature (McGillion, 2004). Later in the 1990s, the Gulf War and its aftermath exacerbated the situation not only in France but all over Europe (Seljuq, 1997). In this highly charged and tense political environment the French public and the media interpreted the wearing of headscarf by French Muslim students as a religious-political statement in defiance of the French principles of separation of church and state. Furthermore, opponents of the headscarf also argued that the Muslim girls were co-opted by Muslim fundamentalist groups who intended to advance their militant political agenda (Begag and Chaouits, 1990).

The headscarf controversy continued in the 1990s amid public demonstrations and law suits. But the matter appeared to be settled in 1996, as an appeal court in the city of Nancy in two separate cases ruled in favor of seven female Muslim students of North African origin, ordering the French government to pay compensation to one student and allow the other six to return to school while wearing the headscarf. But their victory was short-lived, as public opposition to this alleged "Islamic militancy" continued and forced the French government in July 2003 to set up a special investigation commission on religion. Headed by Bernard Staci, the commission heard hundreds of witnesses and published its report in late 2003 recommending twenty three measures to guarantee both the state's neutrality on religion and the equality of religious faiths. In addition to proposed legislation to clarify acceptable religious garb in school, the report also recommended addition of Muslim and Jewish holidays (*Eid-al-Adha* and *Yum Kippur*, respectively) as public holidays; instruction of "religious facts;" teaching "non-state" languages such as Kurdish and Berber in addition to state languages like Arabic or Turkish; and the rehabilitation of "urban ghettoes" where most French Muslim immigrants resided. Acting on the Staci Commission's recommendations in late 2003 the then French President Jacques Chirac proposed a law for constitutional review which was subsequently passed in early 2004 by the French National Assembly by a large majority. But ironically, the proposed law only focused on legislation against "ostentatious religious signs and dresses" which according to the Ministry of Education "whose wearing in public schools leads to the immediate recognition of the wearer's religious belonging, which is to say the Islamic veil, whatever name one calls it, the Jewish Kippa, or a cross of massive dimensions." Yet despite the claim for the law's universality, it clearly focused on the *hijab* or the head covering worn by Muslim women (Silverstein, 2004).

The law banning conspicuous religious symbols in schools became effective in September 2004. But despite divided public opinion its enforcement was rather uneventful. According to one survey taken before the law's passage in February 2004, the law was favored by 69 percent of the population while 29 percent opposed it. Among the French Muslims, 42 percent were supportive of the law while 53 percent opposed it (Anon, 2004). Even among the French Muslim female population 49 percent supported it while 43 percent opposed the law. France is home to the largest Muslim population in Europe outside Turkey, about five million or 8.3 percent of the population (Silverstein, 2004: 3). However, according to an opinion poll taken after September 11, 2001 only about 30 percent of France's heterogeneous Muslim community described themselves as "practicing Muslims;" and the majority of them, or about 58 percent were non-practicing Muslims who can better be described as French persons of Muslim origin (Sondage IFOP, 2001). This might be an explanation for an absence of mass protest after the law's passage. In all, once the law was enforced in schools about 240 female students attended school wearing the headscarf, and reportedly 170 students later accepted to remove it and the rest had undergone "conciliation procedures" (Műller, 2005).

In the absence of an all-out protest against the 2004 law among France's Muslim population and the prevalence of the more "moderate" French Muslim citizens and residents, it is more accurate to define them as a population that consider their faith as an Islamic version of "civil religion," a term coined by the American sociologist Robert Bellah in the late 1960s (Bellah, 1967). This demographic reality begs the question of the reason for the rather harsh reaction by the French government in dealing with the Islamic headscarf. In a search for answers, two issues need to be examined more clearly: France's colonial excursions in the Muslim world particularly in North Africa; and the socio-economic status of Muslim immigrants who have settled in French territories due to colonization, and more recently globalization.

The French Colonial Presence in North Africa

When in 1798 Napoleon Bonaparte was about to invade Egypt, he told his soldiers that they are about to be "engaged in a conquest whose consequences will be incalculable" (Hermassi, 1987: 33). What distinguished the French colonial expedition in Egypt from other European colonizers' conquests was a group of French scientists who accompanied Bonaparte, in an apparent attempt to learn about the history, language and culture of the people who were about to be subjugated. Some have considered this new approach as an indication of Bonaparte's keen interest in, and adherence to one of the main principles of the Enlightenment by acknowledging the common people's basic human and legal rights vis-à-vis the arbitrary power of the dictators and the European aristocracy (Youssef, 1998). But other observers have interpreted it as "propaganda" to cover up the true imperialist (and later colonialist) intentions of the French in their overseas ventures (Cole, 2007). Clearly, the European expansion led to the emergence of an ideology rooted in the paternalistic belief that colonialists had a responsibility to govern and take care of their subjects who allegedly were incapable of doing so on their own. While the Anglo-Saxon colonialists justified their imperial intentions by promoting the "white man's burden," the French colonizers were prone to see themselves as being on a mission to conquer and civilize the colonized people ('*la mission civilatrice*'). Thus while the British were more interested to rule over and control their colonial subjects without forcing them to assimilate to the British way of life, the French did not vie for multiculturalism and considered the French culture superior to all other cultures in the colonies which made it necessary and a "noble" objective to impose it on the colonized (Nasr, 1999: 560–61; Lewis, 1980: 338).

During the 19th century France colonized Algeria, Tunisia, and Morocco in north-west Africa, or what is known as the "Maghreb" (the West). While Tunisia and Morocco were decolonized relatively peacefully in 1956, the Algerians had to fight a bloody war to rid themselves from 130 years of brutal French colonization in 1962. In general, the Muslim "*Magrebin*" proved to be a tough challenge to French colonial ambitions, as they fiercely resented and resisted colonial domination which the French attributed to Islam and its theological doctrine that allegedly condones violence. According to Nasr (1999: 564), "Such Islamic doctrine as jihad, polygamy, strict obedience to religious law (shari'a), and the tendency to introduce Islamic values to public life were seen as evidence of Islam's hostility to progress."

Muslim Immigrants in France

Since the French census enumerators do not ask about religion or ethnic origin, there are no accurate statistics on French Muslims. Estimates for the French Muslim immigrant population range anywhere from 3 to 6 million, but one official estimate in 2000 put the total number at 4,145,000 of which about 3 million were from the Maghreb (see Table 1).

Table 1. Estimated French Muslim Population by the Region/Country of Origin, 2000

Country of Origin	Population
Algeria	1,750,000
Morocco	1,000,000
Tunisia	350,000
Turkey	315,000
Sub-Saharan Africa	550,000
Asia	80,000
Other	100,000
Total	4,145,000

Source: Haut Conseil à L'Intégration, 2000: 26

The most recent government data indicate that in 2004 there were five to six million Muslims in France or about 8–9.6 percent of total population, of which 70 percent have come from the Maghreb (NISES, 2004). France's involvement in Algeria is of particular interest for this study, as the French were not only after economic gain but also total integration of Algeria into France. This led to the declaration of all Algerians as "French" in 1864, and recruitment of Algerian subjects who were then trained to serve as mercenaries fighting alongside the French in their colonial wars.

Historically speaking, the Algerian mercenaries were the first significant group of Muslim immigrants who settled in France. Known as the *harkis*, Algerian soldiers who fought along with the French colonial army to suppress the Algerian revolution were relocated and settled in France after 1962 to avoid reprisal and persecution by the triumphant Algerian resistance army (Haddad, 1999: 604). According to one estimate, there were about 450,000 *harkis* in France, the majority of whom being born and socialized in France (Seljuq, 1997). But the majority of France's Muslim immigrants left their homelands due to France's need for cheap labor during several crucial periods; such as 119,000 Algerians who came to France to work in factories in 1919, and many others who were needed to work in jobs left vacant by war casualties after WWII (Killian and Johnson, 2006: 62). Most immigrants were single men, or men who left their families behind, with inadequate housing and accommodations made available to them. This prompted the French government in the 1950s to build hostels mainly designed to house single men. The economic recession of the mid-1970s forced the French government to temporarily suspend entry of foreign workers, yet another change in immigration policy facilitated the migrant workers' reunification with their families. This led to the so-called 'feminization of foreign population' (*feminization de la population*) from the late 1970s onward (Lequin, 1992). To bring one's family, the policy required migrant workers to prove that they have adequate funds and salaries to support their families, and lodging large enough to house them. Although many workers did not qualify, their spouses often arrived with tourist visas who eventually extended their stay without legal permits (Killian and Johnson, 2006: 63).

The French government does not collect racial, ethnic, or religious data in its censuses, and since the constitution considers everyone to be "French" it follows a color-blind policy that leaves no room for affirmative action programs. Yet there is a consensus that discrimination based on religion, race or national/ethnic origin is prevalent and a fact of life in France, particularly related to the French Muslim population (Mattack, 2005). In the absence of affirmative action policies to support immigrant families; presence of a subtle but persistent racism and disdain for the Muslim *Maghrebi* migrant workers and their families; and a *de facto* segregation of migrant workers in suburban working class neighborhoods around factories in French cities led to a deterioration of quality of life and housing conditions for many of the French residents of *Maghrebi* origin. As a consequence, concentration of Muslim immigrants in self-contained high-rise settlements similar to the "projects" in American cities, and unemployment rates double that of the national average have led to their marginalization in the French society.

In general, there is a prevalent opinion among the ghettoized and marginalized Muslim immigrants that there is a "conscious or unconscious national consensus in France to keep immigrants depressed so that they will always be around to do the dirty, low paid jobs that the French disdain" (Ibid.). This is supported by different studies and official statistics indicating that French Muslim immigrants from the Maghreb have historically had a much lower socio-economic status compared with the rest of the population. For instance, in 1992 French families of North African origin had a much lower rate of home ownership compared with French citizens and other immigrant populations (see Table 2). The findings of another study of immigrants in France indicated that the *Maghrebin* occupied the lowest levels of the social structure by mainly holding manual jobs in factories and construction sector, were poorly educated, and had much higher rate of unemployment compared with the general French population (Tribalat, 1995, 1996). A slow economic growth in France and across Europe in the new Millennium has perpetuated the plight of *Maghrebi* workers and their families, as by 2005 the unemployment rate for those under 25 was 50 percent compared with 22 percent for the country (Matlack, 2005).

Table 2. Home Ownership among French Citizens, Immigrants from North Africa and other Immigrant Groups, 1992

Family Type	Home Ownership Status	
	Own (%)	Rent (%)
French	56	44
Foreign Immigrants	22	78
Immigrants of North African Origin	10	90

Source: Kastenbaum and Vermés (1996: 44)

Within the above context, immigrants of Algerian origin have always been subjected to harsher treatment. According to Naravane (2005) a considerable number of French citizens feel that "Algeria was a part of France and should never have been granted independence;" consider continued presence of Algerians and other immigrants of North African origin as "adding insult to injury;" and who "cannot let go of sentiments of racial and colonial superiority." This particularly places the French of Algerian origin at the center of the *hijab* controversy, and as I will explain in the following sections they represent an ethnic and national identity that challenges the French notion of Republicanism and ethnic identity.

French Republicanism and the Problematic of the Maghrebin Ethnicity

The opposition to wearing religious symbols in schools is based on a French law passed in 1905 that recognizes complete separation of church and state and prohibits the latter from funding or supporting any religion. The French term *"laïcité"* which sometimes is erroneously translated as "secularism," in essence means creating a balance between public order and religious freedom. Related to educational institutions, the 1905 law enforced *laïcité* in schools in order to prevent the anti-democratic influences of Catholicism and the Catholic Church (Vaïss, 2004: 2). In fact, the French government does not have any officially sanctioned racial, ethnic, or religious group classification, and only recognizes individuals as citizens who in turn should pledge allegiance to the Republic. Furthermore, keeping schools as "religion-free zones" lies at the heart of the French idea of citizenship, and schools that are funded and operated by national or local governments are prohibited from endorsing any religious doctrine (Astier, 2004).

France has always promoted "French Republicanism" that is based on individualism and full assimilation of all individuals who have made a political choice of becoming a "French citizen." Recent urban riots and the *hijab* controversy have led some to question the practicality of Republican ideals, yet the Anglo-Saxon/ American model of multiculturalism has not gained official support in France. Those opposed to multiculturalism often argue that allowing various ethnic groups and nationalities to express their "cultural particularities" will lead to the "fragmentation of society into several separate communities," which in turn will ruin "the unity of the nation"(Kastoryano, 2006).

More specifically, the concept of "minority" does not have any relevance to French social relations, as the official policy is to legally and socially unify the population in accordance with the constitutional definition of the French Republic as "one and indivisible" (Open Society Institute, 2002: 71). In addition, France does not recognize rights of groups, and under the constitutional principles of "*läicité*" only individual rights are recognized (Haut Conseil à L'Intégration, 2000). In the context of the European Union, France has signed but not ratified the European Charter of Regional Minority Languages (ECRML), nor has she signed the Framework Convention for the Protection of National Minorities (FCNM) (Open Society Institute, 2002: 72). This is highly problematic for religious groups and immigrant populations who are subjected to overt and covert forms of prejudice and discrimination and yet have no legal and political recourse to address their concerns.

French Muslims come from diverse ethnic and national backgrounds, but in the absence of any official recognition of immigrants' ethnic and religious identity they are all lumped together and recognized as "French Muslims." Being Muslim within the French context of "*läicité*" means being the "other" vis-á-vis the "*Français de souche*" (French by extraction) (Hervieu-Leger, 2000: 80). The French of Algerian origin comprise the most numerically significant immigrant population. But they are also the most prominent population within the context of French colonial history. For instance, Algeria was France's major "settler colony" to which French citizens and their European allies migrated, expropriated land from the indigenous population, and effectively destroyed Algeria's agrarian and nomadic economic, political and social structures (MacMaster, 1997). This led to massive displacement and emigration of Algeria's indigenous population, mostly in search of employment. Since all colonial subjects were considered as French nationals, prior to Algeria's independence from France in 1962 those Algerian migrant workers who went to France did not see themselves as leaving one country to enter another, rather as French citizens entitled to full economic, political and legal rights. However, the French government simply considered them as colonial subjects who were in France as temporary migrant workers. This was also the position of the Algerian government after the independence under two leaders, Ahmed Ben Bella (1962–1965) and Houari Boumediene (1965–1978). While France benefited from a supply of cheap migrant labor, the Algerian governments considered the perpetuation of their citizens' stay in France a product of neo-colonialism that continued to exploit Algerians even after independence (House, 2006).

France's presence and involvement in colonial and post-colonial Algeria led to polarization and radicalization of Algerians both in their home country and in France. During the war of independence most Algerians sympathized with the National Liberation Front (FLN, *Front de Libération Nationale*). In addition, the French of Algerian origin played a decisive role in the Algerian war of independence by siding with the resistance movement during the 1954–1962 period. Since the French ruled Algeria as a settler colony, no Algerian comprador bourgeoisie class in its classic form was created. As a result, after the French defeat and withdrawal in 1962 there was no exodus of Algerian upper class out of fear of being persecuted by the revolutionaries. Instead, some segments of the *harkis*, those Algerians who fought alongside the French army against the FLN were evacuated and resettled in France. But they were mostly of lower class origins, and once in France they were "parked in unspeakable, filthy, crowded concentration camps for many long years and never benefited from any government aid—a nice reward for their sacrifice for France, of which they were, after all, legally citizens." The *harkis'* horrible treatment by the French government added them to the rank and file of other immigrants of Algerian origin who considered themselves second-class citizens after Algeria's war of independence (Ireland, 2005).

During the three decade period after WWI, known as "*les trente glorieuses*" (30 glorious years of prosperity) both the older generation *Maghrebin* and their French-born off-springs were warehoused in high-rise low-income housing structures (HLM, or "Habitation à Loyer Modéré") built in the suburbs of major French cities like Paris, Lyon, Toulouse, Lille and Nice, where most factories and industries were also situated. This effectively segregated the *Maghrebi* workers and their families in urban peripheries ("*les banlieues*") where there were little or no provisions for shopping or leisure activities. Ireland (2005) vividly describes the present living conditions in the French HLM:

> Now 30, 40, and 50 years old, these high-rise human warehouses in the isolated suburbs are today run-down, dilapidated, sinister places, with broken elevators that remain un-repaired, heating systems left dysfunctional in winter, dirt and dog-shit in the hallways, broken windows, and few commercial amenities—shopping for bare necessities is often quite limited and difficult, while entertain-ment and recreational facilities for youth are truncated and totally inadequate when they're not non-existent.

Social Spheres and Maghrebi *Muslim Identity: A New Frontier for Anti-colonial Resistance*

Similar to the American "melting pot" approach, the assimilationist perspective espoused by supporters of French Republicanism assumes integration and cultural adjustment is a necessity for immigrant populations in order to survive in the host culture. But several studies indicate that the social and political conditions under which immigrants exit their country of origin, the social class background, differences in residence environments (i.e., rural vs. urban immigrants), and the socio-economic and political contexts of the host society are all significant variables that contribute to immigrants' ability and willingness to integrate (Chaichian, 1997: 612–64; Portes and Borocz, 1989: 614–620). Studies of identity formation increasingly emphasize its interactive nature in a process of negotiation with other identities. For instance, Hall (1996: 4–5) argues that identities are constructed "through the relations to the Other, the relation to what it is not, to precisely what it lacks, to what has been called its *constitutive* outside that the 'positive' meanings of any term—and thus its 'identity'—can be constructed." Identity formation and its maintenance is often stronger among the groups that have unequal access to a society's social, cultural, political, and economic spheres. On the other hand, those who support the totalizing power of the French Republic, both French and assimilated immigrants, tend to resist and resent such identity formations. Khosrokhavar (1997: 37–38, cf. Open Society Institute, 2002: 77) succinctly describes this reactive tendency in post-colonial France particularly related to the *Beur* (second-generation French Muslims):

> Access to French nationality for Maghrebian youth . . . involves Frenchmen granting to the children of the ex-colonized what was, formerly, the colonizers' exclusive privilege. Frenchmen returning to France from Algeria (*pied-noirs*), Algerians who deliberately chose France (*harkis*) and a considerable number of other Frenchmen accept with difficulty [that] the offspring of the formerly colonized, who refused to belong to the French Empire, now call for French nationality after their parents fought against colonial France. An unresolved historical argument, a feeling that immigrants' membership in the nation is fraudulent, the general feeling that young people with migrant origin reject French civilization by their ostentatious adhesion to Islam—all this generates discomfort, which deepens insofar as it has never been classified or publicly discussed.

The period between 1975 and 1985 has to be considered a transitional period during which a new political discourse emerged in France when both the French government officials and the media identified and recognized the "second-generation" French of *Maghrebi* origin in general and of Algerian origin in particular. Commonly known as the *"Beur"* (Arab) and born in France, they were the sons and daughters of the Maghrebi immigrants. Thus they were not immigrants per se, as they were born into the involuntary status of being a *Maghrebi* with French citizenship. Segregation, discrimination, and subhuman conditions in the suburban ghettoes led to the mobilization of the *Beur* as a new political force who in 1983 organized a march from Lyon's suburban high rise (*Les Minguettes*) to Paris, and demanded to be recognized as French like everyone else (*"comme les autres"*). In her discussion of the roots of urban riots in 2005, Cesari (2005) argues that spatial segregation of the *Maghrebin* in post-colonial France and the tension between the "poor suburbs" (the periphery) and French metropolises (the center) is at the core of any discourse about the merits of the French Republican ideals. Elia (1997: 47) observes that while their parents emigrated to France with the dream and illusion of a better life, the *Beur* generation has to deal with a tense reality of a day-to-day life of

> …[C]ommuting between a Muslim, Arabi-speaking home when tradition up-holding parents reminisce about North Africa as they prepare *cous cous* and *meschwi*, and the streets of the only city they know, the French metropolis with its corner bistros, its secular culture, and the growing racism of Jean-Marie le Pen supporters and Neo-Nazi skinheads.

In general, France's resistance to the French Muslim identity has taken place within a highly gendered post-colonial discourse. On the one hand, young Algerian males are stereotyped as dangerous Islamic fundamentalists, juvenile delinquents, and criminals who allegedly refuse to obey the French civic laws and to integrate (House, 2006; Geesey, 1995: 139). On the other hand, young women of Algerian origin are represented as passive and submissive ("barriers to assimilation") and yet prone to integration and assimilation into secular French society due to their subordinate status within the Maghrebian male dominant culture. Thus the French Maghrebian women "are alternately seen as potential agents of integration or victims of Islamic fundamentalist agendas" (Geesey, 1995: 137). The conservative assimilationist camp in France also holds the position that the *Maghrebi* Muslim women who are subordinate to men will assimilate easier than men, since the latter "stand to lose a significant amount of control over female family members" if the former choose to do so by integrating into modern French society (Schnapper, 1991: 173). As Abdelkarim-Chikh (cf. Geesey, 1995: 144) argues, the characterization of *Maghrebi* women, particularly those married to non-Muslims, as willing agents of assimilation is rooted in the colonial ideology held by French Orientalists who "shed crocodile tears" over women's oppressive conditions both in colonized Algeria and in contemporary post-colonial French society. However, she further characterizes the position as "narcissistic satisfaction evoking a symbolic abduction, or better yet, proof of self-admiration of one's own values, in which the abducted woman is a consenting accomplice" (Abdelkrim-Chikh, 1990: 241). The French assimilationist approach is also problematic, by overlooking the significant role Islamic cultural values play in the lives of *Maghrebi* immigrants, both male and female.

Hijab *as the Last Defensive Wall of the Colonized*

Similar to Judaism, Islam is both a religion and a way of life that extends to all spheres for individuals living in Muslim communities. Both Islam and Judaism are also characterized by *orthopraxy*, or their dedication to correct practices as dictated by each faith (Denny, 1985: 43). Thus religious belonging and upbringing is an inseparable part of a Muslim society's inherited culture. Although in different ways, the "headscarf controversy" in France reflects on the significance of Islamic cultural values for both older generations and the *Beur* (Babés, 1997). As a consequence, regardless of one's level of adherence to Islamic theology Islamic culture continues to remain a strong component of one's identity. There are indications that the percentage of "practicing" Muslims in France has been on the rise since the late 1980s. But findings of a 2001 survey indicated that only 36 percent of French Muslims declared themselves "believing and practicing." The survey also indicated that among the upper-middle class French Muslims practicing families are more numerous than non-practicing ones (Open Society institute, 2002: 76). As Hervieu-Léger (2000: 80) explains, Islamic values for French Muslims are "the only cultural and symbolic good that they can specifically assert vis-à-vis the *Français de souche* ("French by extraction") which enables them, at the same time, to transform exclusion into a voluntarily Assured difference." This voluntary assumption of difference between a French Muslim of *Maghrebi* origin and a person of French extraction is indicative of an identity that has emerged in France as a reaction to the government's policy of total cultural and political domination in post-colonial France.

Another variable that is often overlooked in the popular media reporting and analysis, is the rural and tribal origins of the predominant majority of the French Maghrebin. In her examination of the status of North African female immigrants in France Geesey (1995: 140) observes that most studies focus on their most recognizable differences from the rest of the French society such as "illiteracy, modest or Islamic dress, rural origins, higher birth rates, poverty and physical seclusion." However, most interpretations gloss over the immigrants' rural, and particularly tribal cultural backgrounds, and instead quickly move to criticize the restrictions placed on women based on alleged Islamic teachings, without acknowledging the fact that Islamic movement had strong roots in tribal culture and lifestyle. There are no official statistics on the Maghrebian's rural or tribal origins. But Chaker (2006: 3) estimates the number of immigrants in France who speak Berber (language of the Maghrebians with tribal roots, or the *Kabyle*) being close to 1,500,000 of which 1,000,000 are Algerians and 500,000 are of Moroccan origin. This indicates that almost two-thirds of French Muslims of Algerian origin come from tribal areas.[1]

The Algerian Kabyle also come from a long tradition of fighting colonial domination, a historical reality that has certainly affected their identity both as Algerians and immigrants/citizens in France. It is within this historical context of colonial and post-colonial realities that one has to see the link between Islamic orthopraxy and tribal culture, particularly related to the meaning and utility of the *hijab* for Muslim women. Some studies of the *Maghrebi* women in France have made note of "negative pressure put on female family members

---

[1] The Kabyles are tribal people who live in the highlands of the Atlas Mountains in northeastern Algeria on the Mediterranean Sea. The term Kabyle is a truncated form of the original Arabic word "Al Qabayel" which literally means "tribes." The kabyles are predominantly Sunni-Muslim and speak *Kabyle* which is a *Berber language* mainly spoken by tribal people in Algeria, Morocco, Mali and Libya (see Brett and Fentress, 1997).

who seek changes in their traditional lifestyle and status, even by relatives who are still living in their home country" (Taboada-Leonetti and Lévy, 1978: 168–178). Thus Muslim women are discouraged from adopting "foreign ways," that go against their traditions out of fear of being ridiculed and censured by family members and neighbors (Geesey, 1995: 144). Muslims in general and Arab-Muslim societies in particular depend on a "bipolar" and seemingly harmonious and productive social order that creates two strictly separate, gender-specific spheres—women belong to and are in control of the interior of the home (private sphere) and men are in charge of the exterior world (public sphere) (see Bouhdiba, 1975: 43).

The strict division of male and female spheres of Maghrebian communities in France closely mirrors that of Arab and Kabyle communities in the Maghreb (North Africa). In his study of gender relations in 20th century Algeria, Knauss (1987: 4–5), using the French anthropologist Pierre Bourdieu's analysis, explains in detail the rigid sexual segregation, stratification and patriarchal notion of "male honor" particularly among the Kabyle, or Algerians of tribal origin. Bourdieu (1979: 121–122) depicts a typical gender division among the tribal people:

> The opposition between the inside and the outside is expressed correctly in the sharp division between the women's sphere—the home and its garden... a closed, secret, protected space, away from intrusions and public gaze—and the men's space—the place of assembly, the mosque, the café, the fields and the market.

Algerians have an expression that demarcates this gender-based social-spatial division: "*Que la femme fasse le cous cous, et nous la politique*" (let women make the couscous, and we will take care of politics) (Knauss, 1987: 5). In Kabyle tribal culture the men are also expected to protect women and the intimacy of the family (private sphere) while girls are socialized to expect to be protected by men (see Figure 1). Outside the home, women in most Muslim tribal cultures, including the Kabyle, are not protected by the veil, but an elaborate system of masculine and feminine pathways and public accommodations effectively keep men and women separate. As Bourdieu (1979: 122) explains, it is "in the urban world where men's space and women's space overlap" that female intimacy is "safeguarded by confinement and the wearing of the veil." Thus the veil becomes a protective tool for tribal men who have to confront other

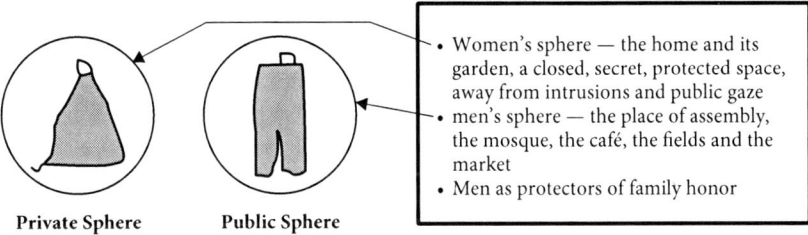

Private Sphere   Public Sphere

Figure 1. Gender-specific spaces in a Muslim Maghrebin rural-tribal culture

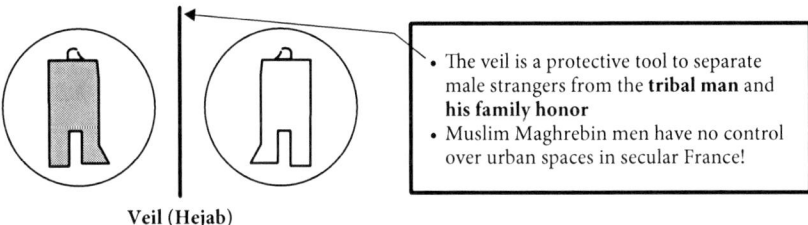

Veil (Hejab)

Figure 2. The veil (hejab) and its function in urban public spheres

men, strangers who may not necessarily belong to their own tribe. In her book *The Veil and the Male Elite*, Mernissi (1991: 85) explains in detail the rationale for the descent of the verse of the *veil* (curtain in Arabic) in the Qur'an, and the fact that it was "not to put a barrier between a man and a woman, but between two men (see Figure 2)." She further argues that the concept of the word *hijab* has three inter-woven dimensions:

> The first dimension is a visual one: to hide something from sight...the second dimension is spatial: to separate, to mark a border, to establish a threshold. And finally, the third dimension is ethical: it belongs to the realm of the forbidden (93).

It is the *hijab*'s third dimension, namely, the ethical that is imperative to the tribal culture of male honor that the Kabyle also prescribe to. Bourdieu (1979: 123) describes how the male members of the Kabyle are socialized to protect not only their women, but also the whole sphere of intimacy including internal family and tribal dissentions and shortcomings from strangers. Clearly, all aspects of the Kabyle's cherished tribal culture are violated within the post-colonial French social context. First, the *Maghrebi* men are disenfranchised, discriminated against and forced to live in dilapidated housing and to take low-paying jobs. They are also effectively cut off from the French political process: they no longer have any control over the public sphere and its associated politics in post-colonial France as they did back in their homeland. Second, women who joined their male relatives in the 1970s, as well as their French-born female offspring (Beur) are forced to live in the public housing complexes in the *banlieus* where there are no protective measures to keep their private spheres separate from the public sphere. This also exerts pressure on *Maghrebi* men who are expected to protect their women and their homes (private sphere) from strangers. Furthermore, *Maghrebi* women's interactions with teachers, social workers and nurses exposes them to the nuances of a secular Western culture which the *Maghrebi* men come to consider as a "plot organized against them to dethrone them from a reign that is increasingly difficult to maintain" (Yahyaoui, 1989: 10). Third, in a tribal cultural context where men and women are expected to uphold endogamous marriages, the French *Maghrebi* women are exposed to the non-Muslim public sphere and have a chance to meet and marry non-Muslim men. Unable to control female spaces in urban France, as they used to do back home, the Muslim *Maghrebi* "parents, brothers, even cousins prevent girls in the family from going out," and when they fail, they "place them under close surveillance" as dictated by their honor code (Begag and Chaouite, 1990: 66). Thus, being themselves subdued and continuously exploited in post-colonial France, the *Maghrebi* men use the *hijab* as the last available cultural tool at their disposal to protect their shattered honor and violated private sphere from a hostile and domineering public sphere that continues to colonize them and their families.

The descent of the *hijab* during the Muslim prophet's time was to protect the private sphere of the family from the dangers of unknown forces in the public urban sphere of Medina. But the resurgence of the *hijab* at the end of the 20th century in many Muslim countries and in post-colonial situations signifies a new era when Muslim societies and populations have not only lost their economic and political independence, but also their cultural identity. The confinement of women by Muslim men is seen as a solution for a crisis of global magnitude. As Mernissi (1991: 99) argues, "protecting women from change by veiling them and shutting them out of the world has echoes of closing the community to protect it from the West." In brief, the French government's handling of the *hijab* controversy and eventual banning of the headscarf in French schools is a clear example of using Muslim immigrant women's bodies as a cultural and ideological battleground to subject the Muslim immigrant population to total submission to France's post-colonial interests; and the Muslim communities' pressure on women to wear the *hijab* in public is their last remaining defensive tool against invasive forces of globalization in the context of the French society.

REFERENCES

Abbink, Jon; de Bruijn, Mirjam and van Walraven, Klaas, eds. 2003. *Rethinking Resistance: Revolt and Violence in African History*. Leiden: Brill.

Abdelkrim-Chikh, Rabia. 1990. "Les Femme Exogames: Entre La Loi de Dieu et les Droite de L'Hommes," *L'Islam en France*, Editions Bruno Ettienne, pp. 235–254.

Abrahamsen, Rita. 1997. "The Victory of Popular Forces or Passive Revolution? A Neo- Gramscian Perspective on Democratisation" *The Journal of Modern African Studies* 35(1): 129–52.

Acosta Reveles, Irma Lorena. 2006. "Balance del Modelo Agroexportador en América Latina el Comenzar el Siglo XXI" in *Revista Mundo Agrario, Revista de Estudios Rurales*. Number 013, Vol. 7, July–December. Centro de Estudios Histórico Rurales de la Universidad Nacional de la Plata, Argentina.

Acuña, R. 2007. *Corridors of Migration: The Odyssey of Mexican Laborers, 1600–1933*: Univ of Arizona Pr.

Affairs, Senate Committee on Homeland Security & Governmental. 2009. *Senators Voice Concerns About SBInet Management and Effectiveness* 2008 [cited May 23 2009]. Available from http://hsgac.senate.gov/public/index.cfm?FuseAction=Press Releases.Detail&Affiliation=C&PressRelease_id=e3910540-0678-4f9d-9143-86513c 10ff5c&Month=1&Year=2008.

Africa All Party Parliamentary Group. 2006. *The Other Side of the Coin: The UK and Corruption in Africa*, retrieved 3/1/2009 at www.africaappg.org.uk.

Alarcón, Rafael. 1995. *Immigrants or Transnational Workers? The Settlement Process Among Mexicans in Rural California*. The California Institute for Rural Studies. U.C. Davis.

Albala-Bertrand, J.M. 1993. *Political Economy of Large Natural Disasters*. New York: Oxford University Press.

Ali, Ashgar. 2006. "A Conceptual Framework for Environmental Justice based on Shared but Differentiated Responsibilities," Tony Shallcross and John Robinson, eds., *Global Citizenship and Environmental Justice*. New York: Editions Rodopi B.V., pp. 41–77.

Alvarez, Sonia E. 1998. "Latin American Feminisms "Go Global": Trends of the 1990s and Challenges for the New Millennium." pp. 293–324 in *Cultures of Politics, Politics of Cultures*, edited by Sonia E. Alvarez, Evelina Dagñino, and Arturo Escobar Boulder, CO: Westview Press.

Amin, Samir. 1976. *Unequal Development*. New York: Monthly Review Press.

Anderson, M. and Collins, P.H., eds. 1992. *Race, Class and Gender: An Anthology*. Wadsworth.

Andreas, Peter. 1998. The Escalation of US Immigration Control in the Post-NAFTA Era. *Political Science Quarterly*: 591–615.

——. 2004a. "The Clandestine Political Economy of War and Peace in Bosnia" *International Studies Quarterly* 48: 29–51.

——. 2004b. "Illicit International Political Economy: The Clandestine Side of Globalization" *Review of International Political Economy* 11(3): 641–52.

Anon. 2004. "The War of the Headscarves," *The Economist* (February 5). http://www .Economist.com/world/Europe/displayStory.cfm?story_id=2404691, accessed 7-4-2008.

Arenal, Electa. 2007. 'Women in the Oaxaca Teachers' Strike and Citizens' Uprising.' *Feminist Studies* 33 (1): 107–117.

Arkibong Bayan. 2009. "Hong Kong OFWs vs ban on direct hiring," 14 February, http://arkibongbayan.or/2009/2009-02-Feb10-HKDhire/hkvsbanFeb10.htm. Accessed 2.14/2009.

Arrighi, Giovanni. 1979. *Imperialismo e Sistema Capitalista Mondiale*, ed. Naples: Liguori.

Astier, Henry. 2004. *The Deep Roots of French Secularism*. http://news. bbc.co.uk/i/hi/Europe/3325285.stm, accessed 7-1-2008.

Augelli, Enrico and Murphy, Craig N. 1988. *America's Quest for Supremacy and the Third World: A Gramscian Analysis*. London: Pinter.

Babés, L. 1997. *L'Islam Positif: La Religion des Jeunes musulmans en France* (Positive Islam: The Religion of Young Muslims in France). Paris: Édition de L'Aube.

Baillard, Dominique. 2008. "Estalla el Precio de los Cereales" in *Le Monde Diplomatique*, South Cone Edition.

Ballentine, Karen and Nitzschke, Heiko. 2003. "Beyond Greed and Grievance: Policy Lessons from Studies in the Political Economy of Armed Conflict." New York: International Peace Academy.

Bandy, J. 2000. Bordering the Future: Resisting Neoliberalism in the Borderlands. *Critical Sociology* 26 (3):232.

Barkan, Steven. 1985. *Protestors on Trial: Criminal Justice in the Southern Civil Rights and Vietnam Antiwar Movements*. New Brunswick, NJ: Rutgers University Press.

Barnett, A. 2007. "Three Faces of the World Social Forum." Open Democracy, (January 30, 2007), Retrieved 1 March 2007 (http://www.opendemocracy.net/globalization-protest/wsf_faces_4297.jsp)

Barreda Marín, Andrés. 2004. 'The Dangers of Plan Puebla Panama.' In Armando Bartra (ed.), *Profound Rivers of Mesoamerica: Alternatives to Plan Puebla Panama*. Mexico City, MX: Instituto Maya, third edition, pp. 131–208.

Barry, Andrew; Osborne, Thomas and Rose, Nikolas. 1996. Introduction. In *Foucault and Political Reason: Liberalism, Neo-liberalism, and Rationalities of Government*, edited by A. Barry, T. Osborne and N. Rose: University of Chicago Press.

Barry, Tom. 1995. *Zapata's Revenge: Free Trade and the Farm Crisis in Mexico*. Boston: South End Press.

Bartra, Armando, ed. 2004. *Profound Rivers of Mesoamerica: Alternatives to Plan Puebla Panama*. Mexico City, MX: Instituto Maya, 3rd edition.

BBC News. 2008. "France Rejects Veiled Muslim's wife" (July 12). http://news.bbc .co.uk/2/hi/Europe/7503757.stm, accessed 7-13-2008.

Beas Torres, Carlos, ed. 2007. *La Batalla Por Oaxaca* (The Battle for Oaxaca). Ediciones Yope Power: Oaxaca, Oaxaca, MX.

Bebbington, Anthony and Thiele, Graham. 1993. *Non-governmental Organizations and the State in Latin America*. London: Routledge.

Begag, Azuz, and Chaouite, Abdellatif. 1990. *Ecartes d'Identité*. Paris: Seuil.

Beirne, Piers. 1980. "Empiricism and the Critique of Marxism on Law and Crime." *Social Problems*, 26: 373–385.

Bellah, Robert. 1967. "Civil Religion in America," *Daedalus*, 96(1): 1–21.

Bello, Walden. 2004. *The Anti-Development State: The Political Economy of Permanent Crisis in the Philippines*. Diliman, Quezon City: University of the Philippines and Bangkok, Thailand: Focus on the Global South.

Bennett, Vivienne. 1989. "Urban Public Services and Social Conflict: Water in Monterrey." pp. 79–100 in *Housing and Land in Urban Mexico*, edited by Alan Gilbert. San Diego: Center for U.S.-Mexican Studies, UCSD.

——. 1992. "The Evolution of Urban Popular Movements in Mexico Between 1968 and 1988." pp. 240–259 in *The Making of Social Movements in Latin America: Identity, Strategy, and Democracy*, edited by Arturo Escobar and Sonia E. Alvarez Boulder: Westview Press.

——. 1995. *The Politics of Water: Urban Protest, Gender, and Power in Monterrey, Mexico*. Pittsburgh, PA: University of Pittsburgh Press.

Berberoglu, B. 2005. *Globalization and Change: The Transformation of Global Capitalism*. Lanham: Lexington Books.

Bernstein, Mary. 1997. "Celebration and Suppression: The Strategic Uses of Identity by the Lesbian and Gay Movement." *American Journal of Sociology* 103: 531–65.

Bieler, Andreas and Morton, Adam David. 2001. "The Gordian Knot of Agency-Structure in International Relations: A Neo-Gramscian Perspective." *European Journal of International Relations* 7(1): 5–35.

Binford, Leigh. 2002. "Remesas y Subdesarrollo en México," in *Relaciones. Estudios de Historia y Sociedad* 90, vol. XXIII: 115–158.

Blau, Judith and Moncada, Alberto. 2005. *Human Rights: Beyond the Liberal Vision*. Lanham, MD and Oxford, UK: Rowman & Littlefield.

Bob, Clifford. 2002. "Political Process Theory and Transnational Movements: Dialectics of Protest among Nigeria's Ogoni Minority." *Social Problems* 49: 395–415.

Bonacich, Edna, and Appelbaum, RP. 2000. *Behind the Label: Inequality in the Los Angeles Apparel Industry*: Berkeley: University of California Press.

Bond, P. 2008. "Lessons of Zimbabwe: An Exchange Between Patrick Bond and Mahmoud Mamdani." Retrieve December 2008 (http://links.org.au/node/815/9693).

Bonilla-Silva, E. 2006. Racism Without Racists: Color-Blind Racism and the Persistence of Racial Inequality in the United States. Lanham, MD: Rowman & Littlefield Publishers.

Borg, Erik. 2001. "Steinbruch Gramsci: Hegemonie Im Internationalen Politischen System." *iz3w* 256.

Bouhdiba, Abdelwahab. 1975. *La sexualité en Islam*. Paris: PUF.

Bourdieu, Pierre. 1970. *Zur Soziologie der symbolischen Formen*. Frankfurt am Main: Suhrkamp.

——. 1979. *Algeria 1960*. New York: Cambridge University Press.

Bratton, Michael. 1989. "The Politics of Government-NGO Relations in Africa." *World Development* 17: 569–587.

Brett, E.A. 1993. "Voluntary Agencies as Development Organizations: Theorizing the Problem of Efficiency and Accountability." *World Development* 24: 269–303.

Brett, Michael, and Fentross, Elizabeth. 1997. *The Berbers*. Blackwell Publishing.

Brewer, R.M. 2006. "Forged in Blood: Black Racial Injustice in the U.S." Lui, et al. editors, *The Color of Wealth: The Story Behind the US Racial Wealth Divide*. New York: The New Press.

Broad, Robin and Heckscher, Zahara. 2003. "Before Seattle: The Historical Roots of the Current Movement against Corporate-Led Globalisation." *Third World Quarterly* 24(4): 713–738.

Browne-Dianis, Judith, Lai, Jennifer, Hincapia, Marielena and Soni, Saket. 2006. "And Injustice For All: Workers' Lives in the Reconstruction of New Orleans." <www.advancementproject.org/reports/workersreport.pdf>

Brubaker, Rogers. 2004. "Ethnicity without Groups," in Andreas Wimmer, Richard J. Goldstone and Donald L. Horowitz, eds., *Facing Ethnic Conflicts—toward a New Realism*. Oxford: Rowman & Littlefield Publishers, 34–52.

Brulle, Robert and J. Craig Jenkins. 2008. "Fixing the Bungled U.S. Environmental Movement." *Contexts* 7(2): 14–19.

——; Turner, Liesel H., Carmichael, Jason and Jenkins, J. Craig. 2007. "Measuring Social Movement Organization Populations: A Comprehensive Census of U.S. Environmental Movement Organizations." *Mobilization: An International Quarterly Review* 12(3): 195–212.

Brunsma, David. 2008. "Disasters in the Twenty-First Century: Modern Destruction and Future Instruction," *Social Forces* 87, No. 2: 983–991.

Bustamante, Jorge. 2007. "La migración de México a Estados Unidos. De la coyuntura al fondo." *Revista Latinoamericana de Población*, Year 1, No. 1, pp. 89–113.

Buttel, Frederick and Gould, Kenneth A. 2006. "Environmentalism and the Trajectory of the Anti-Corporate Globalization Movement," Christopher Chase-Dunn and Salvatore Babones, eds., *Global Social Change*. Baltimore, MD: Johns Hopkins University Press., pp. 269–288.

Cabrera Adame, Carlos Javier and López Gernández, Diana. 2008. "Gastos y políticas públicas en el campo" in *Revista Economía Informa*, Number 350, January-February. Facultad de Economía, UNAM. pp. 52–59. Mexico. Available at: http://132.248.45.5/publicaciones/econinforma/pdfs/350/04cabrera.pdf

Calavita, Kitty. 1983. "The Demise of the Occupational Safety and Health Administration: A Case Study in Symbolic Law." *Social Problems*, 30, No. 4: 437–448.

Calva, José Luis. 1996. "La Economía Nacional y la Agricultura de México a Tres Años de Operación del TLCAN" *Simposio Trinacional de Investigación: EL TLC y la Agricultura. ¿Funciona el experimento?* CIESTAAM, Universidad Autónoma Chapingo and the Texas Agricultural Market, Research Center, Texas A&M University, November, San Antonio, Texas, USA.

Canales, Alejandro I. and Zlolniski, Christian. 2001. "Comunidades Transnacionales y Migración en la Era de la Globalización," in *La Migración Internacional y el Desarrollo en las Américas*. Santiago de Chile; CEPAL, BID, OIM and FNUAP.

—— and Montiel, Israel. 2007. "A World Without Borders." Mexican Immigration, Internal Borders and Transnationalism in the United States." In Antoine Pecoud and Paul de Guchteneire (eds.). *Migration Without Borders. Essays on the Free Movement of People*. Berghahn Books and UNESCO, Oxford and New York.

——. 2008. *Vivir del norte. Remesas, desarrollo y pobreza en México*. Consejo Nacional de Población. Mexico.

Carlsen, Laura. 2004. 'Conservation or privatization? Biodiversity, the global market, and the Mesoamerican Biological Corridor.' In Gerardo Otero (ed.), *Mexico in Transition: Neoliberal Globalism, the State and Civil Society*. London: Zed Books, pp. 52–71.

Carmichael, Cathie. 2005. "The Violent Destruction of Community during the 'Century of Genocide'." *European History Quarterly* 35(3): 395–403.

Carr, Edward Hallett. 2001 [1940]. *The Twenty Years' Crisis, 1919–1939; an Introduction to the Study of International Relations*. London: Macmillan and co. limited.

Castles, Stephen and Miller, Mark J. 2003. [1st edition 1993]: *The Age of Migration: International Population Movements in the Modern World*. London; Macmillan.

Cesari, Jocelyne. 2005. "Ethnicity, Islam, and les Banlieues: Confronting the Issues," *Social Science Research Council*. http://riotsfrance.ssrc.org/cesari/printable.html, accessed 7-14-2008.

Chaichian, Mohammad. 1997. "First Generation Iranian Immigrants and the Question of Cultural Identity: The Case of Iowa," *International Migration Review*, 31(3): 612–627.

Chaker, Salem. 2006. *Berber, a 'Long-Forgotten' Language of France* (translated by Laurie and Amar Chaker). http://www.utexas.edu/cola/insts/france-ut/arcives/chaker_english.pdf, accessed 6-30-2008.

Chambliss, William J. and Mankoff, Milton, eds. 1975. *Whose Law? What Order?* New York, NY: Wiley & Sons.

——. 1980. "On Lawmaking." *British Journal of Law and Society*, Winter, 149–172.

——. 2001. *Power, Politics, and Crime*. Boulder, CO: Westview Press.

——. 2004. "The State, The Legal Order, and Social Problems," pp. 405–418 in A. Kathryn Stout, Richard A. Dello Buono and William J. Chambliss eds. *Social Problems, Law, and Society*. Lanham, MD: Rowman and Littlefield.

Chase-Dunn, Christopher and Babones, Salvatore. 2006. *Global Social Change*. Baltimore, MA: Johns Hopkins University Press.

—— and Hall, Thomas D. 2006. "Ecological Degradation and the Evolution of World-Systems," Andrew K. Jorgenson and Edward L. Kick, eds., *Globalization and the Environment*. Boston, MA: Brill, pp. 231–252.

—— and Kaneshiro, Matheu. 2009. "Stability and Change in the Contours of Alliances Among Movements in the Social Forum Process," David Fasenfest, ed., *Engaging Social Justice: Critical Studies of 21st Century Social Transformation*. Leiden: Brill.

Chassen-López, Francie R. 2004. *From Liberal to Revolutionary Oaxaca: The View from the South, Mexico 1867–1911*. University Park: The Pennsylvania State University Press.

Childress, Stacey M. 2008. Harvard Business School. <http://www.exed.hbs.edu/cgi-bin/wk/5826.html>

Coalition to Stop the Demolition (CSD). 2008. <http://changethegamenow.org/web/index.php?option=com_content&task=view&id=61&Itemid=1>

Cole, Juan. 2007. *Napoleon's Egypt: Invading the Middle East*. New York: Palgrave-MacMillan.

Coleman, M. 2008. Between Public Policy and Foreign Policy: US Immigration Law Reform and the Undocumented Migrant. *Urban Geography* 29 (1):4–28.

Coll-Hurtado Atlántida and Calderón, Godínez; Lourdes, María de. 2003. *La Agricultura en México: un Atlas en Blanco y Negro*. Instituto de Geografía de la UNAM. Mexico.

Collier, Paul and Hoeffler, Anke. 1998. "On Economic Causes of Civil War" *Oxford Economic Papers* 50: 563–73.

——. 1999. "On the Economic Consequences of Civil War" *Oxford Economic Papers* 51: 168–83.

—— and Hoeffler, Anke. 2002. "The Political Economy of Secession" New York: World Bank: 22.

—— and Hoeffler, Anke. 2004. "Greed and Grievance in Civil War." *Oxford Economic Papers* 56: 563–95.

Collins, P.H. 1986. "Learning for the Outsider Within: the Sociological Significance of Black Feminist Thought." *Social Problems* 33: 14–30.

——. 1990. *Black Feminist Thought*. Boston: Unwin Hyman.

Combahee River Collective Statement. 1982. Hull, G.T., P. Bell-Scott, and B. Smith, eds. *All the Men are Black, All the Women White, But Some of Us Are Brave*. Old Westbury, New York: Feminist Press.

CONEVAL. 2008. *Informe de Evaluación de la Política de Desarrollo Social en Mexico*. SEDESOL. Mexico. Available at: www.coneval.gob.mx/contenido/home/2234.pdf.

Coomaraswamy, Radhika. 2002. 'Are Women's Rights Universal? Re-Engaging the Local.' *Meridians* 3 (1): 1–18.

Cornelius, Wayne A. 2005. Controlling 'Unwanted' Immigration: Lessons From the United States, 1993–2004. *Journal of Ethnic and Migration Studies* 31 (4): 775–794.

Corotis, Ross B. and Enarson, Elaine. 2004. *Socio-Economic Disparities in Community Consequences to Natural Disasters*. http://www.ifed.ethz.ch/events/Forum04/Corotis_paper.pdf>

Courville, Sasha and Piper, Nicola. 2004. "Harnessing Hope through NGO Activism." *The Annals of the American Academy of Political and Social Science* 592:39–61.

Cox, Robert W. 1981. "Social Forces, States and World Orders: Beyond International Relations Theory." *Millennium: Journal of International Studies* 10 (2): 126–55.

——. 1998. „Weltordnung Und Hegemonie—Grundlagen Der ‚Internationalen Politischen Ökonomie'", in *Studien der Forschungsgruppe Europäische Gemeinschaften (FEG)*. Marburg: Universitaet Marburg, 142.

Cramer, Christopher. 2002. "Homo Economicus Goes to War: Methodological Individualism, Rational Choice and the Political Economy of War" *World Development* 30(11): 1845–64.

Daase, Christopher. 2003. "Krieg Und Politische Gewalt: Konzeptionelle Innovation Und Theoretischer Fortschritt," in Gunther Hellmann, Klaus Dieter Wolf and Michael Zürn, eds., *Die Neuen Internationalen Beziehungen*, Baden-Baden: Nomos Verlagsgesellschaft, 161–208.

Davis, A. 1981. *Women, Race, and Class.* New York: Random House.

DeGenova, Nicholas. 2002. Migrant" Illegality" and Deportability in Everyday Life. *Annual Review of Anthropology*: 419–447.

Delgado, Héctor L. 2008. "Unions and the Unionization of Latinas/os in the United States." In H. Rodríguez, R. Saénz and C. Menjívar (eds.) *Latinas/os in the United States. Changing the Face of America.* New York, Springer. pp. 369–383.

Delgado-Wise, R, and Marquez Covarrubias, H. 2007. The Reshaping of Mexican Labor Exports under NAFTA: Paradoxes and Challenges. *International Migration Review* 41 (3): 656–679.

Dello Buono, Richard A. 2004. "Critical Perspectives on Law and Society: A Social Problems Approach," pp. 3–18 in A. Kathryn Stout, Richard A. Dello Buono and William J. Chambliss eds. *Social Problems, Law, and Society.* Lanham, MD: Rowman and Littlefield.

Dencik, Lars. 1977. "Plädoyer Für Eine Revolutionäre Konfliktforschung," in Dieter Senghaas, ed., *Kritische Friedensforschung.* Frankfurt a.M.: Suhrkamp Verlag, 247–70.

Denny, Frederick. 1985. *An Introduction to Islam.* New York: MacMillan.

Department of Homeland Security (DHS). 2007. "The Eighteenth Month Anniversary of Hurricane Katrina: Progress Made and Lessons Learned." <http://www.dhs.gov/xprevprot/programs/gc_1173201764934.shtm>

Diamond, Jared. 2005. *Collapse: How Societies Choose to Fail or Succeed.* New York: Viking.

Dierckxsens, Wim. 2008. "Especular con alimentos" Periódico p. 12, May 25, Argentina. Available at: www.pagina12.com.ar/imprimir/diario/suplementos/cash/17-3495-2008-05-25.html

Dill, B. l979. "The Dialectics of Black Womanhood." *Signs*, 4: 553–555.

Disaster Resource Network . 2007. *Disaster Vulnerability Maps.* <http://www.drnglobal.org/maps/disaster-vulnerability>

Domestic Workers United. 2006. *Home is Where the Work Is: Inside New York's Domestic Work Industry.* New York: Domestic Workers United.

Durand, Jorge and Massey, Douglas. 1992. "Mexican Migration to the United States: A Critical Review," in *Latin American Research Review*, 27: 3–43.

Egbert, Jahn; Fischer, Sabine and Sahm, Astrid; eds. 2005. *Die Zukunft Des Friedens Band 2: Die Friedens- Und Konfliktforschung Aus Der Perspektive Der Jüngeren Generationen.* Wiesbaden: VS Verlag für Sozialwissenschaften.

Ehrlich, P.R., and Ehrlich, A.H. 1990. *The Population Explosion.* New York: Simon and Schuster.

El Barzón. 2009. *Bienvenido a Fundación El Barzón A.C.* Website: www.elbarzon.org.

Elin, Nada. 1997. "In the Making: Beur Fiction and Identity Construction," *World Literature Today*, 71: 47–54 (winter).

Engels, Frederick. 1946. *Ludwig Feuerbach and the End of Classical German Philosophy.* Moscow: Progress Publishers.

Erikson, Kai T. 1978. *Everything in Its Path: Destruction of Community in the Buffalo Creek Flood.* New York, NY: Simon and Shuster.

Escobar, Arturo. 1995a. *Encountering Development: The Making and Unmaking of the Third World.* Princeton, NJ: Princeton University Press.

Espenshade, T.J. 1995. Unauthorized immigration to the United States. *Annual Review of Sociology* 21 (1): 195–216.

Estrella, Gabriel; Canales, Alejandro I. and Eugenia Zavala, María. 1999. *Ciudades de la Frontera Norte. Migración y Fecundidad.* Universidad Autónoma de Baja California. Mexico.

Faber, Daniel. 2005. "Building a Transnational Environmental Justice Movement: Obstacles and Opportunities in the Age of Globalization," Joe Bandy and Jackie Smith, eds., *Coalitions Across Borders: Transnational Protest and the Neoliberal Order.* Lanham: Rowman & Littlefield Publishers, Inc, pp. 43–70.

Fanon, Frantz. 1981 [1961]. *Die Verdammten Dieser Erde.* Frankfurt am Main: Suhrkamp Verlag.

Fatton, Robert Jr. 1984. "Gramsci and the Legitimization of the State: The Case of the Senegalese Passive Revolution" *Canadian Journal of Political Science / Revue canadienne de science politique* 19(4): 729–50.

Feldman, Shelley. 1997. "NGOs and Civil Society: (Un)stated Contradictions." *The Annals of the American Academy of Political and Social Science* 554:46–65.

Ferguson, R. 2004. *Aberrations in Black: Toward a Queer of Color Critique.* Minneapolis: University of Minnesota Press.

Fernandez-Kelly, Patricia and Massey, Douglas. 2007. Borders for whom? The Role of NAFTA in Mexico-US Migration. *The ANNALS of the American Academy of Political and Social Science* 610 (1):98–118.

Filosa, Gwen. 2006. "Demolition is Development's Destiny," *Times Picayune,* October 18. <www.cwsworkshop.org/katrinareader/node/224>

Finnegan, William. 2002. "Leasing the Rain," *The New Yorker,* April 8, 2002.

Fix, Michael E., and Tumlin, Karen C. 1997. Welfare Reform and the Devolution of Immigrant Policy. Washington, D.C.: Urban Institute.

Flaherty, Jordan. 2006. "Continuing Crisis in New Orleans' Schools." *Left Turn Magazine,* Fall. <www.cwsworkshop.org/katrinareader/node/68>

Foran, John. 1997. 'Discourses and Social Forces: The Role of Culture and Cultural Studies in Understanding Revolutions,' pp. 203–26 in John Foran, editor, *Theorizing Revolutions.* London: Routledge.

——. 2009. 'New Political Cultures of Opposition: What Future for Revolutions?' In John Foran, David Lane, and Andreja Zivkovic (eds.), *Revolution in the Making of the Modern World: Social Identities, Globalization, and Modernity.* London and New York: Routledge, pp. 430–457.

Foster, John Bellamy. 1999. *The Vulnerable Planet: A Short Economic History of the Environment.* New York: Monthly Review Press.

——. 2002. *Ecology Against Capitalism.* New York: Monthly Review Press.

Frank, Andre Gunder. 1967. *Capitalism and Underdevelopment in Latin America.* New York: Monthly Review Press.

——. 2007. "Entropy Generation and Displacement: The Nineteenth-Century Multilateral Network of World Trade," Alf Hornberg and Carole Crumley, eds., *The World System and the Earth System: Global Socioenvironmental Change and Sustainability since the Neolithic.* Walnut Creek, CA: Left Coast Press, pp. 303–316.

Franklin, D.L. 1997. *Ensuring Inequality: The Structural Transformation of the African American Family.* New York: Oxford University Press.

Fricke, Dietmar. 2000. *Globalisierung Und Bürgerkriege: Eine Theoriegeleitete Analyse Von Globalisierungsprozessen Und Ihrem Verhältnis Zu Regionalen Konflikten.* Berlin: Köster.

Frobel, Folker; Heinrichs, Jurgen and Kreye, Otto. 1978. The New International Division of Labour. *Social Science Information* 17 (1):123–142.

Fukuyama, Francis. 1992. *Das Ende Der Geschichte: Wo Stehen Wir?* München: Kindler.

Galtung, Johan. 1977. "Gewalt, Frieden Und Friedensforschung," in Dieter Senghaas, ed., *Kritische Friedensforschung.* Frankfurt a.M.: Suhrkamp Verlag, 423.

Gamson, William A.; Fireman, Bruce and Rytina, Steven. 1982. *Encounters With Unjust Authority.* Homewood, IL: Dorsey Press.

Geesey, Patricia. 1995. "North African Immigrants in France: Integration and Change," *Substance,* 76/77: 137–153.

General, Inspector. 2008. ICE Policies Related to Detainee Deaths and the Oversight of Immigration Detention Facilities. Department of Homeland Security (DHS).

Giddeon, Jasmine. 1998. "The Politics of Social Service Provision Through NGOs: A Study of Latin America." *Bulletin Latin American Research* 17(3):303–321.

Gilbert, E. and J.R. 2008. *Africa in World History*. Upper Saddle River, New Jersey: Prentice-Hall.

Gill, Stephen, ed. 1993. *Gramsci, Historical Materialism and International Relations*. Cambridge: Cambridge University Press.

Gilley, Bruce. 2004. "Against the Concept of Ethnic Conflict." *Third World Quarterly* 25(6): 1155-66.

Gimenez, Martha. 2009. "Global Capitalism and Women: From Feminist Politics to Working Class Politics," in *Globalization and Third World Women: Exploitation, Coping and Resistance*, edited by Ligaya Lindio McGovern and Isidor Walliman, London: Ashgate Publishing Company.

Giugni, Marco. 1998. "Was it Worth the Effort? The Outcomes and Consequences of Social Movement." *Annual Review of Sociology* 24: 371–393.

——. 1999. "How Social Movements Matter: Past Research, Present Problems, Future Developments." in *How Social Movements Matter* edited by Marco Giugni, Doug McAdam, and Charles Tilly. Minneapolis, University of Minnesota Press.

Glenn, Evelyn Nakano. 1997. "From Servitude to Service Work: Historical Continuities in the Racial Division of Paid Reproductive Labor." In *Feminist Frontiers IV*. (New York: The McGraw-Hill Companies, Inc.)

Glick Schiller, Nina; Basch, Linda and Blanc-Szanton, Christina, eds. 1992. "Towards a Transnational Perspective on Migration." *Annals of the New York Academy of Sciences*, vol. 645.

Gonzalez, G.G. 2006. *Guest Workers or Colonized Labor?: Mexican Labor Migration to the United States*: Paradigm Publishers.

Gordon Nembhard, Jessica. 2008. 'Theorizing and Practicing Democratic Community Economics: Engaged Scholarship, Economic Justice, and the Academy,' in Charles Hale (ed.) *Engaging Contradictions: Theory, Politics, and Methods of Activist Scholarship*. Berkeley and Los Angeles: University of California Press, pp. 265–297.

Gotham, Kevin Fox and Greenberg, Miriam. 2008. "From 9/11 to 8/29: Post Disaster Recovery and Rebuilding in New York and New Orleans." *Social Forces*, 87, No. 2: 1039-1062.

Gramsci, Antonio. 1971. *Selections From Prison Notebooks*. New York: International Publishers.

——. 1978 [1926]. "Some Aspects of the Southern Question," in Quintin Hoare, ed., *Antonio Gramsci "Selections from Political Writings (1921-1926)."* London: Lawrence and Wishart.

——. 2001 [1929–35]. *Quaderni Del Carcere: Edizione Critica Dell'istituto Gramsci. 2 ed.* Torino: Giulio Einaudi.

Greater New Orleans Community Data Center (GNOCDC) *Greater New Orleans Nonprofit Knowledge Works.* <http://www.gnocdc.org/>

Group, The GEO. 2009. *George C. Zoley* [cited May 23 2009]. Available from http://www.thegeogroupinc.com/bios/george.html.

Gupta, Swagata. 2008. UPDATE 1-Corrections Corp posts higher Q2 profit. *Reuters*, Aug 7.

Gutiérrez, Natividad. 2001. 'Over 150 Days of Fox's Indigenism.' *Canada Watch* 8 (6), pp. 113-115.

Haddad, Yvonne Y. 1999. "The Globalization of Islam: The Return of Muslims to the West," in John Esposito (ed.), *The Oxford Dictionary of Islam*, pp. 601–641. New York: Oxford University Press.

Hall, Stuart. 1986. "Gramsci's Relevance for the Study of Race and Ethnicity." *Journal of Communication Inquiry* 10(5): 5–27.

——. 1996. "Introduction: Who Needs 'Identity'?" in Hall, Stuart and Paul de Gay (eds.), *Questions of Cultural Identity*, pp. 1–17. London: Sage.

Hanifi, M. Jamil. 2004. "Editing the Past: Colonial Production of Hegemony Through the 'Loya Jerga' in Afghanistan" *Iranian Studies* 37(2): 295–322.

Hanson, G.H. 2003. What has Happened to Wages in Mexico Since NAFTA? In *NBER Working Paper No. W9563* Cambridge: National Bureau of Economic Research.

Hardt, Michael and Negri, Antonio. 2000. *Empire*. Cambridge and London: Harvard University Press.

——. 2004. *Multitude*. Cambridge and London: Harvard University Press.

Harvey, David. 2007. *A Brief History of Neoliberalism*. New York: Oxford University Press.

Hasan, Zubair. 2007. "Labor as a source of value and capital formation: Ibn Khaldun, Ricardo and Marx—A Comparison." International Islamic University, Malaysia (IIUM). http://mpra.ub.uni-muenchen.de/5989/1/MPRA_paper_5989.pdf

Haut Conseil à L'Intégration. 2000. *L'Islam dans la République*. Paris: La Documentation Français.

Hazma, Mohamed and Zetter, Roger. 1998. "Structural Adjustment, Urban Systems and Disaster Vulnerability in Developing Countries." *Cities Journal*, 15, No. 4: 291–299.

Hegel, Georg Wilhelm Friedrich. 1983. *Lectures on the History of Philosophy*. Englewood Cliffs: Humanities Press.

Held, David, et al., eds. 1999. *Global Transformations: Politics, Economics, and Culture*. Stanford, California: Stanford California Press.

Hemassi, Elbaki. 1987. "French Revolution and the Arab World," *International Social Science Journal*, UNESCO (February).

Henriques, Gisele and Patel, Raj. 2004. 'NAFTA, Corn, and Mexico's Agricultural Trade Liberalization.' Americas Program. Silver City, NM: Interhemispheric Resource Center, January 28.

Hernández, D.M. 2008. Pursuant to Deportation: Latinos and Immigrant Detention. *Latino Studies* 6 (1): 35–63.

Hernandez-Leon, R. 2005. The Migration Industry in the Mexico-US Migratory System. *California Center of Population Research Online Working Paper*: 049–05.

Hervieu-Léger, D. 2000. "Le miroir de L'Islam en France. *Vingtiéme Cièsle*, pp. 79–89 (April–June).

Heyman, JMC. 1995. Putting Power in the Anthropology of Bureaucracy. *Current Anthropology* 36 (2): 261–87.

Hillman, A.L., and Weiss, A. 1999. A Theory of Permissible Illegal Immigration. *European Journal of Political Economy* 15 (4): 585–604.

Hinojosa, Maria. 2008. Prisons for Profit. *NOW* (May 9).

Hoefer, M; Rytina, N. and Baker, BC. 2008. Estimates of the Unauthorized Immigrant Population Residing in the United States: January 2007. In *Office of Immigration Statistics, Policy Directorate, US Department of Homeland Security*.

Hoffman, John. 1984. *The Gramscian Challenge: Coercion and Consent in Marxist Political Theory*. Oxford: Basil Blackwell Publishers.

Homer-Dixon, Thomas. 1999. *Environment, Scarcity, and Violence*. Princeton: Princeton University Press.

Hondagneu-Sotelo, Pierrete. 1994. *Gender Transitions. Mexican Experiences of Immigration*. University California Press.

——. 2007. *Domestica: Immigrant Workers Cleaning and Caring in the Shadows of Affluence*: University of California Press.

Hooks, Bell. 1990. *Yearning*. Boston: South End Press.

Hornborg, Alf. 2001. *The Power of the Machine: Global Inequalities of Economy, Technology, and Environment*. Walnut Creek, CA: AltaMira Press.

——. 2007. "Footprints in the Cotton Fields: The Industrial Revolution as Time-Space Appropriation and Environmental Load Dispacement," Alf Hornberg, John

R. McNeill, and Joan Martinez-Alier, eds., *Rethinking Environmental History: World-System History and Global Environmental Change.* New York: AltaMira, pp. 259–272.

House, James. 2006. "The Colonial and Post-Colonial Dimensions of Algerian Migration to France," *Institute of Historical Research,* University of Leeds. http://www.history.ac.uk/ihr/focus/migration/articles/house.html, accessed 7-14-2008.

Hull, Gloria T., Patricia Bell Scott, and Barbara Smith, eds. 1982. *But Some of Us Are Brave.* Old Westbury, New York: Feminist Press.

Huntington, Samuel P. 1993. "The Clash of Civilizations?" *Foreign Affairs* 72(3): 22–49.

——. 1996. *The Clash of Civilizations and the Remaking of World Order.* New York: Simon & Schuster.

Hussain, Imtiaz. 2006. *Indigenous Groups, Globalization, and Mexico's Plan Puebla Panama: Marriage or Miscarriage?* New York: Mellen Press.

IICA. 2005. *La agricultura, un asunto estratégico. Situación y perspectivas de la agricultura y de la vida rural en las Américas 2005.* Executive Summary. San José Costa Rica. Available at: www.iica.int/Esp/organizacion/LTGC/modernizacion/Publicaciones%20de%20Modernizacin%20Institucional/Informe%20Situacion%20y%20Perspectivas%20de%20la%20Agricultura%20y%20la%20Vida%20Rural%202005.pdf

INCITE! Women of Color Against Violence 2007. *The Revolution Will Not Be Funded: Beyond the Non-Profit Industrial Complex.* Boston: South End Press.

INEGI. 2008a. *Resultados Preliminares del IX Censo Agropecuario 2007.* Mexico. Available at: www.inegi.gob.mx/inegi/default.aspx?s=est&c=10210

——. 2008b. Encuesta Nacional de Ocupación y Empleo (ENOE). Online Database. Available at: www.inegi.gob.mx/est/contenidos/espanol/proyectos/coesme/programas/programa2.asp?clave=081&s=est&c=10784

Institute, Migration Policy. *Legal Immigration to the United States: Fiscal Years 1820 to 2007 (in millions)* 2007. Available from http://www.migrationinformation.org/datahub/charts/final.immigbyyear.shtml.

Ireland, Douglas. 2005. "Why is France Burning?," *Z Magazine,* http://www.zmag.org/znet/viewarticle/5076, accessed 7-17-2008.

James, J. 1997. *Transcending the Talented Tenth.* New York: Routledge.

Jaquette, Jane. 1994. *The Women's Movement in Latin America: Participation and Democracy.* Boulder, CO: Westview Press.

Jean, Francois and Rufin, Jean-Christophe; eds. 1999 [1996]. *Ökonomie Der Bürgerkriege.* Hamburg: Hamburger Edition.

Johnson, Erik and McCarthy, John. 2005. "The Sequencing of Transnational and National Social Movement Mobilization: The Organizational Mobilization of the Global and U.S. Environmental Movements," Donatella Della Porta and Sidney Tarrow, eds., *Transnational Protest and Global Activism.* Lanham: Rowman & Littlefield Publishers, Inc, pp. 71–93.

Jorgenson, Andrew K. 2003. "Consumption and Environmental Degradation in the World-Economy." *Social Problems* 50:374–394.

——. 2004. "Global Inequality, Water Pollution, and Infant Mortality." *Social Science Journal* 41(2):279–288.

——. 2006. "Global Social Change, Natural Resource Consumption, and Environmental Degradation," Christopher Chase-Dunn and Salvatorre J. Babones, eds., *Global Social Change, Historical and Comparative Perspectives.* Baltimore, MD: John Hopkins University Press, pp. 176–200.

Joseph, P.E. 2007. *Waiting 'Til the Midnight Hour: A Narrative History of Black Power in America.* New York, NY: Henry Holt and Company, Incorporated.

Kaldor, Mary. 1999. *New and Old Wars: Organized Violence in a Global Era.* Stanford: Stanford University Press.

Kampwirth, Karen. 2002. *Women and Guerrilla Movements: Nicaragua, El Salvador, Chiapas, Cuba.* University Park: Pennsylvania State University Press.

——. 2004. *Feminism and the Legacy of Revolution: Nicaragua, El Salvador, Chiapas.* Athens: Ohio University Press.

Kaneshiro, Matheu, Kirk Lawrence, and Christopher Chase-Dunn. Forthcoming (2009) "Environmentalists and their Movements at the World Social Forum," Ellen Reese and Jackie Smith, eds., *Social Forums, Movements, and Networks.* London: Routledge.

Kaplan, Robert. 1993. *Balkan Ghosts.* New York: St Martin's Press.

Kastenbaum, Michele, and Vermés, Geneviève. 1996. "Children of North African Immigrants in the French School System," *Intercultural Education,* 6(3): 43–48.

Kastoryano, Riva. 2006. Territories of Identities in France," *Social Science Research Council* (June 11). http://riotsfrance.ssrc.org/kastoryano/printable.htm, accessed 7-14-2008.

Katzenstein, Mary Fainsod, and McClurg Mueller, Carol. 1987. *The Women's Movement of the United States and Western Europe: Consciousness, Political Opportunity, and Public Policy.* Philadelphia, PA: Temple University Press.

Kaufmann, Stuart. 2001. *Modern Hartreds: The Symbolic Politics of Ethnic War.* Ithaca/London: Cornell University Press.

Kearney, Michael and Nagengast, Carole. 1989. *Anthropological Perspectives on Transnational Latino Communities in Rural California.* Working Paper No. 3. Working Group on Farm Labor and Rural Poverty. California Institute for Rural Studies, U.C. Davis.

Keck, Margaret and Sikkink, Kathryn. 1998. *Activists Beyond Borders.* Ithaca, NY: Cornell University Press.

Keen, David. 1998. *The Economic Functions of Violence in Civil Wars.* Oxford: Oxford University Press.

Kelley, R.D.G. 2002. *Freedom Dreams: The Black Radical Imagination.* Boston: Beacon Press.

Kentor, Jeffrey. 2000. *Capital and Coercion: The Role of Economic and Military Power in the World-Economy 1800–1990.* New York and London: Garland Press.

Kepel, Gilles. 2002. *Jihad: The Trail of Political Islam.* London: Belknap Press.

Kaldun, Ibn. 1958. *The Muqaddimah: An Introduction to History.* New York: Pantheon.

Khosrokhavar. Farhad. 1997. *L'Islam des Jeunes.* Paris: Flammarion.

Kiefer, John J. and Montjoy, Robert S. 2006. "Incrementalism Before the Storm: Network Performance for the Evacuation of New Orleans." *Public Administration Review,* 66, No. 1: 122–130.

Killian, Caitlin, and Johnson, Cathryn. 2006. "'I'm not an Immigrant!': Resistance, Redefinition, and the Role of Resources in Identity Work," *Social Psychology Quarterly,* 69(1): 60–80.

——. 2007. *Covered Girls and Savage Boys: Representation of Youth of African Origin in France.* Paper presented at the annual meeting of American Sociological Association, New York.

King, D.K. 1988. "Multiple Jeopardy, Multiple Consciousness: The Context of a Black Feminist Ideology." *Signs* 14: 42–72.

Klare, Michael. 2001. *Resource Wars: The New Landscape of Global Conflict.* New York: Henry Holt.

Klein, Naomi. 2004. "Reclaiming the Commons," in Tom Mertes, ed., *A Movement of Movements: Is Another World Really Possible?* London and New York: Verso, pp. 219–229.

——. 2007 *The Shock Doctrine: The Rise of Disaster Capitalism.* New York, NY: Macmillan Publishing.

Knauss, Peter R. 1987. *The Persistence of Patriarchy: Class, Gender, and Ideology in Twentieth Century Algeria.* Praeger.

Krissman, Fred. 2000. Immigrant Labor Recruitment: US Agribusiness and Undocumented Migration from Mexico. In *Immigration Research for a New Century,*

Multidisciplinary Perspectives, New York: Russell Sage Foundation, edited by N. Foner, R.G. Rumbaut and S.J. Gold: Russell Sage Foundation.

——. 2005. Sin Coyote Ni Patron: Why the "Migrant Network" Fails to Explain International Migration. *International Migration Review* 39 (1):4–44.

Ladner, J. 1973. *The Death of White Sociology*. New York: Doubleday.

Landim, Leilah. 1987. "Non-governmental Organizations in Latin America." *World Development* 15 supplement: 29–38.

Laraña, Enrique; Johnston, Hank and Gusfield, Joseph R., eds. 1994. *New Social Movements: From Ideology to Identity*. Philadelphia, PA: Temple University Press.

Laska, Shirley. 2004. "What if Hurricane Ivan Had Not Missed New Orleans?" *Natural Hazards Observer*, 29, No.2.

Leander, Anna. 2003. *The Commodification of Violence, Private Military Companies, and African States*. Kopenhagen: Copenhagen Peace Research Institute.

Lecocq, Baz. 2004. "Unemployed Intellectuals in the Sahara: The Teshumara Nationalist Movement and the Revolutions in Tuareg Society." *IRSH* 49: 87–109.

Lehmann, David, and Bebbington, Anthony. 1998. "NGOs, the State, and the Development Process: The Dilemmas of Institutionalization." In *The Changing Role of the State in Latin America*, edited by Menno Vellinga. Boulder, CO: Westview Press.

Lenin, Vladimir I. 1905. "Two Tactics of Social Democracy in the Democratic Revolution," in *Lenin Internet Archive*.

——. 1960 [1916b]. "Der Imperialismus Als Höchstes Stadium Des Kapitalismus," in Institut für Marxismus-Leninismus beim ZK der SED, ed., *Werke*. Berlin: Dietz Verlag, 189–309.

——. 1964 [1916a]. "The Military Programme of the Proletarian Revolution," in *Lenin'collected Works Vol. 23*. Moscow, 77–87.

Lequin, Y. 1992. *Histoire des Étrangérs et de l'Immigration en France*. Paris: Larousse.

Lewis, Bernard, ed. 1980. *The World of Islam*. London: Thames & Hudson.

Lewis, Ted. 2008. Linking NAFTA and Immigration. *The San Diego Union-Tribune*, Feb. 29.

Lind, Amy and Share, Jessica. 2003. 'Queering Development: Institutionalized Hetero-sexuality in Development Theory, Practice in Latin America,' in Kum-Kum Bhavnani, John Foran, and Priya A. Kurian (eds.), *Feminist Futures: Re-imagining Women, Culture and Development*. London: Zed Books, pp. 55–73.

Lindio-McGovern, Ligaya. 2004. 'Alienation and Labor Export in the Context of Globalization: Filipino Migrant Domestic Workers in Taiwan and Hong Kong," *Critical Asian Studies* 36: 2, 217–238.

——. 2007. "Neo-liberal Globalization in the Philippines: Its Impact on Filipino Women and Their Forms of Resistance," *Journal of Developing Societies* 23: 1–2, 15–35.

Loomba, Ania. 1998. *Colonialism/Postcolonialism*. New York: Routledge.

Lummis, C. Douglas. 1996. *Radical Democracy*. Ithaca and London: Cornell University Press.

Maass, Alan. 2006. "The Crimes Katrina Exposed." *CounterPunch*, August 30., <www.counterpunch.org/maass08302006.html>

Machiavelli, Niccolò. 2001 [1513]. *Der Fürst*. Frankfurt a.M.: Insel.

Macías Macías, Alejandro and Chávez Humberto, González. 2007. "Vulnerabilidad alimentaria y política en México" en *Revista Desacatos* No. 25, September–December. CIESAS. Mexico. pp. 47–78. Available at: www.ciesas.edu.mx/Desacatos/25%20Indexado/Saberes2.pdf

MacMaster, Neil. 1997. *Colonial Migrants and Racism: Algerians in France, 1900–62*. Basingstoke.

Magazine, Roger. 2003. "An Innovative Combination of Neoliberalism and State Corporatism: The Case of a Locally based NGO in Mexico City." *The Annals of the American Academy of Political and Social Science* 590:243–256.

Marable, M. 1983. *How Capitalism Underdeveloped Black America*. Boston, MA: South End Press.

Marañón, Boris and Fritscher, Magda. 2004. "La agricultura Mexicana y el TLC. El desencanto neoliberal" *en Revista Debate Agrario* número 37, CEPES, Perú. pp. 183–210. Available at: www.cepes.org.pe/debate/debate37/07.%20maranon-i.pdf

Martin, P.L.; Abella, M.I. and Kuptsch, C. 2006. *Managing Labor Migration in the Twenty-First Century*: Yale University Press.

Marx, Karl. 1953 [1867]. *Das Kapital*. Berlin: Dietz Verlag.

——. 1967. *Capital: A Critique of Political Economy*. (Vol. I) New York: International Publishers.

——. 1969 [1845]. "Thesen Über Feuerbach," in *Marx-Engel Werke*. Berlin: Dietz Verlag, 5–6.

——. 1972 [1844]. "Die Heilige Familie Oder Kritik Der Kritischen Kritik: Gegen Bruno Bauer Und Kunsorten," in *Marx-Engels Werke*. Berlin: Dietz Verlag, 3–223.

—— and Engels, Friedrich. 1972 [1848]. "Manifest Der Kommunistischen Partei," in *Marx-Engels Werke*. Berlin: Dietz Verlag, 459–93.

——. 1972 [1852]. "Der Achtzehnte Brumaire Des Louis Bonaparte," in *Marx-Engels Werke*. Berlin: Dietz-Verlag, 111–207.

Massey, D.S.; Durand, J. and Malone, N.J. 2003. *Beyond Smoke and Mirrors: Mexican Immigration in an Era of Economic Integration*: Russell Sage Foundation Publications.

Matlack, Carol. 2005. "Crisis in France: How Welfare State Economies Failed a Generation," *Business Week* (November 21). http://www.businessweek.com/print/magazine/content/05_47/b3960013htm?chan==gc, accessed 6-5-2008.

McAdam, Doug. 1982. *Political Process and the Development of Black Insurgency, 1930-1970*. Chicago: The University of Chicago Press.

——. McCarthy, John D. and Zald, Mayer N. 1996. *Comparative Perspectives on Social Movements: Political Opportunities, Mobilizing Structures, and Cultural Framings*. Cambridge: Cambridge University Press.

McClintock, Ann. 1995. *Imperial Leather*. New York, NY: Routledge.

McGillion, Christopher. 2004. "French Move to Ban Headscarf Veils a Deeper Conflict," *The Sydney Morning Herald* (January 20). http://www/smh.com/cgi-bin/common /popupprintarticle.pl?path=/articles/2004/01/19/1079360695620.html, accessed 1-12-2008.

Mehler, Andreas. 2003. "Legitime Gewaltoligopole—Eine Antwort Auf Strukturelle Instabilität in Westafrika?" in *IAK-Diskussionsbeiträge*. Hamburg: Institut für Afrikakunde.

Mehlum, Halvor; Moene, Karl and Torvik, Ragnar. 2006. "Cursed by Resources or Institutions?" *The World Economy*: 1117–31.

Mella, José María and Mercado, Alfonso. 2006. "La economía agropecuaria mexicana y el TLCAN" en *Revista Comercio Exterior* número 3, volumen 5, marzo. Mexico. pp. 181–193. Available at: http://revistas.bancomext.gob.mx/rce/magazines/89/1/Mella-Mercado.pdf

Melucci, Alberto. 1989. *Nomads of the Present: Social Movements and Individual Needs in Contemporary Society*. Philadelphia, PA: Temple University Press.

Mencimer, Stephanie. 2008. Why Texas Still Holds 'Em. *Mother Jones*, July/August.

Mernissi, Fatima. 1991. *The Veil and the Male Elite: A Feminist Interpretation of Women's Rights in Islam*. New York: Addison Wesley.

Merton, Robert K. 1968. *Social Theory and Social Structure (enlarged edition)*. New York, NY: The Free Press.

Mies, Maria. 1986. *Patriarchy and Accumulation on a World Scale*. London: Zed Books.

Mills, C.W. 1997. *The Racial Contract*. Ithaca, NY: Cornell University Press.

Mitlini, Diana; Hickey, Sam and Bebbington, Anthony. 2007. "Reclaiming Development? NGOs and the Challenge of Alternatives." *World Development* 35:1699–1720.

Mohanty, C.T. 2003. *Feminism Without Borders: Decolonizing Theory, Practicing Solidarity*. Motilal (UK): Books of India.

Molotch, Harvey and Lester, Marilyn. 2004. "Accidents, Scandals and Routines: Resources for Insurgent Methodology," in Rhonda F. Levine (ed.), *Enriching the Sociological Imagination: How Radical Sociology Changed the Discipline*. Leiden, Brill Academic Publishers, pp. 91–106.

Moody K. 1997. *Workers in a Lean World: Unions in the International Economy*. London: Verso.

Morton, Adam David. 2002. 'La Resurrección Del Maíz': Globalisation, Resistance and the Zapatistas." *Millennium: Journal of International Studies* 31(1): 27–54.

——. 2003. "Historicizing Gramsci: Situating Ideas in and Beyond their Context." *Review of International Political Economy* 10(1): 118–146.

——. 2007. *Unravelling Gramsci: Hegemony and Passive Revolution in the Global Economy*. London: Pluto Press.

Müler, Christian. 2005. "France and the Challenge Posed by Islam," *Qantara*, http://qantara.de/webcom/show_article.php?wc_e=476&wc_id=298, accessed 7-14-2008.

Mummert, Gail, ed. 1999. *Fronteras fragmentadas*. Zamora, Michoacán, México; El Colegio de Michoacán/CIDEM.

NAFTA. 1994. Documento available at: www.international.gc.ca/trade-agreements-accords-commerciaux/agr-acc/nafta-alena/texte/index.aspx?lang=en&menu_id=34&menu=R

Naravane, Vaiju. 2005. "Flashpoint in France," *Frontline*, 22(24), November 19–December 02. http://www.flomnet.com/fl2224/stories/20051202000905300.htm, accessed 6-5-2008.

Nash, June. 2006. 'Development Strategies, the Exclusion of Women, and Indigenous Alternatives,' in Max Kirsch (ed.), *Inclusion and Exclusion in the Global Arena*. New York and London: Routledge, pp. 97–127.

Nasr, S.V.R. 1999. "European Colonialism and the Emergence of Modern Muslim Societies," in John Esposito (ed.), *The Oxford History of Islam*, pp. 549–599. New York: Oxford University Press.

New York Times. 2008. "People: Alphonso R. Jackson." March 31.

Newdick, Vivian. 2005. 'The Indigenous Woman as Victim of Her Culture in Neoliberal Mexico.' *Cultural Dynamics*. London, Thousand Oaks, CA and New Delhi: Sage Publications. 17(1): 73–92.

Ngai, M.M. 2004. *Impossible Subjects: Illegal Aliens and the Making of Modern America*: Princeton University Press.

Niggs, Joanne M. and Tierney, Kathleen J. 1993 *Disasters and Social Change: Consequences for Community Construct and Affect*. Disaster Research Center, University of Delaware. <http://www.udel.edu/DRC/preliminary/195.pdf>

NISES. 2004. *Total Population*. National Institute for Statistics and Economic Studies. http://news.bbs.uk/2/hi/Europe/4385768.stm#france, accessed 7-11-2008.

Norget, Kristin. 2005. 'Caught in the Crossfire: Militarization, Paramilitarization, and State Violence in Oaxaca, Mexico,' in C. Menjívar and N. Rodríguez (eds.), *When States Kill: Latin America, the U.S., and Technologies of Terror*. Austin: University of Texas Press, pp. 115–142.

O'Connor, James. 1998. *Natural Causes: Essays in Ecological Marxism*. New York: Guilford Press.

Obach, Brian. 2004. *Labor and the Environmental Movement: The Quest for Common Ground*. Cambridge: MIT Press.

Oberschall, Anthony. 2000. "The Manipulation of Ethnicity: From Ethnic Cooperation to Violence and War in Yugoslavia." *Ethnic and Racial Studies* 23(6): 982–1001.

OECME (Oficina Económica y Comercial de México en España). 2004. *Guía País México*. Published by OECME in Mexico. Available at: www.icex.es/staticFiles/Mexico_7238_.pdf

Olzak, Susan and West, Elizabeth. 1991. "Ethnic Conflicts and the Rise and Fall of Ethnic Newspapers." *American Sociological Review* 56: 458–474.

Omi, M and Winant, H. 1986. *Racial Formation in the United States: From the 1960s to the 1980s*. London: Routledge.

Open Society Institute. 2002. *The Situations of Muslims in France*. http://www.eumap.org/reports/2002/eu/international/sections/France/2002_m_france.pdf, accessed 7-17-2008.

Oyeronke, Oyewumi. 1997. *The Invention of Women*. Minneapolis, MN: University of Minnesota Press.

Pasha, Mustapha Kamal. 2005. "Islam, 'Soft' Orientalism and Hegemony: A Gramscian Rereading." *Critical Review of International Social and Political Philosophy* 8(4): 543–58.

Petras, James. 1997. "Imperialism and NGOs in Latin America." *Monthly Review* 49:10–27.

Philp, Mark. 2008. Political Theory and the Evaluation of Political Conduct. *Social Theory and Practice* 34 (3): 389–410.

Pickard, Miguel. 2004. 'The Plan Puebla-Panama: Looking Back to See What's Ahead.' Americas Program. Silver City, NM: Interhemispheric Resource Center, June 8.

Piester, Kerianne. 1997. "Targeting the Poor: The Politics of Social Policy Reforms in Mexico" in *The New Politics of Inequality in Latin America: Rethinking Participation and Representation* edited by Douglas A. Chalmers, Carlos M. Vilas, Katherine Hite, Scott B. Martin, Kerianne Piester, and Monique Segarra. New York: Oxford University Press.

Piore, Michael J. 1979. *Birds of Passage: Migrant Labor and Industrial Societies*. Cambridge: Cambridge University Press Cambridge.

Piven, Frances Fox, and Cloward, Richard A. 1977. *Poor People's Movements: Why They Succeed, How They Fail*. New York: Vintage Books.

PolicyLink. 2007. www.policylink.org <http://74.125.47.132/u/PolicyLink?q=cache:Q6surAY50lMJ:www.policylink.org/documents/nola_fewerhomes.pdf+katrina&cd=1&hl=en&ct=clnk&gl=us&ie=UTF-8>

Portes, Alesandro, and Borocz, Josef. 1989. "Contemporary Immigration: Theoretical Perspectives on Its Determinants and Modes of Incorporation," *International Migration Review*, 23(3): 606–630.

—— and Rumbaut, Rubén G. 1997 [1ª edición 1990]. *Immigrant America*. Berkeley, California: University of California Press.

——; Guarnizo, Luis and Landolt, Patricia. 2003. *La Globalización desde Abajo. Transnacionalismo Inmigrante y Desarrollo. La Experiencia de Estados Unidos y América Latina*. FLACSO México and Miguel Ángel Porrúa. Mexico.

Pozas Garza, Maria de los Angeles. 1989. "Land Settlement by the Poor in Monterrey." pp. 65–78 in *Housing and Land in Urban Mexico*, edited by Alan Gilbert. San Diego: Center for U.S.-Mexican Studies, UCSD.

——. 1990. "Los Marginados y La Ciudad. pp. 15–58 in *La Marginación Urbana en Monterrey*. Monterrey, Mexico: Facultad de Filosofía y Letras and Facultad de Trabajo Social, Universidad Autónoma de Nuevo León.

——. 1995. "Movimientos Sociales Urbanos." pp. 423–429 in *Atlas de Monterrey*, edited by Gustavo Garza Villarreal. Monterrey, Mexico: Universidad Autónoma de Nuevo León and El Colegio de Mexico: Instituto de Estudios Urbanos de Nuevo León.

Pries, Ludger. 1997. "Migración laboral internacional y espacios sociales transnacionales: bosquejo teórico-empírico." In Saúl Macías Gamboa and Fernando Herrera

Lima (Coordinators) *Migración laboral internacional: Transnacionalidad del espacio social*. Benemérita Universidad Autónoma de Puebla.

Pye, Lucian W. 1998. "Democracy and Its Enemies," in *Pathways to Democracy*. New York: Routledge.

Quarantelli, E.L.; Lagadec, Patrick and Boin, Arjen. 2006. "A Heuristic Approach to Future Disasters and Crises: New, Old, and In-Between Types," (pp. 16–41) in *Handbook of Disaster Research* ed. by Havidàn Rodrìguez, Enrico L. Quarantelli, and Russell R. Dynes. New York, NY: Springer.

Quigley, Bill. 2007. *Lessons Learned by Grassroots Katrina and Tsunami Social Justice Activists*. <http://www.counterpunch.org/quigley05282007.html>

Randall, Margaret. 1992. *Gathering Rage*. New York: Monthly Review Press.

Red Oaxaqueña de Derechos Humanos. 2004. *El Plan Puebla-Panamá, Un Proceso en Marcha, V Informe* (The Plan Puebla-Panama, An Ongoing Process, fifth report). Oaxaca, MX: Red Oaxaqueña de Derechos Humanos.

Reese, Ellen; Chase-Dunn, Christopher; Anantram, Kadambari; Coyne, Gary; Kaneshiro, Matheu; Koda, Ashley N.; Kwon, Roy and Saxena, Preeta. "Research Note: Surveys of World Social Forum Participants Show Influence of Place and Base in the Global Public Sphere." *Mobilization: An International Journal* 13(4): 341–445.

Reichert, Joshua. 1981. "The Migration Syndrome: Seasonal U.S. Wage Labor and Rural Development in Central Mexico," in *Human Organization* 40 (1): 56–66.

———. 1982. Social Stratification in a Mexican Sending Community: The Effect of Migration to the United States. *Social Problems* 29 (4):411–423.

Reitan, Ruth. 2007. *Global Activism*. London: Routledge.

Reno, William. 2003. "Gier Gegen Groll: Nigeria," in Werner Ruf, ed., *Politische Ökonomie Der Gewalt: Staatszerfall Und Die Privatisierung Von Gewalt Und Krieg*. Opladen: Leske + Budrich.

Research Unit for Political Economy (RUPE). 2007. "Foundations and Mass Movements: The Case of the World Social Forum." *Critical Sociology* 33: 505–536.

Robinson, William I. [1996] 1998. *Promoting Polyarchy: Globalization, U.S. Intervention, and Hegemony*. Cambridge, New York: Cambridge University Press.

Robles Berlanga, Héctor M. 2008. *Saldos de las Reformas de 1992 al Artículo 27 Constitucional*. Centro de Estudios para el Desarrollo Rural Sustentable y la Soberanía Alimentaria. June, Mexico.

Rodney, W. 1982. *How Europe Underdeveloped Africa*. Washington, DC: Howard University Press.

Rohrschneider, Robert and Dalton, Russell. 2002. "A Global Network? Transnational Cooperation among Environmental Groups." *The Journal of Politics* 64(2): 510–533.

Rojas Sandoval, Javier. 1992. *Monterrey: Poder Político, Obreros y Empresarios en la Coyuntura Revolucionaria*. Monterrey, Mexico: Universidad Autónoma de Nuevo León.

Romero, José and Puyana, Alicia. 2004. Evaluación integral de los impactos e instrumentación del capítulo agropecuario del TLCAN. Master Document. Available at: http://ctrc.sice.oas.org/geograph/westernh/NAFTA_AGRI.pdf

Rootes, Christopher. 1999. "Acting Globally, Thinking Locally? Prospects for a Global Environmental Movement," Christopher Rootes, ed., *Environmental Movements: Local, National and Global*. London: Frank Cass, pp. 290–310.

———. 2005. "A Limited Transnationalization? The British Environmental Movements," Donatella Della Porta and Sidney Tarrow, eds., *Transnational Protest and Global Activism*. Lanham: Rowman & Littlefield Publishers, Inc, pp. 21–43.

Ros, Jaime and Lustig, Nora Claudia. 2003. 'Economic Liberalization and Income Distribution in Mexico: Losers and Winners in a Time of Global Restructuring,' in Susan Eva Eckstein and Timothy P. Wickham-Crowley (eds.) *Struggles for Social Rights in Latin America*. New York and London: Routledge, pp. 125–146.

Rosenzweig, Andrés. 2005. *El Debate Sobre el Sector Agropecuario Mexicano en el Tratado de Libre Comercio de América del Norte.* Serie Estudios y Perspectivas No. 30. Sede Subregional de la CEPAL en Mexico, Mexico.

Rothman, Franklin D. and Oliver, Pamela. 1999. "From Local to Global: The Anti-Dam Movement in Southern Brazil, 1979–1992." *Mobilization: An International Journal,* 4(1): 41–57.

Saldaña-Portillo, María Josefina. 2003. *The Revolutionary Imagination in the Americas and the Age of Development.* Durham and London: Duke University Press.

Saragoza, Alex. 1988. *The Monterrey Elite and the Mexican State, 1880–1940.* Austin, TX: The University of Texas Press.

Sassen, Saskia. 1998. *Globalization and Its Discontents.* New York; The New Press.

———. 1999. Americas Immigration "Problem." In *Race and Ethnic Conflict: Contending Views on Prejudice, Discrimination, and Ethnoviolence,* edited by F.L. Pincus and H.J. Ehrlich: Westview Press.

Sassoon, Anne Showstack. 2001. "Globalisation, Hegemony and Passive Revolution." *New Political Economy* 6(1): 5–17.

Schein, R.H. 2006. *Landscape and Race in the United States:* Routledge.

Schlichte, Klaus. 2004. "Krieg Und Bewaffneter Konflikt Als Sozialer Raum," in Sabine Kurtenbach and Peter Lock, eds., *Kriege Als (Über)Lebenswelten. Schattenglobalisierung, Kriegsökonomien Und Inseln Der Zivilität.* Bonn: Dietz Verlag, 102–21.

Schlosberg, David. 2004. "Reconceiving Environmental Justice: Global Movements and Political Theories." *Environmental Politics* 13(3):517–540.

Schmidinger, Thomas. 2004. *Arbeiterinnenbewegung Im Sudan. Geschichte Und Analyse Der Arbeiterinnenbewegung Des Sudan Im Vergleich Mit Den Arbeiterinnenbewegungen Ägyptens, Syriens, Des Südjemen Und Des Iraq.* Frankfurt am Main: Peter Lang.

Schnaiberg, Allan and Gould, Kenneth Alan. 1994. *Environment and Society: The Enduring Conflict.* New York: St. Martin's Press.

Schnapper, Dominique. 1991. "La Frace de L'Intégration: Sociologie de le Nation en 1990," *Coll. Bibliotèque des Sciences Humaines.* Paris: Gallimard.

Schock, Kurt. 1999. "People Power and Political Opportunities: Social Movement Mobilization and Outcomes in the Philippines and Burma." *Social Problems* 46:355–375.

Scott, Alan. 1990. *Ideology and the New Social Movements.* London: Unwin Hyman.

Scott, James C. 1985. *Weapons of the Weak.* London: Yale University Press.

———. 1990. *Domination and the Arts of Resistance.* New Haven and London: Yale University Press.

Scott, Jerome and Fishman, Walda Katz. 2007. "America Through the Eye of Hurricane Katrina--Capitalism at its 'Best.' What Are We Prepared To Do?" *Race, Gender & Class,* 14, No. 1–2. <http://www.suno.edu/Race_Gender_Class/journal2003.htm#Vol%2014%20#1-2>

Segarra, Monique. 1997. "Redefining the Public/Private Mix: NGOs and the Emergency Social Investment Fund in Ecuador." pp. 489–515 in *The New Politics of Inequality in Latin America: Rethinking Participation and Representation,* edited by Douglas A. Chalmers, Carlos M. Vilas, Katherine Hite, Scott B. Martin, Kerianne Piester, and Monique Segarra. Oxford: Oxford University Press.

Seljuq, Affan. 1997. "Cultural Conflicts: North African Immigrants in France," *International Journal of Peace Studies,* 2(2). http://www.gmu.edu/academic/ijps/vol2_2/seljuq.htm, accessed 6-5-2008.

Sen, J. and Waterman, P. eds. 2009. *World Social Forum: Challenging Empires.* Montreal: Black Rose Books.

Senghaas, Dieter, ed. 1977. *Kritische Friedensforschung.* 4 ed. Frankfurt a.M.: Suhrkamp Verlag.

Serna Hidalgo, Braulio. 2005. *México: Crecimiento Agropecuario, Capital Humano y Gestión del Riesgo.* CEPAL, Santiago de Chile.

Shapiro, Isaac and Sherman, Arloc. 2005. *Essential Facts About the Victims of Hurricane Katrina*. Center on Budget and Policy Priorities (CBPP). <http://www.cbpp.org/cms/?fa=view&id=658>

Shefner, Jon. 2007. "Rethinking Civil Society in the Age of NAFTA: The Case of Mexico." *The Annals of the American Academy of Political and Social Science* 610:182–200.

Shiva, Vandana. 2003. "Environment and Sustainability. The Living Democracy Movement: Alternatives to the Bankruptcy of Globalization," William Fisher and Thomas Ponniah, eds., *Another World is Possible: Popular Alternatives to Globalization and the World Social Forum*. London and New York: Zed Books, pp. 115–124.

Shultz, Jim. 2003. "Bolivia: The Water War Widens." *NACLA Report on the Americas* 36(3): 34–37.

——. 2005. "The Politics of Water in Bolivia." *The Nation*. Available: www.thenation.com/doc/20050214/shultz.

Silverstein, Paul. 2004. "Headscarves and the French Tricolor," *Middle East Report*. http://www.merip.org/mero/mero013004.html, accessed 4-2-2008.

Singer, Paul. 1975. *Economía política de la Urbanización*. Ed. Siglo XXI. Mexico.

Sklair, Leslie. 2002. *Globalization; Capitalism and Its Alternatives, 3rd Edition*. New York: Oxford University Press.

Smith, Cintia. 2008. "Análisis de la Ideología Empresarial Regiomontana. Un Acercamiento a Partir del Periódico El Norte." *CONFINES de Relaciones Internacionales y Ciencia Política* 4(7):11–25.

Smith, Jackie. 2004. "Exploring Connections Between Global Integration and Political Mobilization." *Journal of World Systems Research* 10(1): 255–285.

Smith, Michael Peter and Guarnizo, Luis E., eds. 1997. *Transnationalism from Below*. Somerset, New Jersey: Transaction Publishers.

Smith, Robert. 1995. *Los Ausentes Siempre Presentes: The Imagining, Making, and Politics of a Transnational Community between New York and Ticuani, Puebla*, Ph.D. Dissertation in Political Science. Columbia University.

Snodgrass, Michael. 1996. *La Lucha Sindical y la Resistencia Patronal en Monterrey, Mexico: 1918–1940*. Monterrey, Nuevo León: A.G.E.N.L.

——. 2003. *Deference and Defiance in Monterrey: Workers, Paternalism, and Revolution in Mexico, 1890–1950*. Cambridge: Cambridge University Press.

Sondage Ifop. 2001. "l'Islam en France et les Réactions aux Attentats du 11 Septembre 2001," *Le Monde/Le point* (October). http://www.ifop.com/Europe/sondage/OPINIONF/islam.asp, accessed 7-4-2008.

Speed, Shannon and Collier, Jane F. 2000. 'Limiting Indigenous Autonomy in Chiapas, Mexico: The State Government's Use of Human Rights.' *Human Rights Quarterly* (22): 877–905.

Squires, G. 1994. *Capital and Communities in Black and White*. Albany, NY: State University of New York Press.

Starn, Orin. 1992. "I Dreamed of Foxes and Hawks: Reflections on Peasant Protest, New Social Movements, and the Rondas Campesinas of Northern Peru." pp. 89–111 in *The Making of Social Movements in Latin America*, edited by Arturo Escobar and Sonia Alvarez. Boulder, CO: Westview Press.

Stephen, Lynn. 1997a. "The Zapatista Opening: the Movement for Indigenous Autonomy and State Discourses on Indigenous Rights in Mexico, 1970–1996." *Journal of Latin American Anthropology* 2(2):2–41.

——. 1997b. *Women and Social Movements in Latin America: Power from Below*. Austin, TX: University of Texas Press.

——. 2002. *Zapata Lives! Histories and Cultural Politics in Southern Mexico*. Berkeley: University of California Press.

Stern, Steve J. 1995. *The Secret History of Gender: Women, Men, and Power in Late Colonial Mexico.* Chapel Hill and London: University of North Carolina Press.

Stout, A. Kathryn. 1989. *The Sanctuary Movement in the 1980s: The Dialectics of Law and Social Movement Development.* Ann Arbor, MI: UMI Dissertation Services.

—— and Dello Buono, Richard A. 1991. "Political Prisoners as an Emergent Contradiction of State Repression." *Humanity and Society.* 15, 4: 338–349.

——. 2004. "Law and Social Change: Bringing Movements into the Dialectic," pp. 19–40 in A. Kathryn Stout, Richard A. Dello Buono and William J. Chambliss eds. *Social Problems, Law, and Society.* Lanham, MD: Rowman and Littlefield.

——. Dello Buono, Richard A. and Chambliss, William J. 2004. *Social Problems, Law and Society.* Lanham, MD: Rowman and Littlefield Pubs.

—— and Dello Buono, Richard A. 2008. "'Natural' Disasters are Social Problems: Learning from Katrina," *Agenda for Social Justice: Solutions 2008,* Knoxville, TN: Society for the Study of Social Problems, pp. 23–27. <http://www.sssp1.org/index.cfm/m/323>

Swier, Mark. 2006. "Other Loves' in the 'Other Campaign." Accessed December 15, 2007 at http://www.narconews.com/Issue40/article1691.html.

Taboada-Leonette, Isabel, and Lévy, Florence. 1978. "Femmes et Immigrées: L'Insertion des Femmes Immigrées en France," *Migrants et Société,* No. 4. Paris: La Documentation Français.

Talcott, Molly. 2008. *Claiming Dignity, Reconfiguring Rights: Gender, Youth, and Indigenous-led Politics in Southern Mexico.* Ph.D. Dissertation, Department of Sociology, University of California, Santa Barbara.

Tarrés, María Luisa. 1998. *Género y Cultura en América Latina.* Mexico City: El Colegio de México.

Tarrow, Sidney. 1998. *Power in Movement: Social Movements and Contentious Politics.* 2nd Edition. Cambridge: Cambridge University Press.

—— and McAdam, Doug. 2005. "Scale Shift in Transnational Contention," Donatella Della Porta and Sidney Tarrow, eds., *Transnational Protest & Global Activism.* Lanham: Rowman & Littlefield Publishers, Inc, pp. 121–150.

Taylor, Dorceta E. 2005. "American Environmentalism: The Role of Race, Class and Gender in Shaping Activism 1820–1995.," Leslie King and Deborah McCarthy, eds., *Environmental Sociology: From Analysis to Action.* New York: Rowman & Littlefield, pp. 87–106.

Taylor, Vera and Whittier, Nancy. 1992. "Collective Identity in Social Movement Communities: Lesbian Feminist Mobilization." pp. 104–130 in *Frontiers in Social Movement Theory,* edited by Aldon D. Morris and Carol McClurg Mueller. New Haven: Yale University.

The Bamako Appeal. 2006. Word Forum for Alternatives, Third World Forum, Forum for Another Mali, EDA, and Others," in Jan Sen and Peter Waterman, eds. *World Social Forum Challenging Empires,* Montreal: Black Rose Books.

Thompson, J. 2007. *Cortina: Defending the Mexican Name in Texas:* Texas A&M University Press.

Tichenor, D.J. 2002. *Dividing Lines: The Politics of Immigration Control in America:* Princeton University Press.

Tierney, Kathleen; Bevc, Christine and Kuligowski, Erica. 2006. "Metaphors Matter: Disaster Myths, Media Frames, and Their Consequences in Hurricane Katrina." *The Annals of the American Academy of Political and Social Science,* 604. <http://ann.sagepub.com/cgi/content/abstract/604/1/57>

Tilly, Charles. 1978. *From Mobilization to Revolution.* New York: McGraw-Hill Publishing Company.

——. 1990. *Coercion, Capital and European States, AD 990–1992.* Cambridge, MA & Oxford: Blackwell.

Tribalat, Michéle. 1995. Faire France: Un *Enquête sur les Immigrés et leur Enfants*. Paris: La Déconverte/Essais.

——. 1996. *De l'Immigration á l'Assimilation; Enquête sur les Population d'Origine Etrangér en France*. Paris: La Déconverte/INED.

Union, American Civil Liberties. 2009. *ACLU Challenges Prison-Like Conditions at Hutto Detention Center* 2008 [cited May 23 2009]. Available from http://www.aclu.org/immigrants/detention/hutto.html.

United Nations Development Program (UNDP). 2004. *Informe sobre Desarrollo Social y Humano Mexico 2004* (Human Development Report of Mexico 2004). Accessed at: http://hdr.undp.org/en/reports/nationalreports/latinamericathecaribbean/mexico/Mexico_2004_sp.pdf.

United States House of Representatives Committee on Government Reform—Minority Staff Special Investigations Division. August 2006. *Waste, Fraud and Abuse in Hurricane Katrina Contracts*. <http://oversight.house.gov/Documents/20060824110705–30132.pdf>

Urban Institute Non Partisan Economic and Social Policy Research. <http://www.urban.org/>

Väisse, Justin. 2004. "Veiled Meaning: The French Law Banning Religious Symbols in Public Schools," pp. 1–6, in *The Brookings Institution: US-France Analysis series*. http;//www.brookings.edu/fp/cusf/analysis/vaisse20040229.pdf, accessed 7-2-2008.

van Apeldoorn, Bastiaan. 2002. *Transnational Capitalism and the Struggle over European Integration*. London: Routledge.

van der Pijl, Kees. 1998. *Transnational Classes and International Relations*. London: Routledge.

Vandergeest, Peter, Pablo Idahosa, and Pablo S. Bose, eds. 2007. *Development's Displacements: Ecologies, Economies, and Cultures at Risk*. Vancouver and Toronto: The University of British Columbia Press.

Vargas, Zaragosa. 2005. *Labor Rights are Civil Rights: Mexican American Workers in Twentieth-Century America*: Princeton University Press.

Vellinga, Menno. 1979. *Economic Development and the Dynamics of Class: Industrialization, Power, and Control in Monterrey, Mexico*. The Netherlands: Van Gorcum Assen.

Veltmeyer, Henry. 2005. "Development and Globalization as Imperialism." *Canadian Journal of Development Studies* 26(1):89–106.

Villanueva, Luis. 2005. "Instituciones, tecnología geo-espacial y eficiencia económica: hacia un catastro rural moderno," in *Revista Agronuevo*, No. 1. SRA. Mexico pp. 21–33. Available at: www.sra.gob.mx/internet/agronuevo/num1/villanueva_enero05.pdf

Waldinger, Roger. 1999. *Still the Promised City?: African-Americans and New Immigrants in Postindustrial New York*: Harvard University Press.

Wallerstein, Immanuel. 1974. *The Modern World-System, Vol. I: Capitalist Agriculture and the Origins of the European World-Economy in the Sixteenth Century*. New York/London: Academic Press.

——. 2000. *The Essential Wallerstein*. New York: The New Press.

——. 2009. "Guadeloupe: Obscure Key to World Crisis" retrieved 5/5/09 at http://hap.bloger.hr/post/-guadeloupe-obscure-key-to-world-crisis-/1269755.aspx

Walsh, Edward; Warland, Rex and Smith, Douglas C. 1993. "Backyards, NIMBYs and Incinerator Sitings: Implications for Social Movement Theory." *Social Problems* 40(1): 25–38.

Walton, John. 1977. *Elites and Economic Development*. Austin, TX: The University of Texas at Austin.

Weinberg, Bill. 2006. 'Atenco: sexual abuse confirmed; airport proposal revived?' *World War 4 Report*. October 10. Accessed December 15, 2007 at http://ww4report.com/node/2619.

Welch, M. 2000. The Role of the Immigration and Naturalization Service in the Prison-Industrial Complex. *Social Justice—San Francisco* 27 (3): 73–88.

Wilson, T.D. 2000. Anti-Immigrant Sentiment and the Problem of Reproduction/ Maintenance in Mexican Immigration to the United States. *Critique of Anthropology* 20 (2): 191.

Witness for Peace. 2007. Forced From Home: U.S. Trade Policy and Immigration. Washington, D.C.: Witness for Peace.

Wood, Ellen Meiksins. 1995. *Democracy against Capitalism: Renewing Historical Materialism*. Cambridge, New York: Cambridge University Press.

Wyndham, John. 1955. *The Chrysalids*. London: Michael Joseph Ltd.

Yahhaoui, Abdessalem. 1989. "Crise d" Identité, Crise Idéologique et Pratique Religieuse; L'Islam en milieu Maghrébin," *Identité, 7–15*.

Yousef, Ahmed. 1998. *The Fascination of Egypt: From the Dream to the Project*. Paris: Harmattan.

Zavestoski, Stephen. 2006. "Local and Global Environmental Advocacy Networks; Responses to the Globalization of Environmental Health Hazards." *International Journal of Environmental, Cultural, Economic and Social Sustainability.* 2: 149–158.

Zerai, A. and Salime, Z. 2006. "A Black Feminist Analysis of Responses to War, Racism, and Repression." *Critical Sociology* 32:501–524.

Zibechi, Raúl. 2007. 'Mexico's Street Brigade: Sex, Revolution, and Social Change.' Americas Program Special Report. Accessed December 15, 2007 at http://americas .irc-online.org/am/4822.

Zlolniski, Christian. 2008. "Political Mobilization and Activism Among Latinos/as in the United States." In H. Rodríguez, R. Saénz and C. Menjívar (eds.) *Latinas/os in the United States: Changing the Face of America*. New York, Springer.

Zugman, Kara. 2001. *Mexican Awakening in Postcolonial America: Zapatistas in Urban Spaces in Mexico City*. Ph.D. dissertation, Department of Sociology, University of California, Santa Barbara.

NAME INDEX

SUBJECT INDEX